Gruesome Looking Objects

The 1898 lynching of Tom Johnson and Joe Kizer is retold in this groundbreaking book. Unlike other histories of lynching that rely on conventional historical records, this study focuses on the objects associated with the lynching, including newspaper articles, fragments of the victims' clothing, photographs, and souvenirs such as sticks from the hanging tree. This material culture approach uncovers how people tried to integrate the meaning of the lynching into their everyday lives through objects. These seemingly ordinary items are repositories for the comprehension, interpretation, and commemoration of racial violence and white supremacy. Elijah Gaddis showcases an approach to objects as materials of history and memory, insisting that we live in a world suffused with the material traces of racial violence, past and present.

Elijah Gaddis is Assistant Professor of History at Auburn University, and the co-director of *A Red Record*, a comprehensive mapping of lynching victims in the American South.

CAMBRIDGE STUDIES ON THE AMERICAN SOUTH

Series Editors:

Mark M. Smith, *University of South Carolina, Columbia*

Peter Coclanis, *University of North Carolina at Chapel Hill*

Editor Emeritus:

David Moltke-Hansen

Interdisciplinary in its scope and intent, this series builds upon and extends Cambridge University Press's longstanding commitment to studies on the American South. The series offers the best new work on the South's distinctive institutional, social, economic, and cultural history and also features works in a national, comparative, and transnational perspective.

Titles in the Series

William A. Link and James J. Broomall, eds., *Rethinking American Emancipation: Legacies of Slavery and the Quest for Black Freedom*

James Van Horn Melton, *Religion, Community, and Slavery on the Colonial Southern Frontier*

Damian Alan Pargas, *Slavery and Forced Migration in the Antebellum South*

Craig Friend and Lorri Glover, eds., *Death and the American South*

Barton A. Myers, *Rebels against the Confederacy: North Carolina's Unionists*

Louis A. Ferleger and John D. Metz, *Cultivating Success in the South: Farm Households in Postbellum Georgia*

Luke E. Harlow, *Religion, Race, and the Making of Confederate Kentucky, 1830–1880*

Susanna Michele Lee, *Claiming the Union: Citizenship in the Post–Civil War South*

Kathleen M. Hilliard, *Masters, Slaves, and Exchange: Power's Purchase in the Old South*Ari Helo, *Thomas Jefferson's Ethics and the Politics of Human Progress: The Morality of a Slaveholder*

Scott P. Marler, *The Merchants' Capital: New Orleans and the Political Economy of the Nineteenth-Century South*

Ras Michael Brown, *African-Atlantic Cultures and the South Carolina Lowcountry*

Johanna Nicol Shields, *Freedom in a Slave Society: Stories from the Antebellum South*

Brian Steele, *Thomas Jefferson and American Nationhood*

Christopher Michael Curtis, *Jefferson's Freeholders and the Politics of Ownership in the Old Dominion*

Jonathan Daniel Wells, *Women Writers and Journalists in the Nineteenth-Century South*

Peter McCandless, *Slavery, Disease, and Suffering in the Southern Lowcountry*

Robert E. Bonner, *Mastering America: Southern Slaveholders and the Crisis of American Nationhood*

Gruesome Looking Objects

A New History of Lynching and Everyday Things

ELIJAH GADDIS

Auburn University, Alabama

CAMBRIDGE
UNIVERSITY PRESS

University Printing House, Cambridge CB2 8BS, United Kingdom

One Liberty Plaza, 20th Floor, New York, NY 10006, USA

477 Williamstown Road, Port Melbourne, VIC 3207, Australia

314–321, 3rd Floor, Plot 3, Splendor Forum, Jasola District Centre, New Delhi – 110025, India

103 Penang Road, #05–06/07, Visioncrest Commercial, Singapore 238467

Cambridge University Press is part of the University of Cambridge.

It furthers the University's mission by disseminating knowledge in the pursuit of education, learning, and research at the highest international levels of excellence.

www.cambridge.org
Information on this title: www.cambridge.org/9781316514023
DOI: 10.1017/9781009082266

© Elijah Gaddis 2023

First published 2023

A catalogue record for this publication is available from the British Library.

Library of Congress Cataloging-in-Publication Data
NAMES: Gaddis, Elijah, 1987– author.
TITLE: Gruesome looking objects :
a new history of lynching and everyday things / Elijah Gaddis,
Auburn University, Alabama.
DESCRIPTION: New York, NY : Cambridge University Press, 2022. |
SERIES: Cambridge studies on the American South |
Includes bibliographical references and index.
IDENTIFIERS: LCCN 2022022768 | ISBN 9781316514023 (hardback) |
ISBN 9781009082266 (ebook)
SUBJECTS: LCSH: Lynching – North Carolina – History – 19th century. |
African Americans – Crimes against – North Carolina – History – 19th century.
CLASSIFICATION: LCC HV6465.N67 G34 2022 | DDC 364.1/34–dc23/eng/20220720
LC record available at https://lccn.loc.gov/2022022768

ISBN 978-1-316-51402-3 Hardback

Contents

Figures

Preface

I want to begin in a way uncharacteristic of historical writing by first remarking upon what this book is not. It is not a story of lynching victims. Tom Johnson and Joe Kizer were murdered publicly and brutally. After years of searching, I can find little more about them than the prejudicial and sensational accounts made at the time. The lives of people shortened considerably by mob violence deserve a full accounting. Their lives were ended by a few, intense hours of violence, and marked throughout by the emergence and intensification of Jim Crow's pervasive inequalities. Neither fact does justice to their stories. So, while I will talk about each of these men and what their deaths came to mean, I will not focus on the circumstances of their lynching. Nor will I reify the trauma of their unlawful executions by recasting the prurient details of their murders as history. Enough Black trauma has been reappropriated for white history and by white historians. A full accounting of lynching and its aftermaths needs to deal equally with the meaning that white communities made of these horrific events.

Nor is this a personal narrative, though it is one that proceeds in some small way from my life. I learned about the contours of this story from the serendipity of historical research. I was shocked – stupidly, I now think – by finding that the double lynching of these two men and the resulting century of history and memory of those events occurred in places that I knew well. Indeed, this story takes place in the very same communities that I grew up in, albeit at a significant temporal (if not always historical) remove. That discovery, and the subsequent unraveling of its long impact, brought me to this story. And throughout, I rely on my own intimate, lived experience of these landscapes to inform my understanding as an historian. These tools of affect and experience should always be a part of our approach as scholars but need not dominate our perspective.

If it is neither of these things then, this *is* a story of the meaning made through objects associated with the lynching of Joe Kizer and Tom Johnson. In the absence of correspondence and little firsthand accounting, I have instead turned to *things* and the stories that they can tell. This is a story that insists on the persistence of the past and its presence as a material, enlivened entity both well before and long after what we would typically mark as the conclusion of an event. In this book, I regard this and other lynchings as historical anomalies, events whose contours span the length of a century or more and materialize again and again and again. We are always immersed in memory, and those of us who write history do our best work when we pay attention to its continuities and its conscious uses in the present. We live in the world lynching made.

Acknowledgments

Scholarship is a collective enterprise, though rarely is one's childhood so directly linked to the work of their career. I have first to thank my parents, Pat and Jay, for purposely nurturing my love of reading and history and incidentally raising me in the landscape where much of this book takes place. My siblings, Zachariah and Hannah, can be commended for leaving me to my books and accompanying me on explorations of our woods and hills. All four of them and now their spouses and children have also contributed immeasurably to my happiness and my success.

Others too helped shape this project unintentionally. Even before the inception of this book, the many archivists in the North Carolina Collection, Southern Historical Collection, and the Southern Folklife Collection in Wilson Library at the University of North Carolina (UNC) provided guidance and crucial connections among sources and people across the state and beyond. The special collections staff at UNC are truly unparalleled in the profession. Archivists and librarians rarely get the credit they deserve as co-creators and so I'd like to enumerate a partial list of those who have helped me immeasurably:

- Bob Anthony and John Blythe (who let me into the warren of Wilson's stacks and invariably knew a source I should look at or a person I should talk to);
- Sarah Carrier and Jason Tomberlin (who answered every question with good cheer and almost alarming speed);
- Aaron Smithers (who made me many reproductions to listen to, and pointed me to sources I'd never heard of);

- Biff Hollingsworth and Chaitra Powell (who explained the workings of the library to me, sought access to people for me, and generally went above and beyond for me).

The nature of this book meant that I mined the depths of important and often underutilized local archives and collections, each of which was crucial for this research. At the Eastern Cabarrus Historical Society, where I spent many hours as a child cultivating my love of history, I have to thank Vickey Cline for giving me complete access to the museum's files as well as lots of local guidance. On the other side of the county, staff at the Cannon Memorial Library Local History Room gamely shared all the information they had and made the kind of excellent suggestions that only professionals immersed in a community's history can. Melissa Lindberg at the Library of Congress Prints and Photographs Division was also exceptionally helpful.

While in graduate school at UNC, I was fortunate to be in a department that was immensely supportive of its graduate students. From the American Studies and History Departments, I assembled an enviable (and overly large) dissertation committee: Bernie Herman, Fitz Brundage, Claude Clegg, Sharon Holland, Seth Kotch, and Patricia Sawin. They spent my entire defense probing one half of a single chapter. That kernel has become this book, and I'm grateful to each of them for recognizing its significance before I did.

Seth Kotch and I embarked on the study of lynching together, and I remain grateful for his guidance and collegiality. Bobby Allen is and has been my best professional mentor. He hasn't read a word of this book, but his influence is everywhere in it. And while I have strayed far from the worlds of early America and contemporary art in which Bernie Herman spends so much time, it is his teaching, his methodologies, and his words that I come back to as a model time and time again. His fingerprints are all over this manuscript, as are his many admonitions. Bernie, I hope I have not lost sight of the objects.

At Auburn University, I have been lucky to be surrounded by one of the most formidable assemblies of southern historians anywhere, and a wide range of colleagues who study places distant in time and space, but in ways that have influenced my own thinking. I am often hesitant to share my writing, but it was enriched greatly by the thoughts of Kate Craig, Xaq Frohlich, Jason Hauser, Guy Mount, Daren Ray, Joel Webb, Diana West, and other members of the Junior Faculty Club. I owe each of them, and all my colleagues, a beer at The Hound and unlimited gratitude. I reserve particular thanks for Christopher Ferguson. Ferg encouraged my idea from its outset and was the first person to read a full draft of this manuscript.

I have also been favored with exceptional student colleagues. To the dozens of students at UNC, Auburn, Xavier, and Jackson State who have collaborated to collect data on lynching victims, I owe immeasurable thanks. At Auburn, many graduate student colleagues have conducted research and asked questions that deepened my insights.

I am grateful for the attention and feedback of audiences when I have presented this material. Colleagues at the American Studies Association, Vernacular Architecture Forum, Memory Studies Association, the Africana Studies Speaker Series at Auburn, and elsewhere were unstinting in both praise and criticism. I owe a particular debt of gratitude to Karen Bassi, Gretchen Henderson, and all of my cohort in the Museums: Humanities in the Public Sphere summer seminar sponsored by the National Endowment for the Humanities.

I have benefited tremendously from the good counsel and editorial prowess of a rotating group of colleagues who initially came together around a table to discuss our dissertations. Trista Porter and Steve Mandrevalis are original members of the group and have seen me through multiple projects and papers. Rachel Kirby, Karen Sieber, and Josh Parshall are later but no less valuable additions. Thanks for letting me monopolize our discussions for years, and for your sharp critiques.

At Cambridge University Press, series editors Mark M. Smith and Peter Coclanis were enthusiastic and responsive. My editor, Cecelia Cancellaro, was both helpful and patient in guiding a first-time author through the process of publication.

I have been able to complete this book because of time afforded me to do so. I had two semesters of leave from teaching, one from my department and one from the College of Liberal Arts at Auburn. This was an essential, generative time for which I am grateful. But I also realize that time to do the work of scholarship is precious in an increasingly market-driven profession.

I marvel alike at those colleagues working in academic precarity who nonetheless manage to produce new research, and at those for whom the demands of teaching or other employment don't allow them to pursue their research projects.

Finally, Andrea. You have never known me without this uncompleted book looming over my shoulder. Now that it is through, may I be as generous a partner and as fierce an advocate as you are.

Introduction

Fragments

Joe Kizer and Tom Johnson were lynched on May 29, 1898. To the extent that we know anything definitive about the event, it is through the fragmentary and circumstantial accounts of the people who murdered them, and those who sympathized with this mob. The same absence masks our understanding of their lives. As is the case with so many other racial terror lynchings, historical evidence offers us only passing insight. Through the lens of history, we can understand how they came to be accused, murdered, and transformed into cautionary tales against Black criminality. Through the auspices of historical scholarship, we might begin to regard them as victims of a profoundly unjust system that reached its nadir at this liminal moment between the end of slavery and the full-scale implementation of Jim Crow apartheid. Both offer us incomplete narratives.

Still, the outline of their story, or at least its ending, is a familiar one. Johnson and Kizer were Black men, working as laborers and living around Concord, North Carolina. Later accounts would hint that the men were lawless, former convicts or at least dishonest. But prior to 1898, they were absent from the official records not just of arrest but of habitation or employment.[1] This is hardly unexpected: Ordinary Black folks rarely bore

---

[1] Almost certainly these characterizations were justifying fictions. A few days after the lynching, one article reported that "Kizer bore a bad reputation. He ran away from Union county with another woman, leaving a wife and three children. It is said that there were several indictments against him there. He came here last December. Johnston came here from Lincoln county and hauled coal for Mr. K.L. Craven last winter. He went to work for Mr. Bonds last March. He had, we learn, the mark of shackles on his ankles"; "A

I

Gruesome Looking Objects

either attention or held official interest without some suspicion of wrong-
doing. As a category, Johnson, Kizer, and countless other Black people
might be often remarked upon, but as individuals they undoubtedly
attracted only passing interest from official chroniclers of their day. Perhaps they eluded much of this attention by design, or maybe it was solely
the product of official disinterest. But as with so many other victims of
lynching, white scrutiny eventually bore down upon them. That attention
came to them by force late in the afternoon of May 29. Thirteen-year-old
Emma Hartsell was discovered by her parents when they returned from
church. She had been sexually assaulted and murdered.

With characteristic speed, Kizer and Johnson were accused. In the
late afternoon, Joe Kizer was apparently headed to town to report the
crime. This caused his employer to become suspicious, uncertain of how
he came to possess knowledge of the incident. The employer held Kizer
and summoned the police.[2] Tom Johnson was detained by a mob of citizens around the same time, though the undoubtedly paltry evidence that
justified his capture with went unreported. The twin posses that helped
capture both of them followed the men into town and remained outside
the jail, "a howling mob" for the next several hours.[3] Sometime between
their arrival at the jail around 8:00, and a bit before 10:00 p.m., the
mob found their way into the prison.[4] As was commonplace in lynchings,
newspaper reports stressed the resistance of the police and jailers, even
reporting the minor injuries that they suffered in their would-be defense.
Using hammer and chisel, the mob broke eight locks, tied ropes around
the men's necks, and proceeded out of town.[5]

Horrible Crime," *The Concord Times*, June 2, 1898. There were other bizarre and seemingly unfounded theories, like the notion that Tom Johnson was actually an alias for
another man wanted on various charges: "Was it Joe Williams?" *Daily Concord Standard*, June 20, 1898. This kind of idle speculation and justification also served to prolong
the story and, presumably, sell more newspapers.
[2] "Judge Lynch at Cabarrus," *Lexington Dispatch*, June 1, 1898.
[3] "A Day of Tragedy," *Daily Concord Standard*, May 30, 1898.
[4] "Cabarrus' Day of Tragedy," *Daily Concord Standard*, May 30, 1898.
[5] In his cultural history of the noose, Jack Shuler notes the difficulty of tying the knot properly, which leads to the supposition that most lynchings would not have had a noose but
rather some approximation of it. This matters in part because it allows us to see the technological competencies of the crowd and to inhabit, however provisionally, their actions
and decisions. I am not dedicating a chapter of this book to the rope or the (likely ersatz)
noose that hanged the men. But as Shuler's example demonstrates, that could well be a
productive area of inquiry in many other lynchings: Jack Shuler, *The Thirteenth Turn: A
History of the Noose* (New York: Public Affairs, 2014).

Joining in the mob were at least two doctors, a minister, and a reporter who documented each step in forensic detail. Once the mob was out of the town proper, they turned by Cold Water Lutheran Church and sought out "a spot suitable for hanging."[6] Their site turned out to be a medium-sized dogwood, a curious choice in a forested area dotted with older growth and populated mostly with larger species of tree. The men were both hanged on the same tree at 10:44 p.m. The two attending doctors pronounced them dead ten minutes later.[7]

Hewing closely to the rituals of lynching, the mob "riddled" the men's bodies with bullets. Those present in the mob, by some calculations up to 2,000 people, had first share of the lynching souvenirs. They took scraps of clothing from the bodies of the men, stripped a cap from Kizer's head, cut pieces from Johnson's brand new suspenders. Other mobs came the next day to share in the ongoing spectacle. They took more keepsakes from Kizer's and Johnson's bodies, stripped branches from the tree, used their penknives to cut off pieces of rope. The dead men were left hanging for a full day before, by routine, the Cabarrus County coroner pronounced them dead from the hands of unknown persons and ordered them buried. No kin or friends came forward to claim the bodies. Joe Kizer and Tom Johnson were buried by two other Black men pressed into service from the chain gang. Charles Barnhart and Ed Williams were the last human hands to touch the two, whether out of obligation or impulse to help them to a final resting place. The men were buried at the county home with no permanent markers on their graves.[8]

But Kizer and Johnson, or at least the popular perceptions created around them, were not yet forgotten. Over the coming months, minor details of their deaths showed up in newspapers state wide. Often these were notes about another souvenir of their lynching being found, or a retrospective judgment about their character and criminality. In short order, the specifics of their lynching were translated into symbols of a larger white supremacist repudiation of Black life. Again, familiar.

[6] "A Day of Tragedy," *Daily Concord Standard.*
[7] "Judge Lynch at Cabarrus," *Lexington Dispatch.* I base the composition of the landscape on the consultation of period maps of Cabarrus County. Of particular use was a map of "Rural Delivery Routes, Cabarrus County, NC" (Washington, DC: Post Office Department, 1921), in the North Carolina Collection, Louis Round Wilson Special Collections Library, University of North Carolina at Chapel Hill, and "Soil map, North Carolina, Cabarrus County Sheet" (Washington, DC: United States Department of Agriculture, Bureau of Soils, 1910), in the collection of the author.
[8] "The Lynched Negroes Buried," *Charlotte Observer*, June 1, 1898; "It's All Over," *Daily Concord Standard*, May 31, 1898.

In November, Emma Hartsell's father wrote a short letter linking their lynching to the cause of white supremacy and the repudiation of Fusion politics. As increasingly more symbolic cultural forms, the imagined figures of Kizer and Johnson showed up in songs and stories, serving as periodic invocations of white nostalgia. Undoubtedly too these memories were invoked on the other side of the color line. There Johnson and Kizer might have served as warning signs and reminders of the brutal savagery underneath the surface of the more quotidian racism of the later Jim Crow years. The stories and objects from their lynching remained a part of everyday life for the better part of a century, even if the men themselves were mostly forgotten.

The result of this speculation was a fragmentary narrative. What we know about Kizer and Johnson comes largely through the lens of their lynching, and from written records that trafficked in stereotype and innuendo. As with the majority of the thousands of victims of racial terror, we know little more than their names and supposed crimes. For many others, we have even less information. The work of historians and sociologists in the past twenty-five years has given us an abstract portrait of both lynching victims and mob members. This has been one way to address the paucity of evidence and the lack of surety: to reconstruct a collective identity through the pieces of evidence that we do have.[9]

Still, these are portrayals and interpretations marked largely by absence. At the center of such reconstructions is the gaping hole of the

---

[9] The historical scholarship on lynching particularly is classifiable through the rough categorizations of aggregate characterizations of lynching and more focused studies of specific elements of lynching. Historians and sociologists have made particular strides in recreating the historical conditions of lynching and of lynching victims. Especially useful for the former approach are W. Fitzhugh Brundage, *Lynching in the New South: Georgia and Virginia, 1880–1930* (Champaign: University of Illinois Press, 1993) and Michael J. Pfeifer, *Rough Justice: Lynching and American Society, 1874–1947* (Champaign: University of Illinois Press, 2004). Likewise historical sociologists have been particularly focused on the documentation and characterization of historical victims of lynching. The most comprehensive of these studies is Amy Kate Bailey and Stewart E. Tolnay, *Lynched: The Victims of Southern Mob Violence* (Chapel Hill: University of North Carolina Press, 2015), which offers a collective, demographic characterization of the Black men killed by lynch mobs. This book follows more closely in the vein of interdisciplinary works in American and African American Studies on the culture of lynching. See Ashraf H. A. Rushdy, *The End of American Lynching* (New Brunswick, NJ: Rutgers University Press, 2012); Jacqueline Goldsby, *A Spectacular Secret: Lynching in American Life and Literature* (Chicago: University of Chicago Press, 2006); Amy Louise Wood, *Lynching and Spectacle: Witnessing Racial Violence in America, 1890–1940* (Chapel Hill: University of North Carolina Press, 2009).

particular, the lack of specificity that in some ways reifies the obliterating violences done by the practice of lynching. Scholars have been far too fixed on interpretation and comprehension of events that were, if not singular, marked by their own neatly formulaic narratives in the form of a structuring violence. Lynchings were and are meant as events that create their own context and build their own historicity. To think that we can begin to comprehend them through narrative, even counternarrative, is to accept both their obliterative logic and their own creation of an historical context. Lynchings were never self-contained events – but they aspired to be. Part of the violence of a lynching was epistemic. Its ritual pageantry, routinized narratives, and other ties to the logics of white supremacy made each lynching a paradoxical event at once particular and part of a larger framework. In turn, these logics inform both the very information that scholars have access to and the means by which we shape our narratives. We have to resist these contemporaneous efforts at record keeping and historical creation and look at lynchings in light of the larger conceptual, material worlds from which they sprang.

I propose that we seek to understand lynching through a praxis of fragmentation. In *Gruesome Looking Objects*, I consider the things associated with the lynching of Tom Johnson and Joe Kizer and the stories attached to them. These objects and object narratives offer multiple, sometimes conflicting ways of understanding lynching both in their contemporaneous context and in the wake of memory during the many years afterward. This is an approach rooted in the methodologies of material culture, a close study of objects extant and destroyed, real and imagined. This method is both a narrative and a material fragmentation: the remains of *things* and of stories that were constructed as complete explanations of the lynching. In *Gruesome Looking Objects*, I will examine objects and object narratives not as a means of pulling together a comprehensible whole out of a fragmented past, but in order to mark particular moments of emphasis. In part, this is reflective of the constellations of meanings that form around objects. As I discuss later in this Introduction, objects cycle in and out of both our notice and their own meaning. But this is also a gesture to resist the narrative wholeness of the lynching and to reflect on the absence of humanity at its core.

ASSEMBLING A FRAGMENTED NARRATIVE

The previous pages outlined the conventional narrative of the lynching of Tom Johnson and Joe Kizer. I use the label "conventional" in two particular senses. It is conventional both in the immediate context of the history of this lynching, and in the context of lynchings more generally. This particular narrative was assembled primarily from dozens of newspaper accounts. These many individual scraps of information though are in reality rearticulations of three major narratives whose details and claims emerged in the immediate aftermath of the lynching. Oral narratives based largely on rumor, innuendo, and stereotype were transformed into fact through their reproduction into print. With each reprinting, they further reified the assumptions of the original articles, and helped make a fixed narrative of the lynching that remained in effect for a century. In this sense, there has been a conventionalized narrative of the lynching that helped dictate local and regional understanding of the events for more than one hundred years. I seek to undermine those conventions by pointing to their origins and dissemination as part of the larger cultural logic of lynching.[10]

By conventional, I also refer to broader conventions of reporting and other narrative retellings of lynching events. The outline of Johnson and Kizer's lynching followed a familiar pattern, both in the way events unfolded and in the way the lynching was talked, written, and thought about. From the initial and grisly reports of a white girl's assault and murder through the abduction, capture, hanging, and ritual defilement of the men's bodies, mob members and readers alike could follow a familiar pattern. As with other lynchings, they made sense of Johnson and Kizer's murders from their cultural knowledge of the existing conventions of crime, punishment, and race that constituted the usual facts of lynching. For all the local particularities of this or any other lynching, it was through this reciprocal process that lynchings were made comprehensible.

This had significant implications for the material culture of Kizer and Johnson's lynching particularly in the years after its commission. White people understood the lynching through the frame of their own experience, one largely mediated by the objects related to it. Johnson and Kizer became mere Black victims, ciphers through which the ordinary processes of the lynching could be projected. Objects came into particular focus during this process of sensemaking. Material forms of information established the conventional narratives of the lynching. In newspaper articles, letters, published circulars, handbills, and other forms of public communication, these conventions circulated throughout North Carolina and well beyond, adding to the accumulated epistemological frameworks of white supremacy reinforced by racial violence.

[10] Goldsby, *A Spectacular Secret*.

People also kept more direct remainders of participation in the lynching. Souvenirs and relics allowed them to place themselves squarely at the lynching, either in memory or in imagination. The retellings that these objects enabled allowed their possessors to center themselves as the subjects of the lynching narrative. Their tales of daring acquisition or routine purchase enforced their role not just as spectators, but as participants. And what I call objects of imagination and memory, ordinary objects transformed into conceptualizing things, allowed people to continue remaking the lynching's legacy. Broader than just objects of memory, these conceptual things normalized the lynching by embedding its meaning in everyday objects. A ballad written, sung, and eventually recorded made the lynching of Kizer and Johnson into a tale of heroism and evil. Mediated through a familiar form and melody, it helped preserve those heroic actions and mythic qualities as a marker of southern authenticity. Tools repurposed from the routines of everyday life and labor were likewise reimagined into avenging weapons. These most quotidian things became mythic symbols in the outsized narratives of the lynching over time.

Throughout *Gruesome Looking Objects*, I turn to each of these categories of object, seeking to unravel one fragment after another of the otherwise neatly woven narrative of Tom Johnson and Joe Kizer's lynching. In a sense, the remainder of this book is an unraveling. The metaphor of textile and production is particularly fitting here. A finished shirt or quilt offers a cohesive whole. But if we pick at the seams, pop the stitches, pull apart the layers, we can see the pieces out of which it is composed. There is an obvious analogy here to the work of historical production. It is less that the appearance of the neat whole is a falsity, and more that the illusion of completeness conceals other ways of understanding. This is why I invoke fragments not solely as parts of a larger whole, but as things themselves.

FRAGMENT AS METHOD

It is always the case that our understanding of the past rests in the fragments of testimony that we can uncover about it. For scholars of material culture, this is particularly true. The basis of our field has been the assumption that objects can reveal pasts otherwise untold. We turn to objects to interpret the lives of people who lived before literacy as we now understand it, who existed without the benefit of means to communicate about their own lives, or who otherwise remain silent in the annals of what we confidently call the historical record. Enslaved people, women, the working classes, all come to be understood in part through the material remains they left behind, the enduring detritus of everyday life.[11]

I hold less faith in objects. This is not because they are a less comprehensive source than written records. Material culture carries different omissions and requires different approaches than the textual sources that are the conventionally assumed basis of historical understanding. My distrust is a distrust of the possibility of our knowing with any degree of certitude about the past, and about the inadequacies of narrative to make the past comprehensible. In this book, then, I use an approach to *materiality* – the objects themselves and their array of cultural explanations and understandings – as a way to tentatively approach the past.[12] This reconstructed materiality is useful in that objects do not just give us evidence of how the world was, but serve too as reminders of how people wanted or imagined the world to be. People did things with words, but they made them with objects.[13]

Objects, and the framework of materiality by which we understand them, are always unstable. This is because they do not remain in one

---

[11] A myriad of examples abound for each of the categories of inquiry, and a great many others, that I offer here. Excellent examples include Bernard L. Herman. *Town House: Architecture and Material Life in the Early American City, 1780–1830* (Chapel Hill: Published for the Omohundro Institute of Early American History and Culture, Williamsburg, Virginia, by the University of North Carolina Press, 2005); J. Ritchie Garrison. *Landscape and Material Life in Franklin County, Massachusetts, 1770–1860* (Knoxville: University of Tennessee Press, 1991); Laurel Thatcher Ulrich, *The Age of Homespun: Objects and Stories in the Creation of an American Myth* (New York: Alfred A. Knopf, 2001); Leland Ferguson, *Uncommon Ground: Archaeology and Early African America, 1650–1800.* (Washington, DC: Smithsonian Institution Press, 1992); Zara Anishanslin, *Portrait of a Woman in Silk: Hidden Histories of the British Atlantic World* (New Haven: Yale University Press, 2016).
In general, historical material culture studies in the American context have most often taken Early America as their subject. I would argue that this reflects an assumption that material objects are less necessary when the written records become more extensive and inclusive of a greater number of people. I disagree with this assumption. Indeed, if scholars of historical material culture are to continue insisting on its methodological distinctiveness, this means extending its scope of inquiry into areas sometimes characterized by an abundance of other source material.

[12] On the concept of materiality, see Daniel Miller, "Materiality: An Introduction," in *Materiality*, ed. Daniel Miller (Durham, NC: Duke University Press, 2005), 1–15. I am also relying here on the work of Bernard L. Herman, who distinguishes between object-centered and object-driven approaches to material culture. The former is perhaps the more familiar, documentary approach that centers a close examination of the object itself. I more often use the object-driven approach in this book, looking to the constellations of meaning and the material worlds created by objects and the perception of them. See Bernard L. Herman, "On Southern Things," *Southern Cultures* 23, no. 3 (2017): 7–13.

[13] I am invoking here the performative vocabularies theorized in J. L. Austin, *How to Do Things with Words* (Cambridge, MA: Harvard University Press, 1962).

place or in the hands of one person, but have multiple meanings as they are imagined, created, inherited, donated, destroyed. The classical approach to this problem in material culture studies was formulated by Igor Kopytoff, who conceptualized the lifecycles of commodities. His "Cultural Biography of Things" regarded materiality as processual, a constant making and unmaking of objects in the marketplace of commodities. This Marxian formulation is comprehensive, though it fails to account for the object's tendency to exceed its designed intention and accrue other meanings.[14] To rethink again the lifecycles of objects is to consider what happens to them as their purpose exceeds the memory of those who created and possessed them. Even the most ordinary objects are palimpsests that retain some trace of each of their prior meanings, and each of their prior owners or users.[15] This is particularly the case with the fraught objects associated with lynchings. Some are so evidently associated with the event that it is impossible for them to lose the original force of their meaning. Visual remainders of racial violence – postcards and photographs – are the most obvious example of this enduring materiality. I am concerned here with more ordinary things, those objects that could pass into the everyday and the mundane, that could become objects of both memory and forgetting.

For this, we have to turn to an approach rooted in the fragmented and incomplete. Among any number of other possible organizing metaphors, this one stands out for its ability to express the condition both of many objects themselves, and of the narratives attached to them. My dual concern here then for both object and object narratives is best expressed in the material fragments of things and the snatches of story that attach to them. By advancing this notion of the fragmentary and fragmented as an approach to history, I am consciously invoking the silences inherent in the production of the past. Michel-Rolph Trouillot reminds us that history has a material basis, but it is the selection, preservation, archiving, and retrieval of the archived object that create History. Narratives accrue at each of these points, making the unitary narrative of the historian

---

[14] Igor Kopytoff, "The Cultural Biography of Things: Commoditization as Process," in *The Social Life of Things: Commodities in Cultural Perspective*, ed. Arjun Appadurai (Cambridge, UK: Cambridge University Press, 1986), 64–92. On the tendency of objects to exceed or otherwise depart from their original, designed function, see Judy Attfield, *Wild Things: The Material Culture of Everyday Life* (Oxford: Berg, 2000).

[15] Susan Stabile, "Biography of a Box: Material Culture and Palimpsest Memory," in *Memory and History*, ed. Joan Tumblety (London: Routledge, 2013), 194–211.

simply another among the accreted fragments of comprehensibility.[16] That makes the process of writing the past seem impossible or pointless, a position I have surely inhabited at times during the writing of this book. But in the later chapters of *Silencing the Past*, Trouillot offers us a way forward. He writes of the three overlapping Sans Soucis, unpacking their various iterations and the meanings that they lent to each other. In this he conceptualizes history as always a product of the moment in which it is written. As creators of the past, we are its contemporaries. Or, as William Faulkner has it, "the past is never dead. It isn't even past."[17]

Following Trouillot, then, we might conceptualize the distinctions between memory and history as a continuum for envisioning the past. American historical scholarship of the past two decades has complicated those boundaries with complex studies of historical memory.[18] I only diverge from that body of work in insisting that we go back to Trouillot's refusal of the distinctions between history and memory. I prefer instead to see the entanglements of history and memory as part of the production of a complicated, unresolved, and incomplete past always in the process of becoming. Particularly useful in this regard are Saidiya Hartman's meditations on the work we can do with "the scraps of the archive," the small pieces of the past preserved largely by accident. Her notion of critical fabulation is one that shows us how to enliven these fragments, to work at the intersections of fiction and history that are always, as Trouillot reminds us, transgressable boundaries.[19]

But Hartman also cautions us against uncritically giving voice to the specters of history without considering the ramifications of the past in the present. Her own approach has been to resist the re-creation of the horrors of the past to instead find the sublimated pleasure amid history's erasures. And other scholarship on the archive reminds us that its

---

[16] Michel-Rolph Trouillot, *Silencing the Past: Power and the Production of History* (Boston: Beacon Press, 1995), 26–30.

[17] This quotation, invoked often as a truism bordering on cliché in southern studies, originally appears in Faulkner's *Requiem for a Nun*.

[18] This historiographical trend has been particularly rich in studies related to the South and to the American Civil War. See for instance Caroline E. Janney, *Remembering the Civil War: Reunion and the Limits of Reconciliation* (Chapel Hill: University of North Carolina Press, 2013); David W. Blight, *Race and Reunion: The Civil War in American Memory* (Cambridge, MA: Harvard University Press, 2002); Karen L. Cox, *Dixie's Daughters: The United Daughters of the Confederacy and the Preservation of Confederate Culture* (Gainesville: University Press of Florida, 2003); W. Fitzhugh Brundage, *The Southern Past: A Clash of Race and Memory* (Cambridge, MA: Belknap Press, 2005).

[19] Saidiya Hartman, "Venus in Two Acts," *Small Axe*, no. 2 (July 2008): 4.

depths often hold not just sublimated voices, but the sublimated horrors of trauma.[20] When we write about lynching, even more than other historical subjects, we reify the subject position of those who were able to tell stories and form histories. In the case of lynching, it is the lynch mob whose most detailed justifications are embedded in the objects and object narratives produced around a lynching.[21] We can push against these origins and read sources against the grain, but I have more in mind here the approach of Ann Laura Stoler who reads "along the archival grain."[22] This approach treats the accumulation of historical objects as a process that offers insight into the structuring logics of a system. Stoler unpacks colonial formations; I will look at the various systems of white supremacy that arose to justify lynching.[23]

Accordingly, *Gruesome Looking Objects* seeks to examine the conditions of the creation and circulation of objects. Through considering objects related to the lynching of Kizer and Johnson, I hope to reconstruct

---

[20] In addition to Saidiya Hartman, both in "Venus in Two Acts" and *Scenes of Subjection: Terror, Slavery, and Self Making in Nineteenth Century America* (New York; Oxford: Oxford University Press, 1997), I am thinking here particularly of the work of Ann Cvetkovich. Cvetkovich invites us to see the archives of trauma as ones that connect the ordinary horrors of life to larger world events. This approach clearly accords with the victims of lynching; Ann Cvetkovich, *An Archive of Feelings: Trauma, Sexuality, and Lesbian Public Cultures* (Durham, NC: Duke University Press, 2003). See also Marisa J. Fuentes, *Dispossessed Lives: Enslaved Women, Violence, and the Archive* (Philadelphia: University of Pennsylvania Press, 2016).

[21] Kidada Williams has been prominent in renewing the calls of early anti-lynching activists to measure lynchings' impact as familial and multigenerational. See Kidada E. Williams, "Regarding the Aftermaths of Lynching," *Journal of American History* 101, no. 3 (2014): 856–858; Kidada E. Williams, "Writing Victims' Personhoods and People into the History of Lynching," *Journal of the Gilded Age and Progressive Era*, 20 (2021): 148–156. https://doi.org/10.1017/S1537781420000584. Quantitative sociologists have also helpfully looked at the material legacies of racial violence, establishing causal links between lynching and, among other ills, homicide and corporal punishment in schools: Geoff Ward and Nick Petersen, "The Transmission of Historical Racial Violence: Lynching, Civil Rights Era Terror, and Contemporary Interracial Homicide," *Race and Justice: An International Journal* 5, no. 2 (2015): 114–143; Geoff Ward, Nick Petersen, Aaron Kupchik, and James Pratt, "Historic Lynching and Corporal Punishment in Contemporary Southern Schools," *Social Problems*, 68, no. 1 (2021): 41–62. https://doi.org/10.1093/socpro/spz044.

[22] Ann Laura Stoler, *Along the Archival Grain: Epistemic Anxieties and Colonial Common Sense* (Princeton: Princeton University Press, 2009).

[23] We might refer to these as white supremacies as a reflection of the changes over time in what often gets portrayed as a unitary ideology. Such an attempt to historicize white supremacy needs to acknowledge the consistencies of its core ideological principle, while also detailing the many uses to which it has been put and changes in its particular articulations.

the constellations of meaning around objects used in the imagination, commission, preservation, and overall comprehension of their lynching. In this approach, I embrace the incomplete view that such fragments might give us. Each of the chapters in this book is centered on one object that was used in the commission, circulation, or memory of the lynching. This necessarily implies an expanded temporal and geographic frame of lynching that moves our understanding of the event itself beyond the few minutes or hours of torture and death and toward a more systematic comprehension of the act of lynching.[24] Lynching was only the most spectacular expression of a pervasive white supremacist culture always poised to erupt into violence. This book views the lynching of Tom Johnson and Joe Kizer within that expanded frame in both time and space. Objects help us bridge that gap. While their meaning, and even their physical form, might change over time, they have an enduring presence. Each object biography in this book then is an attempt to capture the portrait of an evolving thing, anchored always in the structuring violence from which it arose.

VARIETIES OF OBJECTS

The following chapters outline this fragmented and fractured history of the lynching of Joe Kizer and Tom Johnson. In a series of object biographies, I seek at once to undermine the conventional narrative of lynching and to look at the ways it was represented and understood in the worlds of its creation. This work is divided into three sections. Each is based on particular categories of object, rather than strict chronology. This reflects both the evolutions and overlaps in meaning inherent in each of these

---

[24] Several scholars of lynching are useful in formulations of this expanded notion of lynching. Goldsby writes about the expansive "cultural logics" of lynching as it was expressed in textual materials and disseminated across the country. For her lynching then is dependent on these cultural productions for much of its meaning: Goldsby, *A Spectacular Secret*. Ashraf Rushdy also details a larger geographic footprint for lynching as an act, though not for individual lynchings. The complicity model that he outlines in *The End of American Lynching* also implies a wider and shared responsibility for the lynching. See Ashraf H. A. Rushdy, *American Lynching* (New Haven: Yale University Press, 2012). I am using a slightly different expanded definition of lynching, whereby we can understand it as a practice that unfolded in multiple places (the site of the alleged crime, the site of the abduction, the site of the hanging, shooting, or other form of murder) and over a longer period of time (the days afterward when souvenir seekers came to view lynched bodies, the months of speculation and news after, the memory work of preserving explanations in the many years after).

objects, as well as their continued circulation, inheritance, and repurposing over time and across space.

The first section consists of studies of what I call "circulating objects." Here I attend to conventional historical sources through a material culture lens. I first look at the production and circulation of newspaper articles in greater depth in Chapter 1, appropriately named "The Article." This chapter puts the material production of lynching narratives into the contexts of both newsprint and changing notions of regional and national space. Chapter 2, "The Letter," picks up this topic, looking in more depth at the public texts written through the landscape of North Carolina in 1898. Using a public letter signed by Emma Hartsell's father, I conceptualize the larger visual and print cultures that helped people to envision and implement spatial white supremacy.

The following two chapters examine the making of souvenirs and mementos. They focus on the ways in which souvenirs from the lynching of Johnson and Kizer were transformed into symbols and talismans of community memory. Chapters 3 and 4 look at "The Clothes" of Johnson and Kizer and "The Tree" from which they were hanged. Chapter 3 details the frenzy to look for and collect scraps of the men's clothing. As one of the most tangible and direct remnants of the lynching, clothing offered a ready aid to memory. As a substitute for the bodies of the two men, it served as a talisman and gruesome fetish object through which collectors could project their fantasies about the bodies of Black men. In both of these purposes, it was a reliquary object, a remainder and reminder of death and the body. Chapter 4 focuses on the pieces of the dogwood tree preserved by local collectors, and places them within the souvenir culture of the era. This new commercialism saw deeply embedded symbols like the dogwood, long a marker of religious belief, white supremacy, and folk wisdom, turned into regional keepsakes. The long-term uses of the dogwood tree that Johnson and Kizer were lynched on illustrate this passage from reliquary to souvenir collecting cultures, and the commercialization of racial violence.

But the things of the lynching were never merely items on a shelf. In the evolving definitions of Johnson's and Kizer's murders, people used objects to conceptualize, imagine, and remember their meanings. The objects at the center of Chapter 5, "The Hammer and Chisel," were used by the mob to pry open the jail cell of Johnson and Kizer. Their forcible entry to the men's cell took advantage of their familiarity with commonplace tools of everyday life, and at the same time exposed the tensions behind the changing meaning of work in their community.

Nearly simultaneous with this lynching was the opening of the South's first African American owned and operated textile mill. Warren C. Coleman's Concord mill marked a break in a county that had been staunchly agricultural for the previous two centuries and exposed pervasive fears at the prospect of Black equality through the auspices of industrial labor. This chapter focuses on these tools as objects of work that invoked this newly imagined rift at the intersections of race, class, and labor. Those currents of thought are evoked again in Chapter 6, "The Song." This chapter centers on a lynching ballad written in the wake of Kizer's and Johnson's murders and recorded as part of the 1960s folk revival. The single of this song ("The Death of Emma Hartsell") again reimagined the lynching, this time as a marker of personal and regional authenticity for its young, revivalist audience. Paradoxically, as the song's material and performative contexts expanded, they served only to fix an increasingly restricted version of the lynching and its meaning to white audiences, who continued to revel in the materialized emotions of the ballad while ignoring its role in the promotion of racial violence.

I conclude the book by again broadening the lens of inquiry to "Archival Remains" of lynching objects. After following the material and conceptual circulations of these objects for well over a century, I look at their translation into objects of history within archival and museum collections. This final chapter regards these newly institutionalized forms of material knowledge and holds in tension the necessity to document and contextualize the histories of racist violence and the potential that this new placement only serves to recast and legitimate a century's worth of prurient interest into academic inquiry.

I conclude then with a look into the present, and by extension the future. Historical practice is a reminder of the enduring presence of the material worlds I have begun to outline here. One of the main points of this Introduction has been the omnipresence of the material past in our experience of the present. History allows for influence but also continuity. We are contemporaries of the past in both our constant creation of it, and our seeming inability to escape its re-creation. This fact has been made all too clear during the process of my writing this book. The grisly visuals of public spectacle murders of Black people remain omnipresent. Another version of the conventions of narrative that I discussed earlier has been replayed in recent years. One spectacle killing bleeds into another, their details collapsing, and our attention and energy waning when confronted with not just an individual death, but an overwhelming system of deaths. Activists remind us to resist that obliteration with their insistence on a memorial and historical practice of profound power: the articulation of names. Spoken aloud and in common names become almost material, collective evocations of a presence in the face of an absence. And there are other material expressions not just of mourning but of history making: the painting of murals, the pulling down of racist statues. When we enter the names of some of these victims into the historical record – Tom Johnson, Joe Kizer, but also Michael Brown, Sandra Bland, Ahmaud Aubrey, George Floyd, and so, so many others – we are beginning the painful process of writing a more complete past for a different future. Slowly, we are beginning to unmake the world made by lynching.

I

The Article

In his tent city barracks around Jacksonville, Florida, Harry P. Deaton waited for news of home.[1] He and many of his fellow soldiers in Company L were Concordians. Young men away from North Carolina for the first time, these words anchored them to home, family, place. This was even truer as they prepared to fight further afield for the expansion of the American empire. Already, they were uncomfortable in their temporary home. Jacksonville seemed strange to them with its majority African American population, "some of whom are extremely wealthy and live in palatial residences."[2] Not much like home. In Concord, Deaton and his friends might see Black people daily, but would rarely find them residing "on some of the principal streets."[3] With the swagger of the newly enlisted, he assured his readers at home that "they are easily controlled, and the sight of a North Carolina soldier makes them shudder with fear."[4]

This linked bravado and longing for home were shored up by word from friends and family and the news they wrote back in turn. Deaton wrote on behalf of the whole Company to the local paper, sending their greetings to the larger reading community. In turn, they received news back from Cabarrus County in the form of letters, telegrams, and newspapers. More than other missives from home, it was the "news of the lynching of the two negroes last Sunday night" that he and his friends

[1] "Company 'L' Notes," *The Standard*, May 12, 1898.
[2] "Our Boys Vaccinated," *The Standard*, June 9, 1898.
[3] "Our Boys Vaccinated," *The Standard*.
[4] "Our Boys Vaccinated," *The Standard*.

particularly wanted.[5] Apparently, the broad outlines of the events had already arrived, maybe by telegram from the father of their commander, Captain Hill, back in Cabarrus.[6] But the prurient, gory details of the murders could hardly be conveyed in a few, short, expensive words. For Deaton "and at least one half the regiment," hundreds of men at least, the full accounting from "*The Standard* was in great demand."[7]

Deaton and his fellow soldiers were not alone in their interest. Nor were they the most distant group to consume one of the standard newspaper narratives of the lynching. Newspaper articles detailing Kizer and Johnson's lynching went throughout North Carolina, the rest of the South, and reached at least as far as Nebraska and Montana.[8] Indeed, broad consumption of this article speaks to many of the issues about the distribution of accounts of lynching. Newer technologies such as the electric telegram were clearly part of communicating the news of a lynching or potential lynching. Both those excited to invite friends to view the spectacle and those wishing to urge leaders to prevent it conveyed urgent messages via the telegram.[9]

In all likelihood, though, most news of a lynching or potential lynching spread from person to person. This oral transmission allowed for mobs to form and for people to communicate details of place, time, and occasion before, and in the wake of, a lynching. In this sense, the white communal ties underpinning much of the act were preserved and strengthened.[10] But

---

[5] "Our Boys Vaccinated," *The Standard*.

[6] "About Our Boys," *The Standard*, May 26, 1898.

[7] "About Our Boys," *The Standard*.

[8] "Hanged the Suspects," *The Nebraska State Journal*, May 30, 1898; "Outraged and Murdered," *The Butte Miner*, May 30, 1898.

[9] The expense of the telegram only added to its perceived urgency, particularly in cases where it might stop a lynching. By the 1890s, activists were frequently making use of the telegraph to demand action against a potential lynching. See for instance the 1894 telegram from the Anti-Lynching League of Chicago sent to Governor Hogg of Texas ("Texans Resent Chicago Meddling," *Chicago Tribune*, March 24, 1894). In a few instances, these telegrams were preserved in archival records, as is the case with those of activists Walter White and Jesse Daniel Ames who each wrote Governor Sholtz of Florida to protest the probable lynching of Claude Neal: Jessie Daniel Ames, "Telegram to Governor Sholtz," January 30, 1934, Florida Memory Collection, State Library and Archives of Florida; Walter White, "Telegram to Governor Sholtz," January 1934, Florida Memory Collection, State Library and Archives of Florida. Telegrams to and from individual citizens are even more scarce, though references to the practice of sending them abound. See for instance "Invitation Issued by Salt Lake Telegram to Lynching Bee," *Deseret News*, June 28, 1917.

[10] On the role of whiteness and lynching's impact on white communal ties, see Grace Elizabeth Hale, "Deadly Amusements: Spectacle Lynchings and the Contradictions of Segregation as a Culture," in her *Making Whiteness: The Culture of Segregation in the South, 1890–1940* (New York: Vintage, 1999), 199–240.

each of these forms of communication is ephemeral and difficult to track. The most consistent, detailed, and lasting means of news and understanding of a lynching came from newspaper articles, such as the clipping forwarded to the North Carolina soldiers in Florida.

These articles had a variety of narrative purposes, as the uses of *The Standard* account among the Florida soldiers suggest.[11] For the part of the regiment not from Concord or Cabarrus County, the article might have provided them their first knowledge of the lynching. For those locals who had already had the news communicated to them, it allowed them to absorb the details of the lynching in the frame of some of their most immediate and well-known references to place and home. All of its bloody details were juxtaposed against a backdrop of familiar landscapes, the nostalgia of young men longing for home perhaps deepening their appreciation for the story. Though they were just becoming acquainted with the specifics of the murders of Kizer and Johnson, both groups of soldiers were undoubtedly familiar with the contours of the broader narrative from the many other lynchings they had read about in similar newspaper clippings.

The standard conventions of reporting on lynchings were well established by the 1890s. Their repeated tropes and shopworn clichés suggested a readership eager for prurient details that mirrored the sensational tales of cheap fiction and grounded them in the real world.[12] So the news about Kizer and Johnson's lynching was distributed and received in a multimodal, overlapping network aimed at multiple audiences. It traversed first from person to person, then over the wires or via a reporter to a newspaper office, then from publisher to newsstand and doorstep. From there, its news might carry further via a clipping sent to family or friend, or a story recounted in great and specific detail to a neighbor who took the *Times* or the *Observer* and not the *Standard*. Read at home or shared in public, narratives of lynching could become material experiences, allowing people to engage with cultures of both print and nontransactional forms of object circulation. But in a larger sense, the narrative itself was already an object, and one that spanned across space

[11] Menahem Blondheim notes that the nineteenth century saw an expansion of the definition of news from merely the events themselves to the way that they were conveyed: *News over the Wires: The Telegraph and the Flow of Public Information in America, 1844–1897* (Cambridge, MA: Harvard University Press, 1994), 16.

[12] On the subject of both representation in and appeal of dime novels to working people, see Michael Denning, *Mechanic Accents: Dime Novels and Working-Class Culture in America* (London and New York: Verso, 1987).

in a newly connected world and nation. News of the Concord lynching reached into areas that had little frame of reference for the place itself, but that had a complex and complicated understanding of what a lynching was, what it meant, and what it did.

As with the soldiers of Company L, the article had different meanings for its multiple audiences. The very nature of news was changing.[13] For some, the news of Kizer's and Johnson's murders had a largely communicative function, overlaid with their knowledge of the narrative conventions of violence, murder, and excess.[14] For others, it added to the circle of intimate familiarity that a newspaper could cultivate, as with the Concord soldiers and their letters published in the local editions. Not just news, but news of a lynching, could make these connections between and among spaces. Its visceral descriptions and strident moralizing made common cause among geographically divergent white people easy. News of a lynching carried with it an implicit – and often explicit – message of warning for Black people that cautioned them away from the traumatic residue of both specific places and general communities. Its communicative power for white people was equally adept at building commonality and even community across spatial divides. News of a lynching, and particularly the newspaper articles that carried the centralized and standardized narrative of a mob murder, brought together places in a shared network of loathing and triumph, materialized in their circulations, and established a newly expanded network of places built on the violent assertion of a white supremacist spatial ideology. Lynching articles were material objects, but also things with material consequences. These materialized narratives helped define and prolong lynchings, allowing particular instances of racial violence to exist in broadened chronological and geographic frameworks. Such newspaper articles about lynching were at the center of broader material networks. These articles were not simply objects of culture, but things connected to new ways of comprehending and conquering regional and national spatial divides amid persistent local ties. The paradox of the lynching

---

[13] Gerald J. Baldasty, *The Commercialization of News in the Nineteenth Century* (Madison: University of Wisconsin Press, 1992), 8.

[14] On the larger culture of the sensational narrative and its relationship to cultures of violence and modernity, see Lisa Duggan, *Sapphic Slashers: Sex, Violence, and American Modernity* (Durham, NC: Duke University Press, 2000). For cultures of spectacle and violence in the southern United States more specifically, see Michael Ayers Trotti, *The Body in the Reservoir: Murder and Sensationalism in the South* (Chapel Hill: University of North Carolina Press, 2008).

article lay in the tensions between local particularities and standardized modes of production and dissemination. Lynchings were local in scope and brief in duration, but their temporal and geographic impact was far greater. To more fully comprehend how lynching was understood by those participating in the spread of information about it, we have to expand our view of how lynchings unfolded in both place and time.

This chapter thinks about newspaper articles as material cultural objects produced as part of a communicative network. That network taught readers both about individual lynchings and about the broader vocabulary and practices of lynching. Newspapers were not just modes of communication but also functioned as part of the larger networks of travel, transport, performance, and sociality that were remaking the meanings of place, space, and other elements of material culture in lives at the turn of the twentieth century. News of lynchings circulated throughout this network, becoming a commonplace feature of these newly networked lives. Racial violence, and news of it, was embedded in everyday life.

SPACE AND MATERIAL NETWORKS AT THE
END OF THE NINETEENTH CENTURY

The North Carolina mob that formed to lynch Tom Johnson and Joe Kizer lived in a world under transition. Cabarrus was representative of other small places still inheriting the spatial, social, and technological transformations of the last half of the nineteenth century. These were in tension with, and sometimes replacing, the older traditions of oral communication and community cohesion based on proximity. More than simply narrative accounts, these articles were part of a broader communicative network that were, in Jacqueline Goldsby's words, "vital means through which Americans encountered lynching's violence and labored to make sense of its meanings."[15] They were central pieces of larger print and visual cultures that allow us to regard lynching, as a "networked, systemic phenomenon." To build on Goldsby's insights, we might ask what material infrastructures underpinned lynching's pervasive and invasive cultural logic.[16] In other words, what were the systems and networks that allowed lynching to become such a persistent cultural and social fact

---

[15] Goldsby, *A Spectacular Secret*, 33.
[16] Goldsby, *A Spectacular Secret*, 5.

beginning in the last years of the nineteenth century? By looking at the production and circulation of information around Johnson and Kizer's lynching, we can see how embedded lynching became in material life at the turn of the century.

The spatial networks of late nineteenth-century America had their origin in earlier attempts to communicate information across the expanses of region and nation. Most immediately, this trend began with an expanded postal service in the antebellum and immediate postbellum years. The post office went from a little used and inefficient national entity in the early Republic to a network that, by 1870, "linked distant individuals in a web of regular exchanges ... tethering them to networks of institutional power."[17] This growth was important in connecting the expanding nation whose borders were subject to frequent expansions and protracted definitional, logistical, and political arguments.[18] The postal service made people aware of others in the rest of the country with whom they might have little or no physical contact. But it also habituated individuals to the notion of a network.[19] These connecting networks were abstractions, but one that Americans understood through the material practices of writing, addressing, sending, and receiving word from afar.

This radical change was made even more commonplace by the spread of the telegraph and the news wire service. The telegraph and telegram allowed for near-instantaneous communication between individuals.[20] Further, they necessitated the establishment of "the scaling up of contrivances into the spatially extensive and temporally intensive communications networks that have become a hallmark of modernity."[21] The speed of this practice was undercut only by its cost meaning that most people used it only infrequently. Still, it became a technology of everyday life. The more common point of access for this new technology was news communicated over the wire. Though readers may have not paid much attention to the source and mechanism of this spread, they certainly experienced it as part of a national expansion that began in

[17] David M. Henkin, *The Postal Age: The Emergence of Modern Communications in Nineteenth-Century America* (Chicago: University of Chicago Press, 2006), ix.

[18] James C. Cobb, *Away Down South: A History of Southern Identity* (New York: Oxford University Press, 2005).

[19] Henkin, *The Postal Age*, 5.

[20] Roland Wenzlhuemer, *Connecting the Nineteenth-Century World: The Telegraph and Globalization* (Cambridge and New York: Cambridge University Press, 2013), 7.

[21] Richard R. John, *Network Nation: Inventing American Telecommunications* (Cambridge, MA: Belknap Press of Harvard University Press, 2010), 1.

the 1850s, intensified in the immediate aftermath of the Civil War, and reached its peak in the emergence of the Associated Press by the late 1890s.[22] As the media historian Menahem Blondheim notes, "the telegraph line ... promoted equality of knowledge across space."[23]

These technologies of transmission meant that more people got access to uniform news. This was true even as the amount and variety that could be carried across a single line lessened. There was, if not a narrative uniformity of information, at least a significant increase in local stories gone national or even international. Local interests, political or otherwise, no longer needed to prevail in the rush to create a paper of universal content designed for any audience, any reader.[24] As spatial historian Cameron Blevins notes, this approach brought about a "fragmentation of both form and content that changed how a paper ... produced local and regional space."[25] Newspapers, telegraph wires and a better postal service all changed the perception of space among late nineteenth- and early twentieth-century Americans. So too did other physical infrastructures, such as sewers, paved roads, and eventually telephone lines. But it was the railroad that was the most visible sign of progress and of the conquering and linking of spaces. The railroad was not only increasingly dominant physically and visually, but it compelled other forms of geographic measurement to adhere to its metrics of defining, measuring, and valuing space. Railroads did not, as the cliché has it, collapse time and space. Rather, they brought about new equivalencies between the two, with each being measured by the other.[26] New relational measures of space did not collapse old regional distinctions. Instead, they made them all the more potent as signifiers of difference and particularity amid fears about uniformity. In this way, the South and its news were both an ever-larger part of national networks, and identifiably regional and even local.

[22] Susan R. Brooker-Gross, "News Wire Services in the Nineteenth-Century United States," *Journal of Historical Geography* 7, no. 2 (1981): 167–179.

[23] Blondheim, *News over the Wires*, 3.

[24] Cameron Blevins, "Space, Nation, and the Triumph of Region: A View of the World from Houston," *Journal of American History* 101, no. 1 (2014): 122–147; Baldasty, *The Commercialization of News*.

[25] Blevins, "Space, Nation, and the Triumph of Region," 138.

[26] Richard White, *Railroaded: The Transcontinentals and the Making of Modern America* (New York: W. W. Norton, 2011), 146.

These kinds of transformation in the built environment are often tracked through the changes in big cities or newly opened regions of settler colonial expansion. But their modifications and alterations of the spatial order were equally transformative in places like Cabarrus County. The late 1850s through 1870s saw rail lines extended through the heart of the county with large terminals at Harrisburg, Concord, and Glass (later Kannapolis.)[27] Railroads and other infrastructures of spatial modernity were largely tools of growing industry in the interior of the Piedmont.[28] They were slow to penetrate the region as tools used directly in the lives of most residents. But by 1898, they were all omnipresent parts of this new network. The railroad, the postal service, the telegraph and telephone were all present in ordinary people's lives, less as a tool of frequent use and more as a transformative, if often unremarked technology undergirding new means of communication across space. As both a technology and a material object, the newspaper bridged this divide and brought disparate local, national, and global spaces together.

1898 was a crucial year for the local newspaper in North Carolina, the South, and the country. It was perhaps the height of the late nineteenth-century newspaper craze, a little-documented growth that saw community papers in nearly every county seat in the South. The rise of the local newspaper in America and particularly in the South was coincident with the rise of lynchings. While there is not a direct causal link between these two facts, there is a more than incidental connection. Newspapers became the means by which lynching was not just spread but comprehended. The news of the 1898 lynching of Tom Johnson and Joe Kizer shared headline space with America's war against Spain and detailed accountings of local births, marriages, and deaths. Its headline-grabbing, blaring broadcast was rivaled in size and scale only by advertisements for the latest goods arrived in Concord stores from northern and global markets.

---

[27] "*Railroad Map of North Carolina 1900.*" Map. Chicago; Rand McNally, 1900. North Carolina Maps, North Carolina Collection, Wilson Library, University of North Carolina at Chapel Hill; Thomas C. Harris, "Map of Cabarrus County, [North Carolina]," Map, circa 1875, North Carolina State Archives; "W. Alvin Lloyd's Southern Rail Road Map," Map, Mobile, Alabama, 1863, North Carolina Maps, North Carolina Collection, Wilson Library, University of North Carolina at Chapel Hill.

[28] Allen W. Trelease, *The North Carolina Railroad, 1849–1871, and the Modernization of North Carolina* (Chapel Hill: University of North Carolina Press, 1991); Rufus Barringer, *History of the North Carolina Railroad* (Raleigh, NC: News and Observer Press, 1894).

Historians often regard newspapers through the lens of the truism that they are "the first draft of history." But if we regard them as objects in and of themselves we can better understand not just *what* they communicated but *how*. Their role in broader, material, and spatial networks brought lynching into the home and out onto the street, into churches and workplaces, and across the country and world. Newspaper articles tell us how lynching became a material practice, communicated across the places of the country and indexing the broader understandings of racial violence as a central component of contemporary life.

DEFINING LYNCHING

Activists, historians, sociologists, and a great many other categories of thinker have spent many thousands of pages defining lynching. More than a century's worth of thought has gone into defining intent,[29] typology,[30] regional and geographic orientation,[31] impact on community,

[29] What we might now think of as lynching studies began with the work of Ida B. Wells, who resisted contemporaneous explanations and justifications for lynching by looking at its economic motivations. See in particular Ida B. Wells-Barnett, *Southern Horrors and Other Writings: The Anti-Lynching Campaign of Ida B. Wells, 1892–1900*, ed. Jacqueline Jones Royster, 2nd ed., the Bedford Series in History and Culture (Boston: Bedford/St. Martin's, 2016). But we should also note that Wells's explanations were made in response to complex and preexisting notions of what a lynching was and where its justifications stemmed from. In that sense, part of Wells's project was to refute white knowledge and reflect Black knowledge in a more public and systematic way. As Koritha Mitchell's work suggests, Wells and other early Black lynching documentarians and theorists characterized one attempt at explaining the power of lynchings. Mitchell's work documents another strand of that epistemological project in the world of embodiment and performance: Koritha Mitchell, *Living with Lynching: African American Lynching Plays, Performance, and Citizenship, 1890–1930* (Urbana: University of Illinois Press, 2011). Though there has been far less work on more vernacular forms of resistance, Christopher Waldrep's work does hint at this origin point and its long continuation: *African Americans Confront Lynching: Strategies of Resistance from the Civil War to the Civil Rights Era* (Lanham, MD: Rowman and Littlefield, 2009).
[30] Brundage, *Lynching in the New South*.
[31] There were important regional distinctions in the practice and understanding of lynching that recent scholarship has drawn our attention to. While the majority of racial terror lynchings took place in the South, there were both significant precursors to this practice in broader national histories, and significant national and global impacts from the rise of southern racial terrorist lynchings. See for instance Ken Gonzales-Day, *Lynching in the West, 1850–1935* (Durham, NC: Duke University Press, 2006); Nicholas Villanueva, Jr., *The Lynching of Mexicans in the Texas Borderlands* (Albuquerque: University of New Mexico Press, 2017); *Swift to Wrath: Lynching in Global Perspective*, ed. William D. Carrigan and Christopher Waldrep (Charlottesville: University of Virginia Press, 2013).

memory, and social relations.[32] Because lynching is meant as both an act of violence and a symbolic ritual, our understanding of it comes in large part through these efforts at intervention and interpretation. Lynching's meaning exists both in the communicative functions of its violence and through the eyes of the many people who have attempted to explain it. Summarizing much of this scholarship, Ashraf H. A. Rushdy notes that it has

> reoriented our understanding of just when a lynching is, by maintaining that a lynching was not a single focal event, circumscribed in time and space, but a pervasive cultural fact punctuated by serial rituals theatrically celebrating the doctrines of white supremacy that underlie them and make them possible.[33]

What Rushdy does not explicate here are the mechanisms of that pervasive cultural fact. Even before the advent of experts on racial violence, there were vernacular understandings of the practice on both sides of the hardening color line. Lynching as a concept was understood widely by Black and white people alike, for the one a threat, for the other a possibility.

That broader understanding underlay each interaction in the lynchings of Tom Johnson, Joe Kizer, and the many thousands of others likewise victims of mob violence. But the specific lynching, *each* specific lynching, also pushed past the borders defined for it through the distributive spatial properties of the newspaper articles that outlined it. The immediate incident – in this case the torture and murder of two men – is only part of what constitutes a lynching. The geographic frame of lynching is far wider than the immediate location of the hanging, shooting, or other act of violence at its core. People in Butte, Montana were reading about Johnson and Kizer's lynching before those in neighboring Iredell County (or those in Cabarrus who tended to read the weeklies rather than the daily). This collapse of the logic of spatial proximity was commonplace by the end of the nineteenth century. Not just information but tangible things – like the goods shipped by rail – circulated in a kind of illogic that marked space as ever changing and made "the quotidian experience of space one of rapid movement."[34] This undoubtedly was not forefront in the mind of most people reading the articles depicting the lynching of Kizer and

---

[32] Jason Morgan Ward, *Hanging Bridge: Racial Violence and America's Civil Rights Century* (New York: Oxford University Press, 2016).

[33] Rushdy, *The End of American Lynching*, 163.

[34] White, *Railroaded*, 141.

Johnson. But the reciprocal process of passage from place to place, of articles that might both influence and be influenced by one another, suggests the importance of these circulations and the way they influenced what lynching was, and what it is.

Temporally too, the articles circulated the lynching and its terror well beyond the immediate days at the end of May. As Rushdy notes, this broadened the frame of those participating in some sense into the thousands, at least, and ensured the preservation of its central messages for weeks and months in both white and Black consciousness. The Johnson and Kizer lynching was daily news for two weeks afterward, an occasional topic in the few months after that, and still being talked about in local accountings a year or more later.[35] These reminders of the event moved gradually from the newspaper articles to cultural memory shared in both informal kin and friend networks and expressed in other cultural productions. Rather than having what we might regard as a conventional news cycle with a fixed endpoint, it instead became a reference point. The narrative of this lynching spurred debates over its righteousness that spilled out in the regional press. But it also occasioned frequent updates and served as a shared body of knowledge for those familiar with its narrative arc. In this sense a specific lynching could overlap with understanding of the conventions of lynching: what it was, how it was communicated, and what it meant.

At least one newspaper editor understood this intimately. Writing to his Oklahoma audience, he articulated a common justification of spectacle lynching, noting that "the spectacle of a body swinging from a limb by the roadway carries with it a grewsomeness which Negroes for fifty miles around do not forget for a generation."[36] He refers here to the body as an object, a spectacle that had significant power for both white and Black. But many of those who held this event in their memories experienced it through the lens of the local reporter and editor. Accounts of individual lynchings stood in for and in some regard served as firsthand experience. This was all the more the case because of the uniform stylistic standards and narrative conventions of the period. As Lisa Duggan suggests, "it was

---

[35] See, for instance, "Down in Cabarrus," *Wilmington Messenger*, July 13, 1899; "The Lynching Justified," *The Durham Sun*, September 17, 1898; "To Your Tents O Israel!" *The North Carolinian*, October 27, 1898; "Was It Joe Williams?" *Daily Concord Standard*, June 20, 1898.

[36] Quoted in Michael A. Trotti, "The Scaffold's Revival: Race and Public Execution in the South," *Journal of Social History* 45, no. 1 (2011): 108.

first and foremost as newspaper accounts that the events that defined lynching ... became recognizable stories with repetitive plots and characterization."[37] This made accounts like that of the Kizer and Johnson lynching all the more recognizable to both local and national audiences. For some readers, there was the thrill of recognition at a local landmark or person invoked in the familiar narrative. These tied individual lynching articles to a particular place, and perhaps gave them a deeper definitional power that local whites might use in defining their homes. The "Concord Lynching" or the "Cabarrus Lynching," as so many accounts labeled it, invoked a kind of local particularity and even pride: It was their lynching and their home, each unique among the many others in the broadened geographic scope of racial terror in the late nineteenth and early twentieth centuries. But for others, the general outline and their existing knowledge were enough to absorb the few, local particulars. This made the lynching a much broader geographic proposition that would also persist as part of the lexicon of everyday life.

SPREADING THE NEWS

Articles such as those about Johnson and Kizer were part of a broad, distributive network. News of the lynching came amid one of the largest periods of growth in the American newspaper. New dailies, as well as ever more weekly or bi-weekly newspapers, meant that there was a saturation point of overlapping community news with national and international press.[38] The scale of these community newspapers meant that readers might gain insight at the same time into the social visits of their neighbors and the latest news about the invasion and war being waged in Cuba. But beyond the newspaper and its circulation, other technologies of space and communication were changing the material lives of the end of the century, for rural and small-town residents. The paradox of these newspapers – and lynching articles like the ones about Kizer and Johnson – was that they lent an intimate familiarity to local affairs that could be broadcast over hundreds or thousands of miles. All news became global, and all places local.

The daily newspaper first came to North Carolina around 1860. By 1899, the year after the Kizer and Johnson story briefly dominated the

---

[37] Duggan, *Sapphic Slashers*, 32.
[38] Baldasty, *The Commercialization of News*, 123; Blevins, "Space, Nation, and the Triumph of Region," 133.

headlines, there were already twenty-six dailies and many dozens of less frequently published papers throughout the state.[39] Nationally, this period represented the height of saturation of the newspaper in the country. Though eventually the number of readers went higher (both in absolute numbers and as a percentage of the population), there were never more papers than in the years between 1899 and 1904.[40] This growth was part of a larger, national shift. Most histories of the newspaper in America account principally for the large sources in metropolitan areas. But these more localized papers were part of the move toward a consolidation of sources and the Associated Press's (AP) "monopoly of knowledge."[41] Though few of the North Carolina papers that carried the news of the lynching provided news to the AP network, they were nonetheless consumers of that network and other, more localized ones like it.[42] As reportage became an ever more professionalized and impartial field, local newspapers such as the *Daily Concord Standard* tried valiantly to adapt with their own local talent.[43] And they certainly participated in the cultural shift of the period as well. They sought to provide engaging and commercially viable items to their consumers. As with other medium city and small-town papers, those across the Piedmont that carried this news the longest were more inclined toward reportage of the criminal and the sensational than their big city counterparts.[44] But those trends in publishing do not account fully for either the impact of or the interest in articles about lynching. These accountings combined the purposes and topics of the late nineteenth- and early twentieth-century newspaper into a news item seemingly tailor-made to interest readers and sell newspapers. In so doing, they aided the spread of lynching as a practice across space and through the material technologies of the "newly vast world."[45]

Indeed, newspapers of the era obliterated time and especially space in a more fitting appropriation of the cliché about railroads in this era. The newspaper page itself was a patchwork of items that belie any attempts

---

[39] Alfred McClung Lee, *The Daily Newspaper in America: The Evolution of a Social Instrument* (New York: Macmillan, 1937), 716.

[40] Lee, *The Daily Newspaper*, 718–719.

[41] Blondheim, *News over the Wires*, 42.

[42] Brooker-Gross, "News Wire Services in the Nineteenth-Century United States," 174–175.

[43] Joseph W. Campbell, *The Year That Defined American Journalism: 1897 and the Clash of Paradigms* (New York: Routledge, 2006).

[44] Baldasty, *The Commercialization of News*, 123.

[45] Alexander Nemerov, *Acting in the Night: Macbeth and the Places of the Civil War* (Berkeley: University of California Press, 2010), 18.

at historical categorization through the rubric of the time-sensitive event. The space of the page reflected both the editor's whims and his instincts about what might sell papers. A survey of front pages suggests that local news rarely predominated in billing, even when it might in overall column space. This collapse of geographic context was intentional. As Duggan notes, "page layouts organized reports of temporally simultaneous occurrences across dispersed geographies according to principles of relevance and hierarchies of significance."[46] This relational geography held up outside the pages of the newspaper as well. By the end of the nineteenth century, railroads had remade the meaning of space into something at once more abstract and more concrete.

Individual places were no longer marked by the physical distance between them, but rather by the ability to move from one place to the other.[47] Places – and the movement between them – thus became as much a matter of money and access to the infrastructures connecting them as it did to the regional distinctions or other markers of individual spatial particularity. This was most truest of railroads, though not exclusively. These last years of the century were crucial ones for the development of the contemporary news media and transportative infrastructures, but the people living then were also the inheritors of a half century of innovation in expanding the networks of connectivity between places, people, and institutions. David Henkin's observations about "the postal age" in which these people lived – that it linked "distant individuals in a web of regular exchanges and [tethered] them to networks of institutional power" – is equally true of the telegraph, the railroad, and the newspaper.[48] People in this period understood themselves as part of these larger networks in an abstract sense,[49] but also through the real and material set of everyday practices that undergirded those larger structures. This was not merely a conquering of distance, but a new expression of power through the potential to be connected to a place you might have never seen and might never go to.[50] It was the newspaper article that left the least to imagination or symbolism.

---

[46] Duggan, *Sapphic Slashers*, 33.

[47] White, *Railroaded*, 140–146.

[48] Henkin, *The Postal Age*, ix.

[49] Henkin, *The Postal Age*, 5.

[50] Nemerov, *Acting in the Night*, 17. This is also a point that recalls the foundational work of Benedict Anderson, whose notion of the "imagined communities" of a nation state applies with equal relevance to these smaller material, spatial, and conceptual networks: Benedict Anderson, *Imagined Communities: Reflections on the Origin and Spread of Nationalism*, rev. ed. (London and New York: Verso, 2006).

Lynching articles represented an excess: of meaning, of expression, of circulation. In very real and tangible ways, things like regional identity or rural versus urban living continued to matter. But *news* of a lynching might bring together these disparate identities and places through a common intrigue in the subject and taste for the sensational. If we return to Concord and the scene of the lynching, we can see these distributive networks in practice. While much of this book is about more conventional objects of material culture transferred from person to person, the context of the broader material networks through which both news and things circulated is crucial. It is in these circulations that we can best understand both how participation in a lynching exceeded its original location, and how its presence in communities became a persistent fact and reference point. Because newspaper articles are public facing, they also obscure much about the individual feelings and personal narratives told about the lynching of Kizer and Johnson or the many other victims of lynching whose deaths (and only rarely lives) were made into stories to be told. The rapidity with which this happened continues to astound. Within hours of the murder of Emma Hartsell, Kizer and Johnson had been accused, abducted, and murdered. In just a few hours more, a narrative of explanation had been written and was quickly winding its way throughout the country. It is a textbook example both of the organization and intention behind lynchings, and of the significant structures that allowed for the narrative's circulation into the public sphere and the deepest recesses of the home and the individual mind. An understanding that persists over a century later, all in the work of less than twenty-four hours. In this case, its historical significance is inversely proportional to the amount of time the event took. Paradoxically, that brief, intense duration left ample room for further speculation and narrative creation. Both contemporary and historical significance were born from these few moments, a prolonged performance that stretched between the narratives of everyday life and the contours of history and memory (Figure 1.1).

LOCALIZING THE NEWS

May 30, 1898, dawned in Concord, North Carolina with news of "the most tragic day in Cabarrus [county] history."[51] As some residents were going to work, or perhaps going to bed after a long and eventful night, the community's main newspaper, the *Daily Concord Standard*, was

---

[51] "A Day of Tragedy," *Daily Concord Standard*, May 30, 1898.

Daily Concord Standard.

Vol. XI.—No. 2729   CONCORD, N. C., MONDAY, MAY 30, 1898   WHOLE No. 11728

A DAY OF TRAGEDY.

MOST HORRIBLE DAY IN THE HISTORY OF CABARRUS COUNTY--AN ASSAULT--A MURDER--TWO NEGROES LYNCHED.

Emma Hartsell, a Thirteen-Year-Old Girl, Brutally Assaulted Then Killed--Neck Cut From Ear to Ear--A Mob Gathers Around the Jail and Overpowers the Officers--Both of the Negroes Lynched.

The most terrible outrage in the history of Cabarrus or many other counties was committed on Sunday morning about four or five miles from Concord near the Coddle Creek railroad bridge. It is horrible in several respects. The one was the assault, the other the murder, and the last one, which was of course a horrible scene, was the lynching of two negroes.

On Sunday afternoon Mr. S J Hartsell and his wife and several children went to the church to worship and left Emma, their 12 year-old daughter, and also the 6 months-old baby, at home. A while before 3 o'clock Rev. Plyler and another gentleman drove up to the barn to get out of the rain. Being a little baby no one porch they hollered, but got no response from the inside of the house. By this time Mr. Hartsell and family were in sight, coming home. Immediately Mr. Hartsell picked up the little baby and took her in the house. Soon one of the daughters who had been to church walked into the kitchen. Here was a most horrible scene. Emma Hartsell lay there on the floor midst clots of blood. Soon the folks gathered and found that Emma had been killed. Her forehead had a gash cut in it, and she was also cut on the right cheek. But this was nothing. It was soon found that the back of her neck was cut from ear to ear.

Exceptionally soon Dr. Pharr and the people of the community were present. Dr. Pharr examined the body and said that he had reasons to think that a estatic deed had also been committed upon her.

THE VILLAINS CAUGHT.

In a short time the people of the community were informed to the highest extent and were looking for the villain or villains that committed the horrible crimes. They soon found that some one had called at the house of Mr. L S Bonds not far away and had cut two of Mr. Bonds' cows. One of them is cut twice and the other once. Their wounds show that it was done with a sharp instrument, as also do the wounds on the face of the girl. The negroes were both found near Mr. Frank Pharr's.

A CONFESSION TO THE CRIME.

The two negroes caught were Joe Kizer and Tom Johnson. After they were caught, we are informed by quite a number of reliable people of that community, that Johnson acknowledged to the crime, but at the same time said that Kizer got

him to go with him. He was a conspirator but that he had the girl, but that Kizer did the work. This statement is verified by a number, and they can vouch for it.

About 5:30 o'clock Sheriff Buchanan received word of the horrible assault and murder. He, together with a posse of deputies, at once went to the place in No. 11 township. When they arrived Tom Johnson was in the hands of Deputy John Bill. Sheriff at once put Johnson in his buggy and made for the jail here, but was followed the entire distance by a howling mob. Every precaution was made by the Sheriff to get the man to jail and when going through the streets here with his pistol in his hand, was constrained to warn them emphatically that they must not lay their hands upon his prisoner.

As soon as the Sheriff left out in No. 11 township, the remaining part of the mob followed the officers in pursuit of Kizer, and succeeded in capturing him at his home near Mr. Frank Pharr's. Messrs. Pink Misenheimer and Frank Weddington, who were deputized, together with Deputy Bill, brought Kizer here to jail. Another large mob followed these men. But they at last succeeded in getting them behind the bars, though the jail yard was simply a jam of people.

From the time the negroes were brought to town several hundred were standing about and every few moments the crowd would holler for them to release the men and let the crowd take them and lynch them.

OVERPOWERED THE OFFICERS.

The officers tried to quell the angry mob, but this was impossible. The Sheriff and deputies, finding that they were in too large a crowd of spectators, went on the inside and held the doors shut. The mob then began to burst the glass and finally succeeded in knocking the doors open. Sheriff Buchanan was cut slightly by the breaking glass and some one hit Policeman Boger on the arm. But now the officers were overpowered and they were compelled to

give up and let them have their way. But while the crowd in the front of the jail was succeeding in gaining an entrance, some persons had succeeded in getting into the back hall by getting through a window in the dining room. No one was in the back hall to force them back except Jailer Bill.

About thirty-five or forty men proceeded upstairs and commenced to break open the doors to halls and cell. Jas Kizer threatened to kill his mate, Tom Johnson, and for this reason Jailer Bill had to put them in separate cells. The mob, before getting their prisoners, broke eight locks. The work of breaking open the cells was done by sledges, hammers and cold-chisels.

At 10:30 they succeeded in getting the ropes around their necks and hollered for the crowd to give way.

PROCEEDED TO HANGING GROUNDS.

The mob then proceeded out by the old Lutheran church, and out by the Three Mile branch. The mob stopped at the branch to let them talk but they only stopped a short while.

A STANDARD reporter talked to the prisoners as they were being pushed along. Each one would relate some incident, but would let him nothing to amount to anything. They would each describe the first part of the trouble, but when it came to the assault and the murder nothing is worth repeating as each claimed innocence.

Just before going down the Big Cold Water hill the mob turned to the left and proceeded about a quarter of a mile. After arriving at a suitable place for the hanging the crowd stopped. Rev. W C Alexander, who was doing all in his power to ward off the lynching, then spoke to the prisoners. In most emphatic tones he told them that they were now on the verge of being hanged and must now prepare to meet their God and not to dare to tell a lie. But the one's statements only implicated the other, and you could hardly say that they openly denied it, neither did they confess it.

Rev. Alexander arrived at the about 9 o'clock, and from the time he arrived he plead most earnestly with the people not to take these persons from the jail, but to no avail.

Tom Johnson then asked that Rev. Alexander pray for him. Rev. Alexander then prayed for them both. His prayer rendered was most pathetic.

THEY MEET DEATH.

Scarcely had his prayer ended when the negroes were jerked a medium size dogwood tree and

CONTINUED TO FOURTH PAGE.

FIGURE 1.1 Front page of *The Standard* the morning after the lynching of Tom Johnson and Joe Kizer

there to detail and contextualize the still ongoing events. The murders dominated the entire page, sharing space only with three advertisers who undoubtedly wished their attempts at levity had not been bought and paid for ahead of the most sensational news in years. In nearby Charlotte, the front-page headline was hardly more subtle. "A Day of Bloody Deeds" blared comparatively smaller in the big city paper. Its front page was dominated instead by the latest news of the troop apportionments for war in Cuba. But the lynching was still there, spilling out in gory detail for its readers to revel in.

Both papers had turned the events of the previous day into a comprehensible narrative. The lurid and sometimes melodramatic news of these three murders shared space on the front page only with a few advertisements, a reminder of the principal function of the community newspaper in influencing the captive audience of a few thousand who got much of their news and opinions from their daily. The news of a lynching was equally connected to that informative and influencing mission as it was to leaving its readers with a readymade articulation of their own ideologies in the form of a newspaper article.

Gone already was any uncertainty about the guilt of Kizer and Johnson, or any doubt about the righteousness of the mob's work. The shared process of meaning-making was made easier by an extant set of storytelling conventions that reporters could share, and readers would recognize. As more papers picked up the story, they adhered to the specifics of these structures with remarkable consistency. This created a reflexive framework for comprehension, where consumers understood a lynching through the narrative conventions they were familiar with. And then in turn, they applied that understanding to the comprehension of their more localized lynchings. Lynching then became legible as a category of action and comprehension.

Individual accounts relied on a roster of stock figures and narrative elements supplemented with the particularities of the individual lynchings. The outlines of this narrative are relatively simple. They focus a significant portion of column space on the alleged crime, assessing the guilt of the accused men by fiat of racist assumption. In the cases where would-be victims were held in police custody, there was a detailed description of both their abduction from jail and the token resistance put up by some member of the law, framed as their both doing their sworn duty and reluctantly bowing to the greater physical power of the mob. The abduction complete, narratives typically turned to a short explication of the movement to a site selected for the lynching. These held a variety of symbolic purposes (telegraph line, courtyard square, outskirts of the city), but are also often portrayed as a simple matter of convenience. The method of execution came next. The narrative specificity tended to be less detailed than the description of the victim's alleged crime. Accountings of the execution invoked a variety of clichés ("riddled with bullets" being a particular favorite) that were more evocative than descriptive. The article would then generally conclude with some reference to the aftermath of the lynching, typically either a note about the crowds visiting the site or the coroner declaring the deed committed "by the hands of persons unknown."

A systematized reading of lynching articles from the several decades around the turn of the twentieth century shows these same conventions repeated, often word for word. Though in a radically different context from readers of the era, I have read thousands of these articles over the course of this project. Their cumulative impact is to routinize and normalize spectacular violence. In effect, these articles instructed people how to perform their roles in a lynching. This expanded frame of lynching encompassed not just the abduction and murder, but the long tail of participation by both mob members, spectators, souvenir hunters, site visitors, and others taking part in disseminating the message of the lynching. This prolonged performance stretched for weeks, months, and eventually decades. We must regard the lynching's duration in both time and space as something that exceeds the few hours of its commission. The murder and torture themselves were brief but formative. The production of this action into both verbal and written news was only one of the first, overlapping material steps in a much longer process of creating a durable meaning for the lynching. For historians, the duration of an historical event can be measured by its observable traces spread across time and space. In this sense, Joe Kizer and Tom Johnson's lynching persisted for generations from the initial narratives made in the immediate wake of its commission. The first newspaper articles about the lynching can tell us not only how people perceived its violence at the time, but what they did with it in years to come.

Of the articles that constituted a narrative of the Concord lynching, likely the *Observer* account was the one first published. Though the newspaper was only putting out one edition on weekdays, the May 30 masthead noted that it was the morning newspaper. It offers fewer details as well, suggesting both a rush to the printer and an expanded regional audience with a smaller appetite for unfamiliar local names and landmarks. Still, much of the narrative was solidified by the morning's first draft. This account opened with many of the standard journalistic conventions of the era, beginning with multiple and repeated details of Emma Hartsell's sexual assault and murder. It clearly borrowed from the literary conventions of the day. Readers were told of the mob gathering in "shades of night," using the "uncertain, fitful light" of a lantern to aid in their abduction. And in a foreboding, melodramatic flourish, the unnamed author of the article evoked the gory particulars favored by southern religious tradition and penny journalism alike, claiming that "nothing but the blood of the guilty would satisfy them."[52] Predictably, it ends with precisely that: a shedding of blood described in sickening detail.

The article was also referential to its own material process of production, replaying the interchange between print and orality in communication about the lynching. Much of the article was focused on this metanarrative of the rapid spread of information within the communities around the site of the lynching. The author did not indicate the mechanism of this dissemination of information, saying only that by the late afternoon on May 29, "the news had spread rapidly and crowds of both town and country began gathering."[53] The notion that it was town and country people both gathering into a potential lynch mob seems intended to emphasize a shared purpose across what otherwise might be a natural division between rural and urban. But it also revealed that people were traversing a significant distance of the county in order to share this news and their outrage. The lynch mob was thus constituted from a larger coalition of people in the county, an observation that would be expounded upon in later revisions of this narrative to argue for a multiracial, unified community lynch mob (a subject I take up in Chapter 5).

But it also suggests how community rumors and gossip – as one phrase had it. "heard ... from the lips of a young negro" – coalesced into narrative in simultaneity with action. It was nearly as crucial to the constitution of a lynching to tell about it, over and over again. Undoubtedly, this occurred in person as the narrative spread throughout the county and became ever more refined and directed toward the formation of a mob. The *Observer* article does not specify how the news eventually got to its offices in Charlotte, but it seems likely (as with other lynchings) that it came in the form of a tip sent telegraphically from someone on the ground. Indeed, a dispatch a few days later from a Wilmington, North Carolina weekly specified that the "wires brought us the report of a double lynching at

[52] "A Day of Bloody Deeds," *Charlotte Observer*, May 30, 1898.
[53] "A Day of Bloody Deeds," *Charlotte Observer*.

Concord."[54] For readers, there was a seeming equivalency between these multiple ways of communicating the news. Particularly as the story persisted in many newspapers, it took on the more conversational tone and nonnarrative approach of a piece of information delivered impassively and in passing. Shocking violence and prurient, specific detail gave way to casual reporting of yet another lynching. The disjuncture in tone and delivery was hardly unusual to an audience at the time who might see local news juxtaposed with international press, and local merchant advertisements paired with notices of violence, death, and tragedy in their communities and beyond.[55] This was the norm, and one taken for granted in part as a reflection of the necessities of newspaper life, and in part as a continuation of the rich and varied ways in which people had previously received and consumed information.

This spread of the news from person to person mirrored the frenzied, geographically uneven distribution of the article in the new material networks of press associations. On the day of the article's publication, at least three other papers had a full or lightly revised version of the *Observer* story in their papers. The nearby *Greensboro Telegram* reprinted the article in full and noted the original as its source. The Butte, Montana *Miner* and Lincoln, Nebraska *State Journal* both printed smaller summary reports without any attribution.[56] Over the next week, some version of the article appeared in sixteen newspapers. Most were with little alteration, though some smaller regional papers authenticated the news further with commentary from a local traveling nearby who could attest to its veracity from having heard the latest rumors from sources in Cabarrus. The *Messenger and Intelligencer* of Wadesboro, near the South Carolina border, appended a brief note from "Mr. J.S. Lowe [who] came down from Concord this morning."[57] It did little but verify the truth of the facts of the article as he had gotten them from the continued gossip in Concord. This authenticating accounting suggested the continued, negotiated nature of authority between newspaper and oral account, and demonstrated at least some preference for a combination of the two. In the absence of firsthand evidence, people might prefer to hear the news, even secondhand, from someone that they knew and trusted.

54 "Minor Mention," *Weekly Star*, June 3, 1898.
55 Blevins, "Space, Nation, and the Triumph of Region," 139.
56 "Outraged and Murdered," *The Butte Miner*; "Hanged the Suspects," *The Nebraska State Journal*.
57 "Horrible Affair!" *Messenger and Intelligencer*, June 2, 1898.

This was, of course, not the case for the majority of accounts of the lynching of Kizer and Johnson published from the model of the *Observer*. Even in many towns across North Carolina, the news was reported initially with little alteration, the only modifications being the editorial license used in modified headlines and subheadings. Like the original, they screamed and wept on the page, declaring "A Horrible Affair in Cabarrus!" or "The Work of Fiends."[58] Otherwise little altered from the original account, they gave the local newspaper the appearance of authority and an expansive, if anonymous, staff who could cover all the news. Newspapers further afield made even fewer concessions to place, probably assuming that their readership would not know (or care) where Cabarrus was. Accounts in New Orleans, Lincoln, and Butte borrowed routine headlines ("Swung to a Tree," "Hanged the Suspects," "Outraged and Murdered") that reflected the standard vernacular used to describe lynchings. Where they differed, as with the strong headline in the Butte *Miner*, was only in the severity and sensationalism of the language they chose to label the articles with. For these readers, the Kizer and Johnson lynching was just another in a long tally of similar events. This spread and casualization of the news helped routinize it further. One lynching was equivalent to another, in the same way that space and time were likewise now categories of experience as much as structuring realities.

The circulation of the *Observer* narrative built on the reputation and authority of the urban center as a source of reliable news. Its reach was national and relied upon the infrastructures of the wire to circulate its accounting in rapid succession. Less well circulated but equally influential were the more detailed and even more salacious articles from the *Daily Concord Standard* and *The Concord Times*. These articles substituted the speed of the *Observer*'s transmission with a depth of detail and specific appeals to their smaller readership.

Though their spread and persistence were more localized spatially, their influence was clear over a broader span of time and in an intensive geographic area, as Bruce Baker noted in his study of the lynching ballad derived from these events (and covered at greater detail in Chapter 6 of this book).[59] We can measure influence both chronologically and

---

[58] "A Horrible Affair in Cabarrus," *Record and Landmarks*, May 31, 1898; "The Work of Fiends," *The North Carolinian*, June 2, 1898.

[59] Bruce Baker, "North Carolina Lynching Ballads," in *Under Sentence of Death: Lynching in the South*, ed. W. Fitzhugh Brundage, (Chapel Hill: University of North Carolina Press, 1997), 219–246.

geographically. Taken together, these three accounts suggested the reach of newspaper networks. They could be both intensive and expansive by turn, allowing for the broadest possible reach nationally and inciting local debates that made them not just news, but an enduring part of the regional understanding of race and violence.

Both of these more local accounts open with a sustained explication of the results of Emma Hartsell's rape and murder. More speculative than the first account from Charlotte, they try to recreate both the scene of discovery and the assault itself. The *Standard* noted that the examining physician, Dr. Pharr, "had reasons to think a satanic deed had been committed upon her."[60] The *Times* went further, speculating from the same doctor's observations "that she would have died from the effects of the outrage." The editors built their narrative on a forensic level of detail, noting what they presumed to be defensive wounds on her hands and fingers.[61] Both articles sought to deepen the perceived dichotomy between the angelic nature of the white girl and the evil of the Black men. Of Hartsell, the *Times* reported that she "fought heroically for her honor and her life."[62] They might invoke satanic acts, but also invested considerable space in humanizing descriptions of the two men. Tom Johnson and Joe Kizer were not stereotypical fiends or brutes in these accountings. Rather, both papers went out of their way to construct the men's backgrounds and identities as a way of both explaining the crime and more fully condemning them, as the *Standard* did in noting that "Joe Kizer has a very bad name throughout the vicinity."[63] This localized not only the crime, but the intention behind it.

Indeed, both articles made particular appeals to their localized readership. In the case of the *Standard* account, this was largely through detailed references to the landscape that read, and were undoubtedly received by curiosity-seeking locals, as directions to the site of the lynching. Following the tracks of Sunday night's mob (which included the reporter, Wade Barrier), the description noted that "the mob proceeded out by the old Lutheran Church and out by the Three Mile Branch .... Just before going down Big Cold Water hill, the mob turned to the left and proceeded about a quarter of a mile."[64] Here are familiar, almost

---

[60] "A Day of Tragedy," *Daily Concord Standard.*
[61] "A Horrible Crime!" *The Concord Times*, June 2, 1898.
[62] "A Horrible Crime!" *The Concord Times.*
[63] "A Day of Tragedy," *Daily Concord Standard.*
[64] "A Day of Tragedy," *Daily Concord Standard.*

intimate landmarks of locality overlain with the lynching narrative. This article made the already commonplace tenets of a routinized narrative local. Readers could take pride, as some did in the coming months, in "their" lynching. The *Times* article appealed even more openly to local place and convention. The masthead on the day the weekly newspaper printed its deeply reported and detailed accounting of the lynching noted its self-proclaimed status as the chief newspaper for the region. By its own reckoning, it was "the most widely circulated paper ever published" in the nine Piedmont counties surrounding Cabarrus and covering the territory from Charlotte to Greensboro.[65] In this way, it was staking its claim to local influence on par with that of bigger, better-resourced, and more frequently published papers. Likely its decision to rely on what appears to be a significant amount of its own original reporting also had to do with this perceived rivalry.

Kizer, we are told, "ran away from Union County ... [where] it is said that there were several indictments against him."[66] Johnson evidently came to Cabarrus "from Lincoln County and hauled coal for Mr. K.L Craven last winter." His last job – for Mr. Bonds – gave even further details about his allegedly peripatetic nature and perhaps characterized an unsteadiness that had him rumored to bear "the mark of shackles on his ankles."[67] Both of these place-based descriptions were intended in part to characterize each as a kind of badman, people who committed crimes and could not stay in one place.[68] But they also represented a relational geography of locality that matched up with the reading area delineated in the masthead. Union was one of the principal counties of the paper's readership, and itself a growing part of the urban-industrial complex in the central North Carolina Piedmont. Lincoln was just to the west of the nine-county quadrant, but locals there were likely to read the papers from Concord at least as much as those from Statesville, both roughly equidistant from the county seat at Lincolnton. These identifiers seemed to allow the residents of counties where the men had previously lived to take part in the lynching's prolonged performance of guilt and revenge.

On the one hand, those residents might bear some of the blame for not rooting out the allegedly criminal nature of two men. But they might

---

[65] "A Horrible Crime!" *The Concord Times.*
[66] "A Horrible Crime!" *The Concord Times.*
[67] "A Horrible Crime!" *The Concord Times.*
[68] Lawrence W. Levine, *Black Culture and Black Consciousness: Afro-American Folk Thought from Slavery to Freedom* (New York: Oxford University Press, 1977), 122.

also share vicariously in the aftermath of the lynching: the souvenir collecting, the visits to the scene of the hangings, and the revelry associated with the white community's violent work. In this way, the more localized accountings from the *Standard* and the *Times* staked claims for local identification within the expanded spatial awareness of the period. Cameron Blevins has pointed out that other, even larger regional newspapers functioned similarly, crafting an imagined geography that "sounded expansive but ... was in fact quite parochial."[69] Considered as a network, the infrastructure of news, railroads, telegraphs and telegrams, postal service, and the other spatial systems of the late nineteenth century remained, to paraphrase Richard John's words, a porous mesh whose netting left many places excluded and disconnected. Accordingly, "the most relevant spatial unit" for these geographic changes "long remained neither the nation, or even the region, but the locality."[70]

The contours of that locality were not defined strictly by county lines or maps, or even by geographic features. By at least one measure, the distinctions that mattered the most here were symbolic ones, part of the imagined community of this small area in the larger context of the nation. The *Times* made proud mention of the fact that the two men "met their death at the hands of outraged citizens, white and colored, from both town and country."[71] In this description, town and country are significant divisions. We can recognize these as spatial distinctions, and increasingly ones of local identity.[72] The growth of urban-industrial space in the county and subregion made the "sense of inscription"[73] that divided urban and rural a particularly meaningful distinction. To see them united across this divide was ever rarer. But of course, the larger division in Cabarrus, in the Piedmont, in the South, and in the nation was racial. Itself a spatial divide in both reality and imagination, "white and colored" represented the most meaningful marker of geographic difference that the reporters, editors, and audience might imagine. For Black people to allegedly participate in the lynching was to suggest the utter

---

[69] Blevins, "Space, Nation, and the Triumph of Region," 133.
[70] John, *Network Nation*, 9, 11.
[71] "A Horrible Crime!" *The Concord Times*.
[72] Here in particular I am invoking Arjun Appadurai's notion of locality as it is produced through the process of social relations. See Arjun Appadurai, "The Production of Locality," in *Modernity at Large: Cultural Dimensions of Globalization*, ed. Arjun Appadurai (Minneapolis: University of Minnesota Press, 1996), 178–200.
[73] Philip J. Ethington, "Placing the Past: 'Groundwork' for a Spatial Theory of History," *Rethinking History* 11, no. 4 (2007): 483.

criminality of the men lynched and their irrevocable break from and vio-
lation of even this increasingly strict spatial order of Jim Crow. It created
a sense of a united community, one that might briefly invite in Black
people who would willingly excoriate and even expunge others from the
small population within the county. Newspaper articles could make that
sense of community and unified purpose, but sometimes the narrative
failed to live up to reality. In a sense, then, the newspaper article made
community out of the expansive and seemingly unlimited space of the
late nineteenth-century nation. Articles about lynching were not unique
in their capacity to build racial consensus across space, but they were
exceptional as instruments themselves of circulating racial terror, ani-
mus, and even additional violence. The newspaper article relied upon a
network of material distribution that had changed the spatial perceptions
of Americans. But it ended up in many ways reinforcing old hierarchies.
The spatial modernity of lynching articles was one that built upon many
of the foundational tenets of race and place and helped reinforce the
emerging social policies of Jim Crow.

LEARNING TO LYNCH?

What set the newspaper apart from other spatial technologies of transmission was its aim of constructing and circulating narratives. Those narratives
were multiply purposed, sometimes informing, sometimes entertaining,
sometimes modeling and instructing. Lynching articles exposed readers
to the mechanisms and vocabularies of lynching. In highly routinized and
prescriptive forms, they detailed the crime, the abduction, the token resistance of the police, the hanging or shooting itself, and the aftermath, with
its protestations about the sad necessity of the mob's task mixed with
an accounting of the souvenir hunters claiming their prizes. As a literary
form, newspaper articles were entangled in a reciprocal process of shaping consumer desires and responding to them by printing whatever news
might sell. The lynching article was in many ways representative of the
complexities of this distributive material network. It was clearly shaped
by consumer desires for sensation and prurience, and a neat conclusion
to real-life events. It held a broad geographic appeal, but also an intensely
local one. But it did more than meet consumer desire. It expanded it, creating a larger appetite for news of racial violence.

In the remainder of this chapter, I want to think through the ways in
which newspaper articles of lynching both distributed news of racial violence and instructed readers in its specific contours. We certainly know

that the late nineteenth-century newspaper was emerging from a period where it had pedagogical aims: to instruct readers in the proper course for politics, to invite them to read and internalize the lessons of fiction, poetry, and other literature published in brief.[74] Certainly, those inheritances informed the newly expanding community newspapers at century's end as much as the other technological and geographic changes of the preceding half century did. How did those forms extend to the lynching article? Did they allow people to internalize the lessons of lynching and apply them in their own communities, to their own victims of racial terror? These are questions only answerable by speculation. Faced solely with the external, written expression of community belief that is the newspaper, we have to guess at its deeper impacts on individuals in these places. Still, the circulation and excitement over these pages, their virality in the places of the long nineteenth century, suggest a utility beyond simple news or entertainment. We ought to regard lynching articles as pedagogical tools in the mode of the earlier newspaper. Given the expanded definition of lynching that this chapter advances, we can understand newspaper articles as teaching readers how to lynch.

The circulation of Tom Johnson and Joe Kizer's murders in around thirty newspapers was average. Just in North Carolina in the immediate years proximate to this lynching, some lynchings got minimal news coverage, while others traveled across the wires, through the nation, and occasionally beyond. The 1905 lynching of John Moore in the far eastern city of New Bern, North Carolina, spread throughout the state and as far as the *Ottawa Citizen* and the German-language *Volksfreund* of Warrenton, Illinois.[75] In total, 183 papers carried the news of his murder and of the well-known but unprosecuted lynch mob leader who carried a piece of the hanging rope as a souvenir.[76] But other lynchings where a mob or mob members were known or even tried received scant coverage. Robert Chambers, a preacher in the mountain town of Cranberry in Mitchell County, was abducted and lynched in 1896. Seemingly part of the remote world untouched by the vast coverage of the newspapers, rails, and wires, news of his death nonetheless reached nearby Asheville, distant Goldsboro in the eastern reaches of the Piedmont, and as far away as Wisconsin and Minnesota.[77] One newspaper reported the arrest of his

74 Baldasty, *The Commercialization of News*, 3.
75 "Richter Lynch an der Arbeit," *Warrenton Volksfreund*, September 1, 1905.
76 "John Moore," *A Red Record*, lynching.web.unc.edu/the-people/john-moore.
77 "Robert Chambers," *A Red Record*, lynching.web.unc.edu/the-people/robert-chambers.

lynchers, though they were apparently never tried or convicted.[78] But the news only spread to a handful of newspapers, geographically disparate though they were. In both depth and breadth, then, news of a lynching circulated. Yet the mere transmission of information or even of an object belies its ultimate use in the hands of those receiving it.

A few years before Johnson and Kizer's lynching, Dallas County, Alabama, saw a spate of lynchings matched in number and frequency of death only by the massive pogroms in places like Wilmington, North Carolina, or Elaine, Arkansas.[79] From 1892 to 1898, nineteen people were killed in and around the county seat of Selma.[80] Nine of those people were killed within little more than a week in December of 1893. There were at least three separate lynchings of multiple people, unrelated to one another but by proximity and the likely participation of white community members in each of the mobs. The violence was reactive and, at least in the perception of locals, reciprocal. According to the widely reprinted account of the last of these lynchings – those of Ely Lyde, Joseph Lyde, and the surviving A. B. McIver – if the culprits were captured "there will doubtless be another first class lynching party."[81]

There were passing similarities between all of the lynchings. Each was centered on the roads of Dallas County as pursuer and pursued raced around. These chases were rendered in the newspaper accounts in three-mile increments, giving those both local and more distant landmarks to better place the sites of the murders.[82] These articles also related each lynching to the others in the space of the county. The killing of four unnamed men on December 10 "occurred only a mile or two from where

[78] "North Carolina," *The North Carolinian*, May 21, 1896.
[79] I cover the Wilmington massacre in greater depth in Chapter 2. The Elaine Massacre still needs more attention, though there are a few excellent studies that put it in the context of state and regional history, as well as within the broader wave of racial violence kicked off in the "Red Summer" of 1919. See Guy Lancaster, ed., *The Elaine Massacre and Arkansas: A Century of Atrocity and Resistance, 1819–1919* (Little Rock, AR: Butler Center Books, 2018); Grif Stockley, *Blood in Their Eyes: The Elaine Race Massacres of 1919* (Fayetteville: University of Arkansas Press, 2001); Lee E. Williams and Lee E. Williams II, *Anatomy of Four Race Riots: Racial Conflict in Knoxville, Elaine (Arkansas), Tulsa, and Chicago* (Hattiesburg: University and College Press of Mississippi, 1972).
[80] These numbers are based on several sources. While understudied, lynching in Alabama was well documented relative to many other states. This is in part because of Monroe Work and other scholars at Tuskegee Institute (today Tuskegee University), who kept track of lynchings in their state.
[81] "Shot from Ambush," *Pine Bluff Daily Graphic*, December 14, 1893.
[82] "Shot from Ambush," *Pine Bluff Daily Graphic*; "Gruesome Sight," *The Buffalo Enquirer*, December 13, 1893.

the two negroes were lynched last week."[83] It was three men who had been lynched just a few days prior, but that kind of imprecision was inconsequential in accounts much more focused on a broad outline of events. The choice of the author to focus on the more precise geography of the lynchings is telling. It suggests a kind of anchoring in the physical world. This was particularly important when "the matter was kept so quiet that nothing was known of it here until today."[84] The "here" in this instance is nominally Birmingham, where the wire reports originated. But, of course, it is also taken as read by the audience who might think of "here" as Baltimore, Buffalo, or any other of the dozen other cities that the news went to.

This circulation – which was matched or exceeded in each of the 1893 lynchings in Dallas County – is indicative of what textual historian Ryan Cordell calls "viral textuality."[85] The viral text was one reproduced across the networks of nineteenth-century circulation, achieving an importance in contrast to its original form. Most often it was a piece of doggerel or unattributed folk wisdom. The news from Concord and the news from Selma were both viral to an extent, though not in the sense of their temporal persistence. Instead, they burned quickly, making a big impact on front pages for a few months, and then fading into largely unarticulated collective memory.

This returns us again to the replicability of the lynching narrative. Each particular instance would be carried far away from its origin. It might briefly ignite the passions of the reader in Butte or Buffalo, but they would just as likely soon forget it. Those closer to the lynching preserved its details, held them in objects and mementos, and continued to refine and retell the narrative. But for both audiences, these lynchings became a kind of infection, adding to the notion of their own virality. The specifics might fade away, but the general outline and the emotions it aroused remained as part of the affective functions that a lynching served up in its wake. Without equating these acts of readership to those who actively perpetrated the most violent aspects of a lynching, this also suggests a return to the expanded framework for a lynching's

[83] "Lynching of Four Negroes," *Lancaster Intelligencer*, December 16, 1893.
[84] "A Quadruple Lynching," *The Baltimore Sun*, December 13, 1893.
[85] This label stems from Cordell's project (with David A. Smith) called "The Viral Texts Project," https://viraltexts.org. A fuller articulation of the idea appears in Ryan Cordell, "Viral Textuality in Nineteenth-Century U.S. Newspaper Exchanges," in *Virtual Victorians: Networks, Connections, Technologies*, ed. Veronica Alfano and Andrew Stauffer (Basingstoke: Palgrave Macmillan, 2015), 29–56.

definition. The spread of the lynching's news was affective.[86] Building on
the conventions of sentimentality and sensation, it brought readers into
the space of the lynching through the creation of an intimate proximity. Invoking familiar conventions and familiar feelings, lynching articles
spanned the space of the nation to unite each reader in the frame of
participation. Further even than Rushdy's complicity models, this kind
of affective work brought white readers into a fuller comprehension of
the material and social contours of lynching as a practice.

NETWORKS, OBJECTS

Lynching articles held a multiple materiality. They had physical presence – the feel and composition of the paper, the visual layout of the
page, the newspaper spread wide open, spanning a table to display its
full contents, the fulfillment of the detailed narrative exceeding the column inches of the first page alone. These articles also had a distributive
materiality. Attaching to the networks of post and wire, they traveled
across the country from newspaper office to newspaper office, and from
individual to individual. If we return again to the North Carolina soldiers
in Florida, we can see both of these materialities at work.

News of the Cabarrus lynching reached them even before the newspapers did. The age-old oral transmission of gossip and community news
was aided by newer networks that allowed for the rapid transmission of
what had previously been in-person communication. It is not difficult to
imagine the reception of news of the lynching in the barracks of Company L. Their published missives home show a group bored of camp life,
and both too poor and too hesitant to explore their new surroundings.
Prior to their payday a few weeks later, "the boys" of Company L seem
to have spent a lot of their time avoiding the blistering heat and awaiting the routine drills and occasional entertainment in the evenings.[87] The

---

[86] On the affective geographies of nineteenth-century literature, see Naomi Greyser, *On
Sympathetic Grounds: Race, Gender, and Affective Geographies in Nineteenth-Century
North America* (New York : Oxford University Press, 2018).

[87] Though there are only a few mentions of the Concord lynching from the Company L
soldiers, there is ample evidence of their social life at the makeshift "Camp Cuba Libre"
in Jacksonville. I based this account principally on these articles: "Short Items," *Daily
Concord Standard*, June 3, 1898; "Our Boys Vaccinated," *The Standard*, June 9, 1898;
"A Promotion," *The Standard*, June 30, 1898; "Jacksonville Letter," *Daily Concord
Standard*, July 29, 1898; "Boys All Well," *The Standard*, May 19, 1898; "Camp Cuba
Libre," *Daily Concord Standard*, June 18, 1898; "Has a Spanish Hard-Tack," *Daily
Concord Standard*, August 27, 1898.

first news of a lynching must have brought some excitement into a space occupied by the stilted aggression of young military men awaiting action. If, as Deaton claimed, the eventual account of *The Standard* was pored over by most of the Company, the conversation, jokes, gossip, and other oral communication of the lynching were even more intensive. In this, we can see the mutually constitutive role of the oral and the written in establishing lynching narratives. Lynching articles communicated more than just the news. As soldiers passed the article throughout "at least one half the regiment,"[88] each new reader could base their understanding of the story on both the conventions of the genre as they understood them, and the details as they absorbed them. An object passed around this way accrues meaning. Each new reader can see the marks of the previous person, can feel where their sweaty thumb has smudged the ink, or their eagerness has torn a corner of the page. They can have added to the news on the page the emotion of the person passing it to them, or the prurience of circulating an object so purple in its prose, so lascivious in its violent depictions. This embodiment of the article intensified its affective approach. We might see this as a process that externalized that affect, that turned emotion into action. Maybe it spurred the Concord soldiers on to something more than a mere visual presence that made Jacksonville's Black residents shudder in fright.[89]

This is all speculative, of course. But we do know that these complex, multiple materialities lend themselves to material acts. Both in circulation and in physical presence in the hand and with the body, things act as means of remembrance, of loss, of anger, of a variety of emotions that might bubble up and externalize. This chapter has been concerned primarily with the things themselves and their distributive properties. But we might think about these things as leading to and building upon each other to create material acts. It is to the power of objects to incite action that we now turn.

---

[88] "Company 'L' Notes," *The Standard*, 1.

[89] It is worth noting here that Company L were regarded locally as inheritors of the mission of the Confederacy. Their arrival home in April 1899 saw them accompanied throughout town by the county's Confederate veterans. After being prayed over by Reverend W. C. Alexander, the minister who earlier presided over the prayers at Johnson and Kizer's lynching, the soldiers were explicitly linked in a speech to these "survivors of the Lost Cause": "Home Again," *The Standard*, April 27, 1899. This is a process repeated frequently during the course of the Spanish American War, as Caroline Janney notes in *Remembering the Civil War*.

2

The Letter

In October 1898, Sam Hartsell wrote a letter. He was the father of Emma – "Emmie" as he apparently called her – whose violent death had prompted the lynching of Tom Johnson and Joe Kizer in May. His widely reprinted letter was intended as a public notice more than a private epistle. Hartsell adopted both the sensationalist authorial voice of turn-of-the-century print culture and the white supremacist politics of the 1898 electoral cycle. He railed against the Fusionist politics that had propelled a coalition of white Populists and Black Republicans to dozens of state and county offices over the previous four years. And he capitalized on the notoriety of the lynchings of Kizer and Johnson to argue that these politics precipitated his daughter's murder.

But the letter's significance had less to do with its contents than its form. The written text was part of a larger material culture of white supremacy ascendant in 1898. The contours of that materiality ranged from public media like Hartsell's to spectacles of mob violence. These material modes of public address represented assertions of power and control in public space and laid the groundwork for the visual and spatial control of the Jim Crow South.

The lynching of Joe Kizer and Tom Johnson was an act immersed in white supremacist material worlds. To use a phrase prominent in the political discourse that surrounded their deaths, it was an object lesson. The elements of the scene were readily observable and immediately legible to both Black and white audiences: the bodies themselves, the rope and branch, the tree, hill, and other physical, formulaic elements of the scene. They signified warning and terror for Black viewers, revenge and redemption for white ones. Some lynch mobs were not content with the overdetermined symbolism of a ritual murder. They left behind notes on the bodies further explaining their intentions. These pieces of paper were hardly fit to the task of communicating amid the violent chaos of a lynching. But their incongruous display held a message of its own.

The year 1898 saw more displays of racial violence than arguably any other year of the most intensive phase of lynching activity. Throughout the 1880s and 1890s, lynching had already been normalized as an extreme extension of prevalent white supremacist ideology. It was in 1898 that it became a commonplace act of political expression.[1] The preceding years had seen a bi-racial political coalition achieve a tentative political foothold; in North Carolina and across the South 1898 promised to overturn it. Freighted with meaning during Fusion's grasp on the state, this election promised a return to normalcy and the status quo of white dominance. Campaigns rested on the manly duty toward white supremacy, decried the indignities of "Negro rule," and insisted on a white electorate that would, in Hartsell's words, "vote for the protection of our mothers, wives, sisters, and daughters."[2]

---

[1] This coincides with the period that Grace Hale and others have defined as the era of spectacle lynchings. See Grace Elizabeth Hale, *Making Whiteness: The Culture of Segregation in the South, 1890–1940* (New York: Vintage, 1999), 199–239, and Wood, *Lynching and Spectacle*. Both scholars note that spectacle lynchings were always a minority of lynchings, though they carried an outsize symbolic weight. While it is clear that such lynchings conventionally defined as spectacles were comparatively scarce, we need an expanded definition of spectacle. The standard definition assumes a crowd witnessing and participating in the torture and execution of a person, typically firsthand. Of course, as I argue in these first two chapters, we should expand that definition considerably to include the longer arc of participation. Spectacle does not always rely upon firsthand observation. Spectacle lynchings built upon a broader visual culture to make themselves legible, and in their telling and retelling indexed that visual culture repeatedly. In other words, the invocation of torture and murder became stock images of a sort. Spectacle could be retrospective, with later retellings of a lynching invoking this widely understood visual imagery. As we begin to have more microhistorical attention to particular lynchings and particular places where lynchings occurred, we will have a better understanding of how commonplace this kind of visual-invoking process of memorialization was on both sides of the color line. An excellent example of the uses of this kind of visual imagery comes in the titular "hanging bridge" of Morgan Ward's *Hanging Bridge*.

The increasing number of studies that rely upon access to large numbers of digitized newspaper and other accounts of lynching (including my own project "The Red Record") are giving scholars a greater sense of how commonplace it was to write and talk about lynchings, particularly from the 1870s forward. They were a significant part of public discourse. The main caveat here is, of course, that our knowledge of the absolute number of lynchings is still very much restricted by both the creation and preservation of records. That is, we can increasingly expand our approximation of the numbers of people that were lynched as we gain better and more systematic access to numbers, but there will almost certainly always be lynchings that were carried out in secret and unrecorded in anything but familial stories, if at all. We will likely never have a full accounting of lynching by the numbers, and certainly not by the toll it exacted.

[2] "Mr. Hartsell's Letter," *Daily Concord Standard*, October 1, 1898.

And when election day came and went, less like a prophecy fulfilled and more like an inevitability arrived at through the force of shameful will, white men triumphed. Using the force of intimidation and violence, Democrats took back state offices in a rout.[3] In Wilmington, the epicenter of Black majority former plantation districts, that lawful power was not enough. On the barest of pretenses, familiar to anyone conversant in the justifying language of racial violence, they stormed the city.[4]

The connections between each of these political triumphs of racial violence are apparent. They are each imbricated in systems built upon decades of white supremacist culture that evolved into crude political ideology. But there are closer ties too. These events and their linkages are made more comprehensible by understanding the spatial cultures of communication that they created and were created out of. As a companion to Chapter 1, this chapter examines a body of more localized material modes of public address produced from or within the larger frame of lynchings and racial violence in the period. By modes of public address,

[3] Though the defeat of the Fusionist alliance between Republicans and Populists was roundly defeated on election day in 1898, Democrats were not content with electoral victory. After months of violent "red shirt" rallies mimicking those led by "Pitchfork" Ben Tillman in South Carolina, election day saw campaigns of voter intimidation and outright violence. Red Shirts were only the most violent arm of a specific white supremacy campaign contemporaneously referred to as "Redemption" and enacted in the next two election cycles in North Carolina. On the development and execution of these specific white supremacist campaigns, see Leon Prather, "The Red Shirt Movement in North Carolina 1898–1900." *Journal of Negro History* 62, no. 2 (1977): 174–184, https://doi.org/10.2307/2717177, and Robert Howard Wooley, "Race and Politics: The Evolution of the White Supremacy Campaign of 1898 in North Carolina," PhD dissertation, University of North Carolina at Chapel Hill, 1977. Helen Edmonds offers broader context in her work on the Fusion movement in North Carolina, still the definitive document six decades after its writing: Helen G. Edmonds, *The Negro and Fusion Politics in North Carolina, 1894–1901* (Chapel Hill: University of North Carolina Press, 1951).
[4] The coup d'état in Wilmington, North Carolina, is still an understudied event. Despite the efforts of many historians and authors, both the event itself and its representations of the political triumphs of white supremacy remain decentralized from popular understandings of American history. Two recent works, one scholarly, one journalistic, look at both the event and its absence from larger conceptions of history: Margaret M. Mulrooney, *Race, Place, and Memory: Deep Currents in Wilmington, North Carolina* (Gainesville: University Press of Florida, 2018); David Zucchino, *Wilmington's Lie: The Murderous Coup of 1898 and the Rise of White Supremacy* (New York: Atlantic Monthly Press, 2020). They are only the latest monographs about the event, which all too often still gets referred to as a "riot" rather than the calculated seizure of power that it was. The centennial collection of essays edited by historians David Cecelski and Timothy Tyson is still the best if not most comprehensive contextualization of the coup: *Democracy Betrayed: The Wilmington Riot of 1898 and Its Legacy*, ed. David S. Cecelski and Timothy B. Tyson (Chapel Hill: University of North Carolina Press, 1998).

I mean the articles and placards, signs and letters, notices and drawings that were read in and with the landscape of North Carolina. These objects helped people understand the politics of white supremacy through the framework of their own homes, towns, and counties. At the center of this chapter is the public letter that S. J. Hartsell wrote, one of many such objects of public address that circulated in the turn-of-the-century South. Through increased density and demographic change, expanded technologies of distribution, and adaptable forms of print and visual culture, collective communicative practices became a prominent part of public life in this new South. These objects served to mark the physical boundaries and practices of an emergent Jim Crow system.[5] Indeed, in many ways they were materially constitutive of the system itself.

I contextualize these nascent forms of Jim Crow materiality through an examination of the reading practices of handbills, pamphlets, and other new forms of public media, whose rise in the South helped constitute a commercial and discursive public culture. We might think of these as object narratives. By this, I mean that these media were themselves objects and carried text that helped make them more comprehensible to their readers or viewers. My focus here is on the material modes of public address associated with lynching. Sometimes they were very specific and dramatically violent (notes pinned to lynched bodies), at other times less spectacularly retributive (Hartsell's letter of Fusionist rebuke). Taken together, the object categories here constituted a localized public sphere in North Carolina and the broader South. Chapter 1 dealt with the wider networks of circulation within the nation. The circulation of objects and object narratives here is more confined. But it is no less important for that reduced scope. Here we can see the local connected to the transnational, and the emergence of a governing ideology of American white nationalism.[6] These objects are important because they indicate precisely how it was that white southerners came to see, read, and observe the world

[5] I base many of the ideas on this chapter in readings of Elizabeth Abel's and David Henkin's books, each of which conceptualizes ways of reading the signs and other texts embedded in a landscape. See Elizabeth Abel, *Signs of the Times: The Visual Politics of Jim Crow* (Berkeley: University of California Press, 2010) and David Henkin, *City Reading: Written Words and Public Spaces in Antebellum New York* (New York: Columbia University Press, 1998). I depart from their primary emphases on reading with an insistence that we understand these texts as part of larger modes of public address materialized in place.

[6] It is important to note as well that 1898 served as an inflection point for American imperial ideology and the entanglements of race and empire. There are several excellent histories linking American domestic racism with the transnational racial superiority of America's growing empire. See for instance Paul A. Kramer, *The Blood of Government:*

around them. With and from these objects, they built a new world of white supremacy.

The newspaper and the public sphere developed apace in the New South. David Henkin observes that the paper and the city streets had a "shared function as means of advertising through graphic representations laid out in rectilinear patterns for all to see." That overlap took on greater significance in a region where new forms of spatial organization replaced the "vertical structures of supervision and subordination" that had marked plantation slavery.[7] The postbellum North Carolina newspaper was the most important marker of space and authority. As Henkin points out, newspaper layouts both mimicked and documented the proliferation of signs, handbills, and advertisements in and on city streets. This analogy had a deeper resonance in turn-of-the-century North Carolina, where such a spatial organization also mimicked the significant overlapping of object forms then proliferating in the state's physical and conceptual landscapes. The newspaper page was the best point of access for many North Carolinians, who still did not have the experience of urban exploration common to New Yorkers a generation or two earlier. It could at once introduce them to the prominent political and emotional discourses of the day and evoke the sites and experience of the city itself. The newspaper page was an object in and of itself, and a repository for many of the other materials that marked the world of its creation. In a sense, it created a common public sphere. This was a more circumscribed community than the transnational one invoked by Benedict Anderson.[8] But this intrastate material public sphere expanded the boundaries of white commonality. And in 1898, it mobilized the Concord lynching as

---

Race, Empire, the United States, & the Philippines (Chapel Hill: University of North Carolina Press, 2006); Eric Tyrone Lowery Love, *Race over Empire: Racism and U.S. Imperialism, 1865–1900* (Chapel Hill: University of North Carolina Press, 2004). Scholars of southern literature have also made these linkages even more explicit and regionally focused: Peter Schmidt, *Sitting in Darkness: New South Fiction, Education, and the Rise of Jim Crow Colonialism, 1865–1920* (Jackson: University Press of Mississippi, 2008); Harry Stecopoulos, *Reconstructing the World: Southern Fictions and U.S. Imperialisms, 1898–1976* (Cornell University Press, 2008).

[7] Henkin, *City Reading*, 104; Abel, *Signs of the Times*, 4.
[8] Anderson, *Imagined Communities*. There is a larger argument to be made here that this did constitute an explicitly white and Confederate nationalist imagining, but I will leave that claim to other chapters in this book.

an object lesson on the dangers of "Negro rule" and the insistent possibilities of white supremacy.

Sam Hartsell's letter first appeared on the front page of the *Daily Concord Standard* in early October. On later reprinting in other papers, it was overwhelmed by contextualizing introductions and charged instructions for rooting out the influence of the Black voter. But in this first iteration it was more subdued, an almost intimate piece befitting its nominal genre. Addressed to "Mr. A.B. Young, Chairman Co. Dem. Ex. Com," on first glance the letter appeared like more of the abbreviated shorthand of the advertisements alongside which it appeared. But the contents of the letter proper were more affective, a familiar articulation of the epistolary form and its more individual and emotional modes of address.[9] Hartsell outlined the alleged crimes of Johnson and Kizer, emphasizing them as crimes against himself and his family "who were at church worshipping God." He translated this personal harm to a crime against the polity, balancing blame on himself for having "voted the Populist and fusion tickets" with the Black men "who do such deeds." In his estimation, "officers thus elected and the political parties winning elections with him ... will protect him in anything he does." He ended the letter with an explicit appeal "to the white men of North Carolina to vote for the protection of our mothers, wives, sisters, and daughters." Shifting his authorial voice for the last line, he again addressed Young: "use this letter as you please."[10]

This last line suggests the ultimate intention of the note and the form Hartsell was adopting. Clearly from the first, it was intended more as a public statement of political affiliation than an actual letter. In this – as I discuss elsewhere in this chapter – Hartsell was hardly alone. Letters of Fusionist refutation written to the white male public were their own minor genre during the election of 1898.[11] Nor was it unusual as a political letter. Hartsell clearly did not intend the letter to be private, and this formal artifice only made it seem a more intimate mode of address to the thousands of white men who read it in the paper, received it as

[9] On the affective qualities of intimate address, see many of the essays in *Epistolary Histories: Letters, Fiction, Culture*, ed. Amanda Gilroy and W. M. Verhoeven (Charlottesville: University of Virginia Press, 2000).

[10] "Mr. Hartsell's Letter," Daily Concord Standard.

[11] See for instance "Brunswick Populists," *The North Carolinian*, September 29, 1898; "Why He Left the Populists," *News and Observer*, September 18, 1898; "Appeals to His Fellows," *Salisbury Evening Sun*, September 17, 1898. The formulaic language and pleas to rejoin the Democrats seem to have clearly influenced Hartsell's own letter.

a broadside, or heard about it from a friend. This was a familiar and widely agreed-upon illusion: Politicians and other public figures had used this form of address to create civic intimacy for at least a century beforehand and continued to do so well afterward. Former Governor Thomas Jordan Jarvis similarly appealed to white male voters toward the end of his career (and life) a decade later. In his 1908 letter to the men of Pitt County, he addressed himself to an imagined "Dear Sir." He was more of a seasoned politician than Hartsell (or the Democratic operatives who may have helped him write his letter), but used similarly emotive appeals. Jarvis asked that Pitt County voters cast their ballots for North Carolina's temperance amendment in large part out of obligation to their families: "I now appeal to you, to each of you ... to do your duty in the fear of God and in love for humanity. With faith in your manhood and in your devotion to home, to county and to duty, I look for noble action on your part."[12] Jarvis's letter was reproduced as a pamphlet, a nod to the commonplace overlaps in form.

Hartsell's letter followed a similar pattern of reception, though it is unclear if it was reproduced specifically as a pamphlet. Regardless, Hartsell clearly intended it as a piece of direct political propaganda. The letter was dated and reprinted on the same day, suggesting coordination with both local newspaper editors and its nominal addressee.[13] Other editors capitalized on that purpose for their readers. Hartsell's text was reprinted with various references to his former and current political leanings: "Voted as a Fusionist," "He Comes to the Democrats," "Joined the White Man's Party." Just as prominent were framings of the personal cost Hartsell paid for his votes: "A Touching Appeal to the White Men of the State," "A Touching Appeal to White Men of N.C.," "He Paid the Penalty." Hartsell's letter was reprinted often, with newspapers liberally borrowing both others' titles and explanation of the letter's context. Thus, the reception of the letter was framed by the local and state political situation in each of these papers, with editors expounding further

[12] Thomas Jordan Jarvis, "[Letter] May 20th, 1908, Greenville, N.C. [to the Men of Pitt County]," Greenville, NC, 1908. North Carolina Collection, Louis Round Wilson Special Collections Library, University of North Carolina at Chapel Hill.
[13] Indeed, the local paper of record, *The Daily Standard*, explicitly denied that they or Democratic politicians had written the letter. In responding to these charges they noted: "We learned that Mr. Hartsell was going to write a letter and we went to see the nature of it ... We found Mr. Hartsell nearly done writing the letter. Though we had to wait to get the letter from Mr. A.B. Young we secured and published it"; "Let Them Assert It," *Daily Concord Standard*, November 3, 1898.

on the nakedly political messaging of the original letter. This was particularly the case in Wilmington, where Hartsell's missive was frequently recirculated in the weeks before the election in the service of that city's virulent white supremacy campaign.[14]

One particularly good example of this comes with the aforementioned "He Paid the Penalty," a highly editorialized printing of the letter in the October 7 edition of Wilmington's *Weekly Star*. The commentary focused on the observed veracity of Hartsell's letter, claiming that "everyone who reads the State papers knows that ... this species of crime has been fearfully frequent and horribly increased." As if to illustrate this, Hartsell's letter was surrounded with both this prefatory commentary and dozens of other news items all of which focused on the dangers of "Negro rule" and Fusionist collaboration. Some of these were short local pieces – pledges of Redemption or violent death in Richmond County, or the "white men united" in Nash. Others were longer commentaries on the statewide situation – condemnations of Cy Thompson and Marion Butler for collaborating with Black voters, or of other white men who had deserted the Populists. In their organization of the page, editors were clearly articulating the relationship between Hartsell's letter and these other texts. This mediation implicated all of the authors and events in a uniform message. By pairing the visceral, emotional impact of Hartsell's letter with observed accounts of other supposedly dire abuses of political power in the state, editors built on existing expectations and mobilized them for the political advancement of white supremacy.

Whatever his specific intentions, there is no denying Hartsell's fervent commitment to his newfound white supremacist ideology. In seeming recognition of his status as a martyr of Fusion politics, he was elected as president of one of the local chapters of the White Government Union.

---

[14] The circulation of Hartsell's letter, and its reframing for a variety of localized political agendas, went throughout the state and beyond. In some cities (like Oxford and Wilmington) it was continually reprinted. Always, its framing combined personal and emotional appeals with the responsibilities of electoral politics. See "A North Carolina Campaign Document," *The Vicksburg Herald*, October 6, 1898; "A Touching Appeal to the White Men of NC," *The Morning Post*, October 2, 1898; "A Touching Appeal to the White Men of the State," *The Enterprise*, October 13, 1898; "A Touching Appeal to White Men of NC," *Oxford Public Ledger*, October 6, 1898; "A Touching Appeal to White Men of NC," *Oxford Public Ledger*, October 13, 1898; "Appeal to White Men of N.C.," *The Wilmington Messenger*, October 18, 1898; "A Touching Appeal to White Men of N.C.," *The Semi-Weekly Messenger*, October 21, 1898; "He Paid the Penalty," *The Weekly Star*, October 7, 1898; "Mr. Hartsell's Letter," *The Concord Times*, October 6, 1898; "Voted as a Fusionist," *Asheville Citizen Times*, October 3, 1898.

This was a short-lived supremacist political organization aimed at capturing back the white Populist wing of Fusion voters, a movement that Hartsell and many other working-class white men had been part of. The minutes from one of the Union meetings Hartsell prevailed over saw him urging his fellow members to make testimonies against Fusion similar to his own public admission. At least one attendee also turned to the language of guilt and redemption, claiming "that if God would forgive him for it, he would never be guilty of the same anymore and he would stand up for white supremacy by voting a straight Democratic ticket."[15] Hartsell and his cohort had the zealotry of new converts. And in all likelihood, their commitment did not end there. Though it's impossible to place Hartsell among the poll-watching groups that sought to intimidate Black voters in 1898, it seems likely that he and his Union formed their own mob that day. Hartsell would be a documented participant in other civic expressions of anti-Black vigilance in the following years. In at least two instances over the next decade, he was partially responsible for capturing Black men accused of crimes.[16] It seems plausible that his vigilantism originated in 1898, a year filled with anti-Black violence. Whether or not this is true in his specific case, we know that word, image, and deed overlapped repeatedly in the white supremacy campaigns of North Carolina in 1898. Racial violence stemmed from communicative objects like Hartsell's. And in the height of the year's terror, racial violence became itself a mode of communication.

These texts are, of course, only part of a larger genre of commonplace public address. These objects were particularly adept at bridging the gap between official proclamations or laws and personal political

---

[15] "They're Now Democrats," *Daily Concord Standard*, October 24, 1898. The organization's founding documents were reprinted in one of the white supremacist papers of record, *The Wilmington Star*, as a means of promoting the founding of chapters statewide: "For White Supremacy," *The Wilmington Star*, August 27, 1898.

[16] In a broad survey of Concord area newspapers for twenty years from 1890 to 1910, Samuel J. Hartsell is twice identified as assisting with arrests of Black men. In 1899, he "aided in the chase" a deputy made in seeking a Black man apparently wanted for an indeterminate crime stemming from a loud "festival." This man hunt and arrest were in the vicinity of Hartsell's house, which perhaps lends some explanation to his participation; "An Attempted Escape," *Daily Concord Standard*, November 18, 1899. Likewise in 1907, Sam Hartsell was one of two men who "brought Abe Allison a negro ... wanted for another and more serious assault" to jail. They apparently arrested him in township 3, again in the proximity of Hartsell's house, though this time without the collaboration of police. Two instances do not necessarily make a pattern, but they are also likely an underrepresentation. Hartsell's continued connection to this kind of vigilantism is, I think, worthy of mention; *The Concord Daily Tribune*, June 27, 1907.

opinion. Visually, they stood out on the page with their mix of attention-grabbing headlines of the newspaper and the personal address of the letter. They were neither and both. These public modes of address drew on both the familiarity of older forms, and the relative novelty of the new, wider forms of circulation. Their designed intentions are clearer than our understanding of audience reception. Perhaps eventually, the formulaic pathos of these public letters wore thin as readers got accustomed to their repetitive appeals. But we can also return to the analogy of the sign and the city street. Novelty gives way to ubiquity, and ubiquity often to habituation. We cannot always create a direct line between observation and action because historians cannot read the thoughts that play out from intention to event. But we can judge from objects and words turned into action. And in 1898, North Carolina's political discourse centered on *things* and the lessons to be learned from them.

OBJECT LESSONS OF THE 1898 ELECTION

The political struggles of the mid-1890s seemed to coalesce in the lead-up to the 1898 election. The tenuously united voting bloc of Republicans and Populists – typically called Fusion – was competitive in statewide races since its formation ahead of the 1894 elections. Post Reconstruction, the mostly native-led Republican party found little success. The tentative victories of the insurgent Populists failed to match the rapacious growth of the Grange from which many of its members came after its 1887 formation.[17] Together, they managed to win big in the 1894 elections, wresting control of the North Carolina General Assembly and reaffirming the possibilities of an ascendant, cross-racial, working-class collaboration. How they exercised that newfound power, particularly amid the difficulties of a fraught partnership, inspired significant commentary and speculation in the years immediately afterward. Today, the Fusionist electoral bloc seems like little more than a passing fad, a movement whose aims far outstripped the reality of the times it came from. But in 1898, Fusion seemed like a looming threat to the desires of much

---

[17] Edmonds, The Negro and Fusion Politics, 32–42; Steven Hahn, *The Roots of Southern Populism: Yeomen Farmers and the Transformation of the Georgia Upcountry, 1850–1890* (Oxford University Press, 1983); "A Directory of the Granges in North Carolina, 1877," Documenting the American South Digital Collections, North Carolina Collection, Louis Round Wilson Special Collections Library, University of North Carolina at Chapel Hill.

of the white electorate. Scores of newspaper commentaries urged people to gather material evidence of what they perceived as the corruption and stupidity of this new coalition governance. The prevailing idea of this campaign was that Black men and their white enablers were physically transforming the state, and evidence of Fusion's misrule was written on the landscapes of its growing cities.

The first great historian of Fusion, Helen Edmonds, called the 1898 election a "picture campaign."[18] The newspapers and the world that year both seemed full of images calculated to give their viewers a better picture of the material and political worlds they inhabited. Both the Populism of the 1890s and the eventual violent Democratic opposition were spurred on by the resurgence of partisan newspapers.[19] Far from simply cataloging the news, these party papers functioned as distributors of both written declarations and vivid imagery. The most prominent of this white supremacist propaganda came from the newspaper magnate Josephus Daniels, who distributed 100,000 "supplements for the Democratic papers of the state containing cartoons, pictures of Negro officeholders," and accounts of the supposed abuses of their offices. Daniels and his many collaborators and employees produced a uniform visual message that literalized the monstrosities of Black political power. In daily front-page illustrations, Daniels's specially employed cartoonist rendered exaggerated portraits of the supposed terrors of this rule. Most famous was the vampiric characterization of "Negro rule." These heightened visuals were received with even more in-depth reports of the political situation in cities throughout the state. These were grounded in observation of the built environment and cultural landscape and read as a counterpoint to the fantastical imaginings of these illustrations. They were no less exaggerated for their supposed veracity.[20]

These warnings and admonishments most often came in the form of brief "object lessons" printed in prominent newspapers across the state.

[18] Edmonds, The Negro and Fusion Politics, 144.
[19] Leonidas L. Polk, the early head of the Farmers Alliance in North Carolina, was editor of *The Progressive Farmer*, which formally endorsed the Populist platform in 1892. His successor, Marion Butler, was editor of *The Caucasian*, which likewise became a mouthpiece for the party. This was an unusually fertile era for the political newspaper in North Carolina, with Josephus Daniels's *News and Observer* doing significant work for the Democratic Party. See Edmonds, *The Negro and Fusion Politics*, 32–50.
[20] Edmonds, *The Negro and Fusion Politics*, 145. For an overview of the political cartoons of Norman Ethre Jennett during the 1898 campaign, see Rachel Marie-Crane Williams, "A War in Black and White: The Cartoons of Norman Ethre Jennett & the North Carolina Election of 1898," *Southern Cultures* 19, no. 2 (2013): 7–31.

As Sarah Anne Carter has shown, the form of the object lesson was a prevalent one throughout the nineteenth century. Originally, these were fairly simple classroom exercises. These lessons proceeded from a single object and broadened out into an exploration of the abilities of the senses to observe and process the world.[21] It was a pedagogy rooted in a faith in description and observation of objects to reveal the realities of the world. Though the phrase has become little more than a cliché, editors and letter writers in 1898 used it in reference to the lessons of their childhood and the simplicity of learning from studied observation. In their estimation, the abuses of Black officeholders and their white allies were clear enough that even a child could comprehend them.

In particular, these object pedagogies sought to bridge the gap between rural majority North Carolinians and the supposed problems of life in the cities. They relied upon old dichotomies of rural and urban space, and a growing association of the city with both progressive modernity and Blackness. They also mediated between the representational visuals of newspaper print and the world they sought to distill into vivid imagery. These printed object lessons vouchsafed as an authority on the state's decline for those who might not stray far from the relative isolation of their rural homes.

The earliest object lessons of the 1898 campaign came in June with a detailed observation of the condition of Elizabeth City under its Fusion leaders. The article is full of inscrutable local references like the condition of "Poindexter bog" (a main street in supposedly poor repair). Under current rule, the street remained "an unsightly monument to the piebald representatives of the good name of the town."[22] This still evolving form held some subtleties of expression and characterization. But increasingly, newspapers became more open in their contempt for African American leaders and their allies. Editors took ever greater care to remind readers of the self-evidence that surrounded them. By September, one of the Wilmington newspapers observed that the election cycle prompted "numerous object lessons ... showing the results of negro rule in North Carolina. They are apparent to every man who walks the earth with his eyes and ears open."[23] For these editors and

[21] Sarah Anne Carter, *Object Lessons: How Nineteenth-Century Americans Learned to Make Sense of the Material World* (New York: Oxford University Press, 2018).
[22] "An Object Lesson," *The Weekly Economist*, June 17, 1898, 2; Fire Insurance Map, Sanborn Map Company, Elizabeth City, Pasquotank County, North Carolina, June 1891, University of North Carolina Libraries.
[23] "Another Object Lesson," *The Weekly Star*, September 30, 1898, 1.

other commenters, the squalor of their cities was an obvious indicator of what they marked as a twin laziness and aggression brought about by Black leadership and empowered Black people. This observation both stemmed from and reinforced white superiority: "The *white* man who can read a story like that without indignation must be a cold blooded miscreation" [emphasis in the original].[24] In this way, whiteness became another bodily faculty to add to the five senses. Its affordances included a clear-sightedness and perceptibility that apparently eluded others. Calling the 1898 election cycle a campaign of white supremacy underscores these facts. These object lessons based their condemnation of Blackness and African American leadership on a valorization of whiteness. Using the isolation of a single viewpoint, they posited a fix to their world's problems that could only be found in a wholehearted embrace of white superiority.

Though the *News and Observer* was the leading voice in the visual white supremacy campaign of 1898, the Wilmington papers took the lead in advocating the in-person "ocular demonstrations."[25] They posed a counterpoint to the Raleigh paper's reliance on exaggerated cartoons and realistic drawings of Black politicians. The form of visuality put forth by the Wilmington papers insisted on embedded, bodily observation, even if it had to be secondhand from a trusted white source. Accounts of visits to the cities as sites of power supposedly revealed the misrule inherent there. The Wilmington *Star* noted that "Mr. P.G Sellers of Brunswick County" renounced his membership in the Populist party after he "visited Wilmington and had an ocular demonstration" of "negro swagger, arrogance and insolence." Similarly, J. D. Allred of interior Randolph County "had doubts about the representations made as to negro office-holding." His solution was to "go to Raleigh, visit the public institutions, and see for himself." He too recommitted "to the ranks of the white man's party" after this visit, which the paper reported as a demonstration.[26] These accounts of the credulous rural resident visiting the urban population center and being converted by what he saw struck a chord in the fractious political environment of 1898. Long-standing white resentment of even miniscule Black power met with growing distrust of urbanization and industrialization. Accounts of these visits played on both. Likewise, they re-created in miniature the experience of the city's arrangement of space.

[24] "Another Object Lesson," *Wilmington Morning Star*, October 8, 1898.
[25] "Convincing Object Lessons," *The Weekly Star*, October 7, 1898.
[26] "Convincing Object Lessons," *The Weekly Star*, 2.

City residents might be subject to the whims of Fusionist rule, but they also had more ready access to the handbills, signs, advertisements, and other visual ephemera that could channel their anger into action. Those object forms relied on a particular arrangement of space, where people would happen by them. In the absence of the spatial experience of the urban public sphere, newspapers created a visual and experiential world for their readers.

These many dozens of near-daily newspaper accounts sought to bridge the gaps between representation and replication. In this usage, newspapers were not material sources as such, but instead served as a frame through which readers could see the world and comprehend or even participate in both large visual spectacles and subtler observed signs. The technological limitations of the newspaper were evident in this framing. Though the earliest photographs had already been printed in papers both at home and abroad, the inexpensive reproduction of photographic images had not yet made it to southern newspapers.[27] So, descriptions had to suffice to create an embodied knowledge. Looking at cities and marking the supposed signs of decay was an important, but passive form of visuality and object-oriented learning. Returning to Hartsell's letter, we can see its overlaps with these object narratives. They both relied on the declamatory conceit of public media of address. Hartsell's letter was not epistolary in any meaningful sense: No one could reply to it, and there was no possibility of exchange in its one-sided address. These object lessons were similarly self-contained and one-sided. Like other material modes of public address, their readership was passive and prescribed. A reader could choose to vote for the politician on the sign, attend the show on the handbill, buy the piece of furniture on the advertisement. These object lessons were similarly transactional, as their framing as pleas to good white men suggested. White readers were left without a rhetorical choice: They could either believe the material evidence they were presented and recommit to white supremacy, or risk losing their status as white men. In this way, visual observation and spectacle came to define the commitment to white supremacy. When we view lynching within this broader context, we can see how it built upon the structures of material white supremacy already so commonplace in the post-Emancipation South.

[27] On the history of photographic reproductions in newspapers and other media, see Michael L. Carlebach, *The Origins of Photojournalism in America* (Washington, DC: Smithsonian Institution Press, 1992).

READING LYNCHING'S LANDSCAPE

The visuality of spectacle lynching was undeniable. The immediate shock of seeing dead bodies forced a visceral reaction: of fear and trauma for Black viewers, of pleasure or at least satisfaction for many white viewers. Photographs and postcards carried much of the retrospective weight of a lynching.[28] But those visual spectacles only had the impact they did because people knew how to view them, and where to place them within their understanding of media circulations and meaning. The object world of the Concord lynching, and of racial violence in the period more broadly, was one populated by things that bridged the gap between the written and the seen. These moments of media encounter – with handbills, printed notices, public letters – were not new, but were newly prominent in reordered southern geographies. They bore an increased ubiquity amid changes in both the built and perceptual environments of this new South. These media encounters, what I call here modes of public address, acted

[28] Though this chapter is primarily about reading cultures and *visuality*, there is a rich literature on the visual cultures of lynching postcards and photography that has influenced my own insights here. Some are cited elsewhere in this text as well, including Harvey Young's work, in both article and book form. His was some of the earliest and remains among the most trenchant theorizations of Blackness, performance, and visuality: Harvey Young, *Embodying Black Experience: Stillness, Critical Memory, and the Black Body* (Ann Arbor: University of Michigan Press, 2010) and Harvey Young, "The Black Body as Souvenir in American Lynching," *Theatre Journal* 57, no. 4 (2005): 639–657. Sandy Alexandre's work remains perhaps the most important intervention into our understanding of the often mentioned but little understood lynching postcard: Sandy Alexandre, "Out on a Limb: The Spatial Politics of Lynching Photography," *Mississippi Quarterly* 61, no. 1–2 (2008): 71–112 and Sandy Alexandre, *The Properties of Violence: Claims to Ownership in Representations of Lynching* (Oxford, MS: University Press of Mississippi, 2012). The most prominent chronicle of lynching postcards, photographs, and other visual representations is still *Without Sanctuary: Lynching Photography in America*, ed. James Allen (Santa Fe: Twin Palms, 2000). The book and traveling exhibition of the same name operate under the assumption that exposure to these photographs will render the viewer shocked, disgusted, and ultimately moved to action. As both the unremarked ubiquity and preservation of these images, as well as the rest of this book, make clear, I remain uncertain that this collection does not also invoke the prurient pleasure of the white supremacist regarding these images of torture. They also fail, in my view, to arouse anything more than a provocation toward reaction, rather than action (a point made by Susan Sontag around images of death and violence generally: Susan Sontag, *Regarding the Pain of Others* (New York: Picador, 2003), especially 34). More recently Marcus Wood has examined the lynching postcard as both collected object and visual symbol situated in a cultural archive defined by enslavement: Marcus Wood, "Valency and Abjection in the Lynching Postcard: A Test Case in the Reclamation of Black Visual Culture," *Slavery & Abolition* 34, no. 2 (2013): 202–221. He finds a tentative possibility of agency within this photographic archive, an unintended veneration of

as framing devices for the comprehension and normalization of lynchings and other forms of racist violence. They allowed spectators to "read" this white supremacist violence into the landscape. In this way, the lynching of Tom Johnson and Joe Kizer spread its influence throughout the state and served as one of the pillars of the permanent spatial and conceptual changes to North Carolina and the broader South. Hartsell's letter was part of an archive read in the new landscapes of white supremacy.[29]

Life in the post-Emancipation South was ordered in part through visual apprehension and comprehension. On a routine level, this meant that the average southerner might read more of the textual and visual material surrounding them than had the previous generation. This was especially true in the growing cities of the region where advertisements blanketed the newer and taller buildings. Cities were transformed by print cultures and circulation practices that saw printed material rise to

the Black people who were so easily murdered but are so difficult to excise. His argument is compelling when applied to the individual photograph read closely. As a collection (or, indeed, as a show), they lose some of their particular narrative power and become chroniclers of varied means of torture and execution (as Wood recounts with his personal history of reception of *Without Sanctuary*). Perhaps the most compelling intervention into lynching photography is the intersection of historical scholarship and artistic expression represented in Ken Gonzales-Day, *Lynching in the West*. His work resituates an assumption about the purpose and victims of lynchings. The book sprang from his photography in his series "Erased Lynchings." This project recenters both active and passive mobs as the subjects of photography, recasting their images as the subject of what otherwise often appear as almost pornographic displays of excessive violence. While indebted to the research and insights of each of these scholars, my own work here looks at a larger visual and material culture by which we might understand these photographs and other objects people sought to circulate.

[29] My use of framing here should be taken as a reference to the context of paratextuality formulated by Gerard Genette and expounded upon in studies of early modern print culture in particular. In this chapter I am primarily concerned with what Genette calls "epitext," the positioning of the reader to understand the text through a variety of social and cultural preconditions. In effect, I am here considering landscape as a form of epitext. Peritext refers to the more formal or even official modes of framing for a piece of writing: front covers, dedication pages, introductions, author's or editor's notes. Scholars of literature, and recently of history, have greatly expounded upon the interpretation of peritext, but have done less so with epitext. Perhaps this is because Genette himself leaves it as a matter peripheral to his main argument and intention. Regardless, it is a way to understand the material world and its relationship to reading practices, a task that I at least begin to accomplish here. In addition to Genette, I am particularly relying here upon Christopher Tomlins's application of paratextuality to the evidence of the Nat Turner case. His "speculative history" is an excellent model of the preconditions with which readers of all sorts approach objects of history and memory. See Gérard Genette, *Paratexts: Thresholds of Interpretation*, trans. Jane E. Lewin (Cambridge, UK: Cambridge University Press, 1997); Christopher L. Tomlins, *In the Matter of Nat Turner: A Speculative History* (Princeton: Princeton University Press, 2020).

FIGURE 2.1 Turn-of-the-twentieth-century Concord, North Carolina, with a proliferation of urban texts. North Carolina Collection, University of North Carolina Library at Chapel Hill

a new level of ubiquity. Structures made of sturdy materials and built to greater heights held advertisements for tobacco and colas, headache medicine and flour.[30] People might read notices in the newspaper or find them tacked to telegraph poles or painted on walls. Advertisements similarly occupied this shared territory. In Concord, where Johnson and Kizer were abducted, urban and industrial growth helped transform the place from a town to burgeoning city (Figure 2.1). True to that transformation, turn-of-the-century images of its main streets are overflowing with visual media of public address. Images of Union Street from both north and south show a still unpaved main street filled with these texts. At every level there are permanent signs and temporary banners, painted advertisements and temporary handbills. They are both monumental and human scaled, appealing to the walker, the rider, or even the viewer of a postcard or photograph. This new reading landscape inaugurated southerners fully into a national consumer society and habituated them to mass media reading practices. The South was an increasingly commercialized economy, and the growth of both regional and national brands infused city life with these constant signs and symbols, what Henkin calls "the spectacle of public life."[31]

But the density of this imagery in the South was not confined to the cities alone. As Chapter 1 suggests, newspapers, railroads, telegrams,

---

[30] Helpfully, North Carolina's historic architecture and changes in the built environment are among the best documented in the nation. Catherine Bishir's landmark volume *North Carolina Architecture* extensively details these changes across the state. See Catherine Bishir, *North Carolina Architecture*, portable ed. (Chapel Hill: University of North Carolina Press, 2005).

[31] Henkin, City Reading, 10. On many of the changes to the built environment of Wilmington specifically in this period, see Mulrooney, Race, Place, and Memory, 111–173.

and even telephones wound their way into the once-backcountry of places like Cabarrus County. Residents there were exposed to these proliferating advertisements, semi-official proclamations, and other public modes of address. And they read them through the frames of their own experience of place. Indeed, one of the characteristics of this new textual and material culture was an emphasis on the rural and urban divide. Readers of the hundreds of newspapers in circulation in 1898 saw depictions of the city that furthered their own identification of their particular, local South as the purest form of regional identity. As I discuss elsewhere in this chapter, the "object lessons" of the reading culture of 1898 were the burgeoning North Carolina cities. For rural readers, these urban spaces were visualized as literal cesspools, run by the incompetent Fusion of white liberals and freed Black men, both bent on their own vision of a remade South. Reading about the urban world in their rural or small-town communities, white rural people came to view cities as exemplars of the corruption that they associated with Fusion and "Negro rule." But they were not immune from the handbills and circulars that crowded telegraph poles, community stores, and trees at crossroads and other gathering spots. And, after the advent of Jim Crow segregation, these same small communities saw their borders and physical resources policed by the semi-official Jim Crow signage that served as the successor to this earlier generation of public, material modes of address.[32]

Life in this South was one of constantly reading and being read. In Henkin's antebellum New York, public spaces were at least theoretically designed for the abstract masses. The texts affixed onto or constructed into the built environment there "could be addressed anonymously, impersonally, and without reference to particularities of status." This was never the case in the South. There, and increasingly in these years around the turn of the century, race and class were visibly sutured. Any person perceived to be Black aroused additional and intensive scrutiny. In this way the implied authority of signs, handbills, public notices, and commercial advertisements was made all the more complex by the very racialized practices of looking, seeing, and categorizing. The texts represented a dispersal of power. For white people, this only reconfirmed their assumptions of their own supremacy and authority. For Black people, it meant an objectless and pervasive power expressed in both what they looked at and how they were

---

[32] See Abel, *Signs of the Times.*

looked at.[33] The anonymous democratization of material, authorial power implied by these new public media expressions marked itself in public space in much the same way that more recognized material objects (houses, Lost Cause memorials) did.[34] Those were clear, material expressions of white supremacist power. But the literal signs and symbols of these landscapes were equally potent in communicating a generic, all-encompassing hegemony.

White supremacists capitalized on that power and made their own cause all the more pervasive through it. In this way, lynching was both a cause and a symptom of the white supremacy of the era. It proceeded from and often combined with the objects people read through the frame of their respective landscapes. And in its spectacularity and sheer affective violence, it both called upon and overwhelmed the practices of landscape reading that southerners had absorbed in the generation after the Civil War. The callousness of "reading" bodies, people, in this way cannot be underestimated. What Marcus Wood calls "the unspeakable subject of lynching" was one expressed through visual and written media, up to and including the bodies of victims themselves. Other scholars have regarded that bodily objectification. I am interested in how these media encounters, this reading of and with the remade southern landscape, served as a frame for white southerners' understandings of the lynchings that they witnessed. To better understand the spectacles that they sought to create through lynching, we should strive to comprehend the everyday visual and material markers that came to populate their worlds.[35]

---

[33] Henkin, *City Reading*, 10. We might reflexively refer to this arrangement of space using the terms of the Foucauldian panopticon. But that would ignore the dispersal of this spatial power as it was arranged and experienced. Power here was distributed from above, below, and particularly from *beside*. The implied power of the billboards, advertisements, and signs was reinforced for Black people by the white man or woman they passed on the street who, with one look, could both comprehend their racial status and order them off the sidewalk or into the road. On these forms of looking and the dispersal of power, see Nicholas Mirzoeff, *The Right to Look: A Counterhistory of Visuality* (Durham, NC: Duke University Press, 2011), 7; Robyn Wiegman, *American Anatomies: Theorizing Race and Gender* (Durham, NC: Duke University Press, 1995), 21.

[34] There is an excellent and fairly comprehensive literature on the landscapes of commemoration in this period of the South. See for instance Catherine Bishir, "Landmarks of Power: Building a Southern Past, 1885–1915," *Southern Cultures* 1, no. 1 (1993): 5–45; Brundage, *The Southern Past*; Cox, *Dixie's Daughters*.

[35] Wood, "Valency and Abjection in the Lynching Postcard," 205. As objects and forms move from innovative to commonplace, their increasing ubiquity marks a habituation to new practices. In times and places like the turn-of-the-twentieth-century South, people

CIRCULATING PRINT CULTURES

The earliest precursors of what would become the Jim Crow system were attempts to extend the intimate familiarity and casual surveillance of the plantation world to new spaces. New license for mobility precipitated segregation as an "[attempt] to counter a world in which people increasingly moved beyond the local and thus the known by creating racial identity anonymously as well."[36] Official segregation followed these informally enacted practices slowly, but when it did, it adopted the preexisting vernacular of signs, handbills, and notices already extant throughout much of the South. Few of the material means of public address were new object forms. Things like political handbills and letters had a long history in North Carolina prior to the 1898 election cycle. Extant copies of these handbills are relatively scarce, but clearly illustrate the evolution of intertwined print and visual cultures that evolved throughout the course of the nineteenth century. The production, and more importantly the circulation, of these material modes of public address defined and delimited a civic sphere based on whiteness.

If surviving archival materials are any indicator, the early nineteenth-century Democrat Charles Fisher was a prolific pamphleteer. A brief public letter circulated early in his career establishes a broad audience: the still newly conceptualized general "public." Indeed, a crucial piece of this pamphleteering was the definition of its own audience. Fisher addressed the biggest possible constituency. Anyone reading the text, or having it read to them, could assume themselves a recipient of his message, provided that they had the hope of eligibility to vote. Like Hartsell several decades later, Fisher sought to create an intimate proximity

could reimagine their world together through intensive engagement with shared cultures of reading. Media historian Lisa Gitelman calls this process "socially realized structures of communication ... a ritualized collocation of different people on the same mental map"; Lisa Gitelman, *Always Already New: Media, History, and the Data of Culture* (Cambridge, MA: MIT Press, 2006), 7. In other words, habituation comes after adaptation and is underpinned by social as much as technological shifts. An apt comparison for this late nineteenth-century moment might be the adaptation to first radio, then television, in the next several decades of the twentieth century. Of course, the even more recent advent of the internet and digital cultures is all the more present in the consciousness of historians now. The means by which novel forms become embodied, often literally, is an ongoing area of interest to media scholars. This is particularly so amid the proliferation of digital cultures of communication and authorship. On this topic, see Alan Liu, "Imagining the New Media Encounter," in *A Companion to Digital Literary Studies*, ed. Susan Schreibman and Ray Siemens (Oxford: Blackwell, 2008), 3–25.

[36] Hale, *Making Whiteness*, 135–136; Abel, *Signs of the Times*, 4.

across a broad category of citizenry. That civic audience became more circumscribed and limited, depending on the year or the occasion, when the title "freemen" was attached as a salutation. It is difficult to track the intensity of circulation of these materials, but clearly they represented a means of communication that increasingly delimited itself on the basis of citizenship and voting rights. The modes of address here are particularly important. Many of these pamphlets and circulars were attacks on an opposing candidate. Yet in what we now expect as commonplace in political advertising, they were universally addressed not to the opposition, but to the citizenry as a whole.

This strategy invited the reader into common cause with the writing politician. We might see this as restrictive, or as a more intimate form of bridging the gap between public figure and public. Already, these objects represented an emerging genre form that skirted the lines of various forms of authority. These were not epistolaries in the usual sense of communicating private news. Nor were they official proclamations of someone holding political power. Rather, they were intended to state implicitly held views and jockey for popular support by confirming a constituent's opinions. They shared that functionality with emerging modes of visual advertising.[37] Shorter and less intensive of language or purpose than contemporary pamphlets – like Wilmingtonian David Walker's *Appeal* – these handbills served as both a mode of address and a kind of advertisement.[38] They helped create a larger culture of public address that repurposed familiar forms. Hartsell and his Democratic collaborators would have been very familiar with these circulars as both implied recipient (Hartsell) and author. These modes of public address exhibited authority in and of themselves. Not expressions of authorial power, they had both vaguely defined audiences and a distributive authority that came from their circulation itself.[39]

---

[37] It's also important to note that advertisements and particularly tracts and handbills owe a great deal of their evolution and ubiquity to the evangelical religious movements of the early nineteenth century. See David Paul Nord, *Faith in Reading: Religious Publishing and the Birth of Mass Media in America* (Oxford: Oxford University Press, 2004).

[38] Its own kind of material mode of address, Walker's *Appeal* should be understood not just as a pamphlet or other print work, but within the broader material context I am outlining here: David Walker, *Walker's Appeal, in Four Articles: Together with a Preamble to the Colored Citizens of the World, but in Particular, and Very Expressly to Those of the United States of America* (Boston: Printed for the author, 1829).

[39] In early Republican North Carolina, these imprints were apparently already an established form judging by the preservation of some early examples, such as two from nearby Salisbury in 1804: Stokes Montfort, "To the freemen of the counties of Rowan,

Material texts like these also helped to define the physical space of the polity. Much of early American urban space was littered with these kinds of declamatory political, commercial, and public objects. That pattern persisted and intensified in the postbellum urbanizing South. In 1868, Wilmington saw a rash of "sepulchral notices" posted in prominent public places. Adopting the mythical language of the nascent Ku Klux Klan (KKK), these bulletins addressed the new constitutional attempts at universal male suffrage. Undoubtedly, they were intended for both Black and white passersby who might alternately despair or thrill at the "wonderful attraction in mystery" of language that newspaper editors tried to parse. People who encountered the signs across town knew how to read its jargon because of the attention given to the KKK and its mythic-literary pretensions from their very birth. Their incomprehensible, faux-learned rhetoric parodied authoritative, official notices. What white people could read as light parody or simple entertainment was legible to Black readers as a new articulation of control over the space of the city and the broader public sphere. Newspaper editors understood that, comparing the KKK and its space-claiming notices to the Union leagues that had "gathered every vagabond darkey from the Potomac to the Rio Grande." Wilmington was typical of the constant attention given to the KKK and its literary pretensions written in public space. A front-page, reprinted article called the Klan's language unequaled "since the dark, dismal, and ghastly times of Shakespeare." The stakes of these distributed notices were historic then, a salvo in the contestation over claims to public space that was constantly being enacted in these immediate postwar years. The same editors who bemusedly and obsessively reported the Klan's public writings angrily condemned people "marking over with indecent words and sentences, all available public places." Like other graffiti, these markings and phrases clearly had subversive intent and radical potential. Like the KKK handbills, they were directed at no one and everyone at once. This

---

Randolph, and Cabarrus in the state of North-Carolina," Salisbury: 1804, in the North Carolina Collection, Louis Round Wilson Special Collections Library, University of North Carolina at Chapel Hill; Stokes Montfort, "To the freemen of the counties of Rowan, Randolph and Cabarrus; in the state of North-Carolina: Fellow-Citizens," Salisbury, NC: 1804, NC Collection. And the form was still common at least into the 1860s: J. G. Ramsay, "Circular: to the freemen of the Eighth Congressional District," North Carolina: October 16, 1863, NC Collection. The aforementioned Charles Fisher either had a long enough career and/or sufficient resources to have a relatively large number of these ephemeral documents authored by him preserved in archives. The North Carolina Collection at UNC holds circulars spanning thirty years from him: Charles Fisher, "To the Public," 1815–1817, NC Collection.

proliferation of public addresses written onto the landscape could seem simply like a debate without sides or stakes. But for the empowered Klan, it was only one part of a strategy of asserting power over the public spaces of Wilmington. A report a few days later told of a "mysterious horseman ... making a rapid circuit" of a working-class neighborhood at 1:30 a.m. The night-riding Klan was backing up its written words. This kind of intimidation overpowered the passive rhetoric of writing in public space, re-inaugurating symbolic acts of terror as a way of literally emplacing power.[40]

The period of post-Emancipation contestation over public and civic spaces was a brief one. Over the next generations, the definitions of public place and belonging changed with the advent of industrial capital, urban growth, and the attendant rise of new forms of political power.

The best example of this comes from so-called mill villages, worker housing where all nominally publicly shared space was company owned. In these facsimiles of a public sphere, mill owners used public notices as an extension of their power (Figure 2.2). The owners of the White Oak mill in Greensboro distributed broadsides in 1909 that regulated workers' yards through the auspices of a contest. The bold printed "NOTICE!" at the top of the page made the assurances that "our desire is merely to help beautify the village and we want everyone to help" seem false. It is an object whose creator was keenly aware of both the visual impact of its design and its placement in quasi public space. Requests to coop up chickens, plant bulbs and seeds to "beautify the village," and compete for the "neatest kept premises" were thinly disguised regulations. The notices posted around the intentionally self-contained

[40] Henkin, *City Reading*; "Mysterious," *The Wilmington Morning Star*, March 24, 1868, 3; "'Thrice the Brindle Cat Hath Mewed,'" *The Wilmington Morning Star*, March 24, 1868, 1; "K.K.K. the Spirits Moving," *The Wilmington Morning Star*, March 25, 1868, 1; "Mysterious Horseman," *The Wilmington Morning Star*, March 28, 1868, 3. Both Margaret Mulrooney and William McKee Evans mention this incident in passing: William McKee Evans, *Ballots and Fence Rails: Reconstruction on the Lower Cape Fear* (Chapel Hill: University of North Carolina Press, 1967), and Mulrooney, Race, Place, and Memory, 99–100. Mulrooney in particular suggests that this was the work of the nascent Ku Klux Klan. Likely it was a group building upon the notoriety of what was still a small organization from Tennessee obsessed with its own culture of literate nonsense. Elaine Frantz Parsons's study of the early Klan complicates the narrative obsession with this new group as manifested in the articles cited above with the realities of its nonexistent national infrastructure. Groups like the one in Wilmington were performing the spectacle of secrecy they associated with the KKK, a performance that fit neatly within the urban visual media of the day: Elaine Frantz Parsons, *Ku-Klux: The Birth of the Klan during Reconstruction* (Chapel Hill: University of North Carolina Press, 2015).

NOTICE!

Prizes will be awarded as usual this year for the best front yards and neatest kept premises.

In planting vines and shrubbery at the various houses, the company does not mean or intend to take the control or arrangement of the front yards away from the occupant. Our desire is merely to help beautify the village, and we want every one to help in his own way toward this end.

Flower seeds, grass seeds, and bulbs will be distributed as usual, dates of distribution to be posted later.

Every one who desires his front yard to be plowed will please give his name to Miss Richardson at once.

It is particularly requested that everybody who has chickens keep them cooped up or else in enclosed wire yards.

The following prizes will be awarded :

One First Prize	$15.00
Two Second Prizes	10.00
Five Third Prizes	5.00
Ten Fourth Prizes	3.00
Ten Fifth Prizes	2.00
Fifteen Sixth Prizes	1.00

Those who received first or second prizes last year will not be allowed to compete for these prizes this year. They may, however, compete for third prize or lower.

WHITE OAK COTTON MILLS.

March, 1909.

FIGURE 2.2 An example of the broadside announcements commonplace in southern mill villages

confines of the mill village only exaggerated their power as proclamatory objects. These mill-owned villages replicated the regulatory space of the urban grid in miniature.[41] Handbills and other notices then served as more than advertising or even quasi-regulatory objects. They had a particular pedagogy embedded in their encounters. Their observed visuality was meant to instruct and discipline. The White Oak flier was one that both taught its viewers how to regard their own and their neighbor's lawns and instructed them in how to achieve an ideal of boss-directed perfection.

These pedagogies were increasingly commonplace in turn-of-the-century North Carolina. Though they would continue to be prominent

[41] Much of the literature on postbellum southern urbanism rightly focuses on race and its spatial regulations. Works like those by Hanchett and Delaney also usefully outline, at least by implication, the classed dimensions of this new development: David Delaney, *Race, Place, and the Law, 1836–1948* (Austin: University of Texas Press, 1998); Thomas W. Hanchett, *Sorting out the New South City: Race, Class, and Urban Development in Charlotte, 1875–1975* (Chapel Hill: University of North Carolina Press, 1998).

technologies of control well into the twentieth century, it was in the election year of 1898 that these media forms reached their height.[42] That year's political contests saw arguably the most violent suppression and revocation of voting in the long history of such indignities in the United States. The year 1898 was marked by both visual and written evocations of political misrule, and violent material markers of its revocation. These spectacles of public order and disorder borrowed most obviously from the rise of spectacle lynching over the course of the two previous decades. Never isolated from the larger material worlds of its enactment, the material culture of lynching too was emmeshed with modes of media and public address.

PUBLIC COMMUNICATION ON THE BODY

The most obvious examples of these forms of public address came in the interstices of urban space. As discussed above, they were calculated to reframe urban experience and served as a spectacle of roving authorial presence and implied authority. They were at once objects laden with meaning and overdetermined with their excessive force of often extraneous expression. This need – both to write on the landscape and to have its visual force be legible to those viewing it – was not confined to the city streets or the newspapers. Its most vivid expression came in the notes left at lynching sites or pinned to lynched men's bodies.

These notes were excessive things, texts of justification and threat that offered a written gloss on a message that was already viscerally apparent at the scene of a lynching. In a survey of several hundred lynchings across several southern states, I found roughly a dozen instances of explanatory

---

[42] Later examples from the North Carolina Piedmont include other handbills, fliers, and ephemera that further complicate the balance between power, politics, and advertising. A fairly straightforward example of political pamphleteering from an older tradition was distributed in Burlington in 1947: "To the Voters of the City of Burlington," Handbill, Burlington, NC, 1947, North Carolina Collection, Louis Round Wilson Special Collections Library, University of North Carolina at Chapel Hill. Complicating matters was the city's reputation as a city comprised of individually run mill villages whose dispersed power lay mostly in the hands of mill owners and managers. More complicated still is the handbill from 1960s Raleigh: "Don't Buy at These Stores: Woolworth's, McLlellan's, Walgreen's, Efird's, Kress', Hudson-Belk's," Raleigh, NC, 1960, North Carolina Collection, Louis Round Wilson Special Collections Library, University of North Carolina at Chapel Hill. It comes from a marked place of disempowerment, but boldly asserts a boycott message in its simple wording and design. It is at once anti-advertisement and appeals to moral authority in the longer tradition of other such public notices.

notes left on lynched bodies. They spanned from the 1880s to the 1910s. Given the representation of notes in many of the visual illustrations of lynching (cartoons for instance), it seems likely that the practice was far more commonplace than this seeming paucity might suggest.[43] Regardless, the number of these notes belies their importance. Like other such objects of public address, they articulated the principles of an otherwise unstated set of practices and assumptions. We know that lynching was underlain by the increasingly articulable ideologies of white supremacy, but the specific justifications of the practice were generally carried in the spectacle that they assumed. To add this written justification and explanation, then, was to put voice and space to the shared assumptions of a lynching and what it meant to do. These notes were aberrant objects that made the unwritten norms of lynching visible. They give us material access to the composition of a lynching, to the shared formulaic understanding of its practices. In combination with the other circulated accounts of lynching, these notes represented their own pedagogies, instilling in white audiences instruction, explanation, and justification. These notes were nominally intended for Black audiences. But like Hartsell's letter or Fisher's circulars, their stated form was far different from their actual use. Dead bodies were themselves more than sufficient means of communication for African American audiences. Already primed by routinized surveillance and violence, they needed no further warning about the dangers of white mobs. These overdetermined media then were intended primarily for white audiences who would build further commonality and solidarity from these unwarranted notes of intent.[44]

[43] The motif of the lynching note was ubiquitous in editorial cartoons. The rise of these notes is coincident with what Amanda Frisken has defined as the height of the visual "lexicon of anti-lynching activism." Before the commonplace distribution of photography, Black-run newspapers like *The Freeman of Indianapolis* or the *Richmond Planet of Virginia* produced detailed and pointed cartoon illustrations condemning lynching. As with other cultural practices of lynching and anti-lynching, it is hard to know whether these illustrations mimicked extant rituals of mob violence, or helped create and reinforce them. Part of the vernacular of these cartoons though were depictions of notes left at lynching sites. Certainly some of the earliest anti-lynching cartoons identified by Frisken depict explanatory signage. One such, "Some Daily or Rather Nightly Occurrences in the South," shows an anonymous lynched body with a prominent "Miss. K.K.K" sign attached to the trunk of the lynching tree: Amanda K. Frisken, "'A Song without Words': Anti-lynching Imagery in the African American Press, 1889–1898," *Journal of African American History* 97, no. 3 (2012): 264; "Some Daily or Rather Nightly Occurrences in the South [Cartoon]," *The Freeman*, September 21, 1889, sec. 4.
[44] I am relying here on the literature on formulaic composition and oral narrative in the fields of folklore and cultural anthropology. Oral transmission of both narrative and performance standards within speech and expressive communities seems the closest analog

The earliest instance of a note pinned to a lynched body that I can locate in North Carolina came with the murder of politician and community leader Wyatt Outlaw in 1870. The note left to be discovered on his body referenced both similar means of public address and the parodic historical language of the KKK. The mob clearly intended this note as part of the larger symbolic apparatus of the lynching. After seizing Outlaw from his home, its members hanged him to an elm in the Alamance County courthouse square. In so doing, they invoked the authority of the legal, public executions that traditionally took place in this spot. But the mob was also capitalizing on the role of the public square as a venue for public address. Those involved only added to that reading of the scene with the note they left pinned to Outlaw's body. The phrasing of the simple message was intentionally anachronistic: "Beware ye guilty parties both black and white." Its mock-antiquated, mock-legalistic English claimed both history and authority. That historicity served as an additional authenticating and authoritative measure. There was an irony in the creation of this object being embedded in that imagined history. Its message was to the particular moment, and to the rising power of white and Black allied Republicans during Reconstruction. Lynching would continue to evolve as a mode of specifically racialized terror, but notes were constructed with claims to different forms of universality.[45]

A little more than a decade later, two separate lynching victims in neighboring North Carolina counties had similar notices pinned to their bodies by mobs. The note left at the site of Archie Johnson's hanging proclaimed: "Our wives and daughters must be protected." Two years later, the cause for John Boggan's murder was elaborated slightly: "This man makes a full confession. Our women must be protected." The notes were already conforming to a recognizable style and uniform intention. They differ in content, though arguably not in intent, from the notice left on Outlaw's body. Both notes supplement the immediately readable violence of the lynching with a justifying framework. As lynchings were

to the circulation and entextualization of belief that I write about here. See the work of Dell Hymes and particularly his early theorization of the linkages between spoken word and performance: Dell Hymes, "Breakthrough into Performance," in *Folklore: Performance and Communication*, ed. Dan Ben-Amos and Kenneth Goldstein (The Hague: Mouton), 11–74. Also of particular use here is Michael Pfeifer's articulation of the rituals of lynching. See in particular *Rough Justice*, 44–49.

[45] This sign is documented in several instances, including "The Outrage at Graham," *The People's Press*, March 18, 1870; "Impeachment," *The Southern Home*, March 7, 1871.

increasingly explained as protections of white femininity, these notes and their reportage in newspaper and oral accounts helped spread that justifying logic.[46] More interesting is their relationship to each other. While their message is hardly original, even in a moment when the particular language and iconography of spectacle lynching were still being defined, they are clearly influenced by one another. Perhaps this is because both mobs shared some participants. More likely I think is that they were the result of a reading and circulation of the text. Some mob members might have seen the note at Johnson's lynching in person. Some may have heard about it from friends at the lynching. Most others undoubtedly read about it in newspaper accounts. Both the original object and its facsimiles then served as initiators of a localized print culture. Like other material modes of public address (advertisements in particular come to mind), they capitalized on well-known local events and understandings in a *thing* that both referenced and built on its prior references. Notes pinned on bodies then become reciprocating objects.

These notices circulated in other ways too. Notes are clearly visible in photographs of the bodies of Virgil Jones, Robert Jones, Thomas Jones, and Joseph Riley of Russellville, Kentucky, and of Nease Gillespie, John Gillespie, "Jack" Dillingham, Henry Lee, and George Irwin in Salisbury, North Carolina.[47] Each of these photographs was a commercial production aimed at local and regional distribution. Undoubtedly, there were many other victims with notes attached to their bodies whose photographs have not survived in private collections or public archives. Their purchasers or recipients likely could not read the reproduced notes, though they could refer to their transcription in newspaper accounts. In this way the visual and the written formed an equivalency as they did elsewhere in these kinds of public reading practices. They built on and extended the urban landscape reading of the period.

---

[46] On the linkages between femininity and lynching, see in particular Crystal N. Feimster, *Southern Horrors: Women and the Politics of Rape and Lynching* (Cambridge, MA: Harvard University Press, 2009) and Jacquelyn Dowd Hall, *Revolt against Chivalry: Jessie Daniel Ames and the Women's Campaign against Lynching*, rev. ed. (New York: Columbia University Press, 1993).

[47] "The lynching of five African American males, August 6, 1906, Sailsbury [sic], NC," lithographed photo postcard, in *Without Sanctuary: Lynching Photography in America* (Sante Fe: Twin Palms, 2000). A fuller explication of this lynching – and this image – in community memory appears in Claude Andrew Clegg, *Troubled Ground: A Tale of Murder, Lynching, and Reckoning in the New South* (Champaign: University of Illinois Press, 2010).

The best example of these overlapping practices is in the physical spaces and social contexts these lynching notes were placed in. They mingled with different kinds of public notices, pinned to trees, poles, or other gathering places. The tree Augustus Goodman was hanged from was littered with tattered papers, including a worn notice for an event to celebrate President Theodore Roosevelt, and advertisements for the Bainbridge Furniture Company and Sutherland Cane mills.[48] Clearly, the site of his death was already a community gathering spot. These other materials of public address were posted in overlapping patterns there. Conducting the lynching and then leaving his body there ensured that people would see them and read them in the context of community space. They might read his body too as a kind of overdetermined message of vengeance and terror.

Unlike many other lynching victims, Goodman did not have a visible note of explanation pinned to his body. Missing too, or at least not visible in the surviving, damaged photograph of the lynching scene, are advertisements for the Bainbridge production of Thomas Dixon's *The Clansman*. The story whose film version a decade later would be one of the most inflammatory justifications of racial violence in American history had just ended a run on the stage in Bainbridge.[49] Like the advertising handbills it might have accompanied on the oak where Augustus Goodman was lynched, its clearly articulated message was received by the white citizens of the town. Headlines the day after the lynching claimed that the "Drama Inspires Negro Lynching." Locals were apparently "wrought up to a high pitch of anger against negroes by the presentation of Thomas A. Dixon's play."[50] This and other newspaper accounts made a direct connection between the racial violence acted out on the playhouse stage and the actual lynching of Goodman.

[48] "The Lynching of Augustus Goodman, November 4, 1905, Bainbridge, Georgia," card mounted print, *Without Sanctuary: Lynching Photography in America* (Santa Fe: Twin Palms, 2000).

[49] The play that would become D. W. Griffith's racist epic, *The Birth of a Nation*, was itself an enormously popular work of drama. Touring shows were put on throughout much of the United States and, like the movie later, inspired waves of protest by African American citizens. See for instance "Colored Protest against a Play," *Arizona Republican*, October 23, 1906. As the white press later would, these protestors clearly linked the play to acts of racial terror. On the broader reception histories of the drama and its role in crafting white supremacist entertainment, see Stephen Johnson, "Re-Stirring an Old Pot: Adaptation, Reception and the Search for an Audience in Thomas Dixon's Performance Text(s) of The Clansman," *Nineteenth Century Theatre & Film* 34, no. 2 (2007): 4–46; Maxwell Bloomfield, "Dixon's 'The Leopard's Spots': A Study in Popular Racism," *American Quarterly* 16, no. 3 (1964): 387–401.

[50] "Drama Inspires Negro Lynching," *Chicago Tribune*, October 30, 1905.

We have to view these often-repeated claims with the knowledge that they were partially rooted in justification and explanation for the actions of lynch mobs.[51] They reveal a self-perception and acknowledgment that Goodman's murder, like so many other lynchings, was immersed in local media cultures. Far more than just a backdrop for his death, they were (and were seen as) both an integral cause and the carrier of much of the lynching's meaning. They suggest too that lynch mobs and commenters were aware of the parallels between symbolic and actual violence. But, even reading these newspaper accounts with the skepticism they deserve, we can see that lynching was in part a grand imitation of actions read about in newspapers, seen in photographs, or witnessed on the stage.[52]

This reading of a lynching site was one that contemporaries around the turn of the century were well versed in. Their assumptions about location, method, and justification were increasingly confirmed by visual evidence and written accounts of particular lynchings. In this way, the material aftermath of lynchings and the news of their happening helped form an object-centered epistemology of racial violence. In other words, an object lesson. Writers could confirm the facts of a case, but they did it through firsthand accountings and appeals to the shared formulaic assumptions of the objects, places, and actions that constituted a lynching.

In a widely covered 1894 lynching in north Alabama, Ed Felton, Fayette Deloney, and Emmet Deloney were captured and killed after a conflict with a local white landowner. After their abduction from protective custody, they were hanged "from a county bridge a few blocks away from the jail." The mob then "quietly dispersed, leaving the bodies hanging to one of the beams of the bridge."[53] This mob compounded its message further. Some days after the mass lynching, the group "pasted ... sensational white cap notices" around town. They were put on "electric light poles" around Tuscumbia as a warning against "dark deeds ... such

---

[51] Accounts of the lynching that emphasized this explanation appeared in several newspapers: "Lynching Laid to 'The Clansman,'" *The Minneapolis Journal*, October 30, 1905; "Drama Inspires a Lynching," *Muscatine News-Tribune*, October 31, 1905; "Telegrams Tersely Told," *The Beatrice Daily Express*, October 31, 1905; "The Clansman," *Chillicothe Morning Constitution*, November 1, 1905.

[52] On anti-lynching plays, see Mitchell, *Living with Lynching*. Also useful on the subject of visual imagery and the historiographical context of lynching photography generally and the problematics of *Without Sanctuary* particularly is Amy Louise Wood, "Without Sanctuary: The Symbolic Representation of Lynching in Photography," *Journal of the Gilded Age and Progressive Era* 20, no. 1 (2021): 87–94.

[53] "An Alabama Lynching," *Fair Play*, April 28, 1894.

as burning, stealing, etc."[54] These had the same dual audiences as the bodies hanging from the bridge, or the notes pinned to bodies. Nominally for Black residents, their direct communication to that audience was less important than the fact of their existence. Black residents would have received the message without need of further written interpolation. For the most part, those noticing and consuming these written messages would be the mob members' fellow white citizens. Given that actual audience, the postings were more symbolic than communicative. This was an assertive, aggressive address to coincide with the character of "rough justice." The notices also functionally expanded the site and message of the lynching from a specific location to a much wider sphere of influence. As with Hartsell's letter a few years later, they helped expand the local context and claims of influence for this lynching.

This point is underscored by yet another Alabama case. In Lee County, the murderers of John Ross identified themselves in a note pinned to his body as "100 determined men." They attempted to preserve the symbolism of his hanging body and make the threat of their actions explicit. The mob pinned a note to Ross's body that read "whoever cuts him down will suffer his fate." And besides the note fixed on his back, they left a letter at a community church four miles distant, letting parishioners know that they had hanged Ross from the tree used in a lynching the previous year.[55] These actions suggested an insistence on the persistent symbolism of the lynching in localized parlance. The repurposed tree helped frame this new lynching, and the explanatory note made sure that this intentionality was not disguised. Neither note was informative. Like handbills, advertisements, and street signs, they marked space. As objects, these notices and the bodies they adhered to were ephemeral. But they were persistent things, as the interrelationship between individual lynchings and the qualities of the illustrated portrayal suggest. The ephemerality of the object itself gave way to incorporation into the formulaic object narratives of lynching, and eventually into landscapes of memory marked by both preservation and willful forgetting.[56] Communication in public space, and conceptual claims to an all-white version of the public sphere, marked the materiality of lynching's spread.

---

[54] "White Cappers Give Warning," *Montgomery Advertiser*, May 4, 1894.
[55] "Lynching of George Hart," *The Times*, November 9, 1887.
[56] On the processes of both memorialization and forgetting at/in sites of trauma, see the work of geographer Kenneth Foote, particularly Kenneth Foote, *Shadowed Ground: America's Landscapes of Violence and Tragedy* (Austin: University of Texas Press, 1997).

In photographs, mobs pictured with both the body and the applied note posit themselves as an extension of the anonymous public authority embedded in such objects. They seem outside the bounds of city, town, or plantation, but such an assertion of power, control, and the power to label was at the very heart of lynching's visual terror. This confluence was represented best in the world of the newspaper, which combined written and visual forms into objects of observation, circulation, and education.

MOB VIOLENCE AND MATERIALIZING WHITE SUPREMACY

Unsurprisingly, the long trail of Joe Kizer's and Tom Johnson's murders got caught up in the spectacle of everyday life in 1898 North Carolina. Hartsell's letter apparently brought the lynching back to prominent attention in the broader region. But it was viewed skeptically through the exaggerated rhetoric of the campaign, what Fusionist supporters labeled as "Democratic Lies." Rumors circulated that the lynching of Johnson and Kizer was among these lies and that they "did not commit that terrible deed in Cabarrus and were not hanged." This charge came from a man in Davidson County, perhaps the strongest foothold of Republicanism in the Piedmont, and as the *Standard* noted, just one county away from Cabarrus.[57] A Concord resident had to defend the honor of his county, but only convinced his interlocuter of the truth of the lynching when he assured the man "that [he] saw with his own eyes."[58] The omission of the object ("it," the lynching) is revealing, even if unintentional. It suggests not only that the unnamed Concordian was there and viewed the lynching, but that his act of witness went further. He was someone who *saw* with his own eyes, irrespective of party platforms or Democratic, Republican, or Populist rhetoric. That implicit appeal to visual independence and visual supremacy underlay much of the campaign for white supremacy in 1898. If white men could see and then act without the mediation of political parties or newspaper editorials (never mind their being guided to this supposed independence by those same sources), they would act to take back the state. The acts of everyday life were marshaled here as evidence of a broad conspiracy to destroy whiteness. The

---

[57] "The Biggest Democratic Lie Yet," *Daily Concord Standard*, October 19, 1898. According to Edmonds, Davidson was solidly Republican from 1876 to 1896, a rarity for majority white counties; Edmonds, *The Negro and Fusion Politics*, 25.

[58] "The Biggest Democratic Lie Yet," *Daily Concord Standard*.

1898 election then turned those selfsame quotidian actions into spectacle, moving from everyday action to violent displays of power.[59]

When election day came, groups of white men clad in the intimidating garb of the Red Shirt terrorist movement surrounded the polls.[60] Whether their attempts at intimidation or the various forms of fraud and suppression were successful, Democratic voters viewed their physical intimidation as yet another example of the power of the spectacle in the world.[61] The party's handbook for the 1898 election is full of both observations about the disorder of Black rule, and the necessity for "white people unite[d] to stop it." Party leaders invoked "the press and the pulpit ... thunder[ing] against lynch law," but pledged that "no law has ever been written and no law ever can be written, drastic enough to compel an Anglo-Saxon to consent to place his wife and children under the rule of the black man from Africa."[62] Elections then mattered as little as other illegitimate laws. As with lynching, the basis of the law was redefined as the sole expression of white patriarchal power and community. White men had only to look around them to see that, and to notice the immediate impacts their own acts of intimidation, violence, and terror might have.

This was the operative logic of what white supremacist writers dubbed "the Wilmington Revolution" of November 10–11.[63] Groups of organized white men, radicalized by the campaign of the previous several months, gathered on the morning of November 10. Their first action

---

[59] On the Red Shirt movement see Prather, "The Red Shirt Movement in North Carolina."

[60] Prather, "The Red Shirt Movement in North Carolina," 179–180.

[61] Paul D. Escott, *Many Excellent People : Power and Privilege in North Carolina, 1850–1900*, The Fred W. Morrison Series in Southern Studies (Chapel Hill: University of North Carolina Press, 1985), 241–262.

[62] State Democratic Executive Committee of North Carolina, "The Democratic Hand Book. 1898. Prepared by the State Democratic Executive Committee of North Carolina," Handbook. Raleigh, NC, Edwards & Broughton, 1898, 48, 91, North Carolina Collection, Louis Round Wilson Special Collections Library, University of North Carolina at Chapel Hill.

[63] My account of the event variously called the Wilmington revolution (by white supremacists), the Wilmington race riot (by the few white historians who wrote about it until recently), or the Wilmington massacre/Wilmington coup d'état (by more recent historians), comes largely from the official centennial accounting of the events. Despite its problematic categorization of the event in its title and some crucial omissions, it is still the most comprehensive accounting of the timeline of the events of November 1898. Mulrooney's *Race, Place, and Memory* places those events in a much broader spatial and temporal frame that was likewise useful here. See LeRae Umfleet and 1898 Wilmington Race Riot Commission, "1898 Wilmington Race Riot Report," Raleigh, NC: North Carolina Office of Archives and History, 2006.

was to destroy the building of the city's only Black newspaper and put its editor, Alexander Manly, on the run. They justified their actions as a response to an editorial Manly had written decrying the justifications for lynching and referring to the consensual sexual relationships between white women and Black men. True to the sensationalist practices of the year, Daniels's *News and Observer* brought the editorial to prominence months after its initial publication. The destruction of Manly's *Record* was a clear example of the formulaic symbolism of racial violence. Burning it – and then posing in front of its charred remains – recalled the events of lynching and literalized the many attempts to obliterate other forms of messaging in the wake of white supremacist violence. These same mobs of white men then roamed the city streets, forcibly laying violent claims to public spaces, African American neighborhoods, and the entirety of the city. Some of their leaders eventually installed themselves in place of the elected local officials, completing and formalizing the assertion of their own authority. This was public address too, stripped of any of its niceties and relying on only the most violent materialization of its messaging.

Unsurprisingly, the scarce accounts of the coup d'état in the city are significantly split along racial lines. Alfred Moore Waddell, one of the figureheads of the massacre and the man who installed himself as mayor, focused his remembrances a few years later on the pacific qualities of the multiple days of violence. His memoirs concentrated on recuperating his image from the part he played in the massacre. Waddell noted that "legally and technically it may be properly" termed a riot, "but not in the usual sense of disorderly mob violence." According to his account, "an army officer who was present and witnessed it [said] it was the quietest and most orderly riot he had ever seen or heard of." This was a familiar trope. Accountancy of lynchings, including that of Johnson and Kizer, frequently emphasized the orderliness and high social status of those comprising the mob. After the Concord lynching, newspapers observed both that there had been no drinking among the lynch mob, and that the group was composed of "our best citizens."[64]

---

[64] Alfred Moore Waddell, *Some Memories of My Life* (Raleigh, NC: Edwards and Broughton, 1907), Special Collections Library, East Carolina University. Accounts of the orderliness and good social status of the crowd were written up multiple times, including in "A Day of Tragedy," *Daily Concord Standard*, May 30, 1898 and "That Cabarrus County Lynching," *Henderson Gold Leaf*, June 23, 1898.

This emphasis on the observed calmness of the situation is deeply in contrast with that of Reverend J. Allen Kirk. Kirk was a local African American leader who lived through the massacre in Wilmington. Like Waddell, Kirk refers to the authority of someone else's visual witnessing of the riot. In his case, it is because he was sheltered with his family in the "Colored Cemetery" on the outskirts of town, fearing seizure and sending messengers back and forth for news. Unlike so many observers of the political landscape in 1898 North Carolina, he was not permitted to see with his own eyes, though his secondhand observations are no less forceful for that. He writes of the white women and children taken from the violence, calling it a "great sight to see them marching from death and the colored women, colored men, colored children, colored enterprises, and colored people all exposed to death."[65] Kirk also reported other visual testimony from his vantage point as information gatherer, like the "eye witness [who saw] an army of white citizens mobilized in the old field back of Tenth street."[66] His own eventual escape via cart and railroad only made him more aware of the pervasiveness of visual scrutiny combined with the actionable technologies of the day. As he sat on the train, awaiting discovery and sure violence, he reflected on the "organic strength" of the white supremacy movement: "The telegraph, the telephone, and even it seems the very railroad train knows how to move against the Negro in this matter."[67] Violent surveillance was so pervasive, Kirk found himself in an environment literally enlivened to his capture and potential torture. This was a materialized white supremacy, a world apparently hostile to even the existence of Black life. And it was those most powerful technologies of space and information that carried this violent potentiality.

Reflecting on the aftermath that Kirk fled from, Waddell invoked a postcoup calm. He wrote of the time since his own forcible ascension to the office of mayor as one of calm in "the historic city of Wilmington." His continued mayoral tenure in the years since saw "the old town suffer no calamity and moved steadily and rapidly along the path of peace and

---

[65] J. Allen Kirk, "A Statement of Facts Concerning the Bloody Riot in Wilmington, N.C. Of Interest to Every Citizen of the United States," Wilmington?, North Carolina, 1898, Documenting the American South Digital Collection, Louis Round Wilson Special Collections Library, University of North Carolina at Chapel Hill, https://docsouth.unc.edu/nc/kirk/kirk.html (accessed April 16, 2022).

[66] Kirk "A Statement of Facts," 5.

[67] Kirk, "A Statement of Facts," 14.

progress."[68] Waddell's observations showed a marked contrast to the alleged realities of Fusion rule in North Carolina's cities. All was happy and calm in his world, with white order restored. But Kirk's observations show the more lingering impacts of the terror. Without even the minor security of any Black elected officials, North Carolina became again a place full of implied threats and hazards. The biggest object lesson of all, at least as contemporaries read it, was the seizure of Wilmington. If the previous months of materialist lessons were a primer on misrule, the coup d'état in Wilmington was a lesson designed both to reinforce white supremacy and to send a material reminder of violence to Black populations: "The only act decreed which was outside the bounds of the law being one of stern necessity to teach an object lesson for the safety and good name of wives and daughters. This was the destruction of the *Daily Record* office."[69] Such was the ordinary logic of white terroristic violence, identical to the justifications used in lynching. Necessary by dint of its desired impact, the coup was legal in the eyes of those who regarded it as a "radical revolution accompanied by bloodshed and a thorough reorganization of social and political conditions."[70] Waddell's visual and spatial logics were ones based on his own perception of both custom and necessity.

The cycle of visuality and violence renewed again. With the theoretical threat of "Negro rule" vanquished, the state turned more fully to the customary, spatial instantiation of white supremacist political ideology. Among the most visible markers of Jim Crow were the quasi-public directives applied to any shared space in the form of signs. Jim Crow was not implemented and enforced by these media alone, but they were the most frequent material reminder of this new reign of terror. Like earlier signs and media of public address, they relied on implied authority and arbitrary racial discrimination. These new spaces again expanded the power of the segregated public sphere into any place where Black people might go. Segregated space was no place in particular, and everywhere, all at once. As Elizabeth Abel notes, "race and space were constructed in relation to each other through words tacked directly to the built environment."[71] Never innocuous, the visuality of these signs relied for its even deeper impact on the terror instilled through actions like the lynching of Kizer and Johnson

---

[68] Waddell, *Some Memories*, 246, 245.
[69] "The City Pastors," *The Morning Star*, November 15, 1898.
[70] Waddell, *Some Memories*, 242.
[71] Abel, *Signs of the Times*, 14–15.

or the massacre in Wilmington. This was more pervasive then than even seeing anti-Black signs marking the boundaries of propriety and action under the implied threat of recriminative violence. Instead, Kirk invoked a profound spatial terror. This potential violence was abstract and pervasive, a part of the connective tissue of the technologies making the "modern" world. This was clearly a large part of the intention of racial violence, like that planned and executed at large scale in Wilmington, or in its more circumscribed form in Concord. What emerged from these efforts was a civic sphere dictated by the tenets of white supremacy and built on racial violence.

3

The Clothes

In the end, the mob stripped Tom Johnson and Joe Kizer even of their clothing. By patchwork, individual people took scraps of shirts and pants, lengths of Johnson's new suspenders, and any other piece of fabric that they could tear, pry, or cut from the dead men's bodies. The grasping touch of members of this mob was familiar, intimate even. They probed the men's bodies as part of the rituals of the lynching, claiming their place and commemorating their presence there. More than any other trophies taken from the site of the lynching though, they took pieces of clothing as reminders of the men themselves. Clothes signified bodies – guilty bodies, condemned bodies – but never the actuality of the people who once wore them.[1] Articles of clothing and the scraps of cloth taken from them were part of a collecting culture in the South. Objects taken from lynching sites and claimed from lynched bodies sit at the interstices of souvenir and relic, as I discuss in this paired set of chapters. This mode of collecting and display translated the intimacy of Victorian domestic reliquary practice to the public realm while still reserving the most secretive memory practices to the confines of the home. Lynching relics helped make the memory of death material, and the celebration of suffering public.

---

[1] I use aftermaths here in reference to the important work of Kidada Williams, who asks that we think about the multiple unfolding scenarios that stretched out in the wake of a lynching. She refers principally to the intergenerational trauma of lynching for Black families and Black communities. To that, I add the other aftermaths that I refer to here: the more immediate materializations of proof, and the white reliquary practices. Each stretches the temporal frames of lynching, and demands that we see both individual lynchings and the broader practice not as single events, but rather as an ongoing immersion in a violent racial history not yet past. See Williams, "Regarding the Aftermaths of Lynching."

These scraps of clothing collected and preserved toed the line between the ordinary and the spectacular, between the quotidian objects people made to surround themselves and the symbolic objects that helped structure their understanding of that world. Clothing is a physical repository for our selves. In the one sense, we fashion ourselves after the clothes that we wear, whether they be items we choose to don, garments prescribed to us by status, or some happy medium between the two. But they contain us in other ways as well. They become soaked with our sweat, stained by our blood, shaped to our form, suffused with our smells. Even after we are gone, our clothes stay behind, ghostly casts of the body that once was.[2]

As trophies taken from the scene of a lynching, clothing served as both symbol and archive. As whole articles of worn apparel, Johnson and Kizer's clothing was regarded as an indicator of their racial and social status and weighed as tangible evidence of their guilt. Once collected from the men's bodies, these objects evoked a material world of signs and symbols. The intimate act of taking clothing from the body, then, is one that builds upon the meaning overlain onto that body and the clothes that clad it. Clothes are a stand-in for what and who we are. They are also a projection of the capacities of our bodies and our deeper selves, the things people imagine us doing and being capable of doing. Physically, worn clothing holds the traces of its wearer's activity. The rumples and stains, creases and tears are proof of both long wear and the immediate events that caused them. A rip might come from a single motion, but it was made possible by many hours of wear, with and against the body. Clothing is an indicator of both immediate event and longterm activity, an archive of both momentary action and many long hours. In this way, clothing is a repository of unique complexity. Clothes represent both single events and a longer duration, objects that are both particular and more abstract.

Indeed, these particular objects were overlain with wider perceptions of clothing and the statuses that it held. For Kizer, Johnson, and generations of Black men before and after them, the clothing they wore was an expression of the social status they were confined to, or a marker of their aspirations. Clothing both defined and delimited. And through this process of definition, clothing became the closest substitute for the body itself, and

---

[2] Peter Stallybrass, "Worn Worlds: Clothes, Mourning, and the Life of Things," in *Cultural Memory and the Construction of Identity*, ed. Dan Ben-Amos and Lilian Weissberg (Detroit: Wayne State University Press, 1999), 27–44.

the readiest symbol of the person who once wore it. As an artifact taken from a lynching site, clothing became a relic of the lynched body.[3]

Relics were a lingering particularity in the years around the turn of the twentieth century. The reliquary culture of the South represented a materialization of affect that surpassed the simplistic characterizations of sadness and mourning. Instead, these relics represented a complexity of emotions, materialized and claimed by their collectors. Reliquary objects were things of particular significance, though made of the most commonplace materials. They surpassed terrestrial origins by connecting their owners to the unseen and unknowable worlds that objects seemed to offer a conduit to. They were things that connected their possessors to a personal, particular past. Relics were a material expression of longing. Most often relics were made to mourn for a lost loved one, or in admiration of a celebrity. But the relic represented broader claims to ownership over the bodily signifiers of a distant person. For its possessor, the relic claimed some small part of the person disconnected from them by the distance of time, death, or celebrity. Lynching relics did not mourn death. They commemorated and celebrated it. The same was true of other relics in this period, as nineteenth-century practices evolved into a new memorial material culture that served, paradoxically, as both a bulwark against modernity and an embrace of it. Reliquary objects did the work of bridging these gaps, injecting a legitimizing historicity into new configurations of white supremacy and racial terror.

---

[3] I am building here on a relatively small but enormously generative body of work at the intersections of fashion studies, material culture, history, and early modern world studies that all seek to theorize worn clothing as an archive of materialized memory. Particularly useful in this regard has been the work of Peter Stallybrass, both alone (in his meditations on the clothing of his close collaborator Allon White, cited earlier) and with Ann Rosalind Jones (on early modern investiture and bodily inscription); Stallybrass, "Worn Worlds"; Ann Rosalind Jones and Peter Stallybrass, *Renaissance Clothing and the Materials of Memory* (Cambridge, UK; New York: Cambridge University Press, 2000). On clothing as a material object of archival value more generally, I have found works by Leora Auslander, Carole Hunt, and Ellen Sampson particularly useful: Leora Auslander, "Deploying Material Culture to Write the History of Gender and Sexuality: The Example of Clothing and Textiles," *Clio. Women, Gender, History*, no. 40 (2015), https://doi.org/10.4000/cliowgh.716; Carole Hunt, "Worn Clothes and Textiles as Archives of Memory," *Critical Studies in Fashion & Beauty* 5, no. 2 (2014): 207–232, https://doi.org/10.1386/csfb.5.2.207_1; Ellen Sampson, "Creases, Crumples, and Folds," *Fashion Studies Journal*, no. 2 (2017). Finally, I found clothing historian Hilary Davidson's meditations on grave clothes as archaeological and historical categories of evidence useful in thinking about the practices of burial and survival of clothes made for the dead: Hilary Davidson, "Grave Emotions: Textiles and Clothing from Nineteenth-Century London Cemeteries," *TEXTILE* 14, no. 2 (2016): 226–243, https://doi.org/10.1080/14759756.2016.1139383.

MAKING SOUTHERN RELICS

The trajectory of reliquary culture seemed almost destined for the heightened displays of public emotion associated with southerners in the nineteenth century. In a society already obsessed with its own mythologizing, the many deaths of the Civil War created a cult of loss.[4] To be sure, southerners were not alone in crafting, preserving, and keeping material markers of the dead or even of memorializing the act of death itself.[5] But their adaptation of reliquary culture persisted well beyond its prominence elsewhere. In the years after the Civil War, much of the white South was transformed into a culture obsessed with commemorating both loss and death. People built on the reliquary cultures of the Victorian era to transform their civic and public places into sites that celebrated sacrifice and mourned loss. This commemorative material culture helped order white society. Lynching relics went further. They served as both individual and collective, personal and private reminders of the white South's foundational violences. The course of the nineteenth century saw a transformation of relics. This was a shift that happened in many societies, though it was concentrated in those worlds most touched by death and loss. Relics became substitutes for the absent bodies of loved ones, the unattainable bodies of celebrities, and, as I argue here, the bodies of lynching victims and other racialized people.[6]

[4] The particularities of behavior in the antebellum South have long been a topic of interest for historians of the region. On the linkages between violence, honor, and the culture of death and punishment, see Bertram Wyatt-Brown, *Southern Honor: Ethics and Behavior in the Old South* (Oxford: Oxford University Press, 1983). More recent work has redefined the place of death in southern and American cultures, particularly during the Civil War and its aftermath. See for instance Drew Gilpin Faust, *This Republic of Suffering: Death and the American Civil War* (New York: Alfred A. Knopf, 2008); *Death and the American South*, ed. Craig Thompson Friend and Lorri Glover (New York: Cambridge University Press, 2015); Franny Nudelman, *John Brown's Body: Slavery, Violence, and the Culture of War* (Chapel Hill: University of North Carolina Press, 2004); Mark S. Schantz, *Awaiting the Heavenly Country: The Civil War and America's Culture of Death* (Ithaca, NY: Cornell University Press, 2004).
[5] As I will note throughout this chapter, the material culture of death is a topic rich for both research and speculation. Other sources delve more deeply into particular periods, but Elizabeth Hallam and Jenny Hockey, *Death, Memory, and Material Culture* (Oxford: Berg, 2001) does a particularly good job introducing the topic within the Atlantic World.
[6] Simon Harrison extends our understanding of relics with his study of the culture of trophy hunting in the American Civil War, noting that southerners collected relics from the bodies of northern soldiers as a kind of proto-ethnological practice. Though he does not dwell on their classification as relics, he does make note of the wide usage of that phrase in the period: Simon Harrison, "Bones in the Rebel Lady's Boudoir: Ethnology, Race, and Trophy Hunting in the American Civil War," *Journal of Material Culture* 15, no. 4 (2010): 385–401.

Relics as they were redefined in the eighteenth and particularly nineteenth centuries built on their origins as sacred objects associated with
sainthood. But they became things of more immediate, often domestic
intimacy that represented a tension between celebration and mortifica-
tion of the absent bodies they stood in for. Though there were certainly
continuities, these later object rituals primarily marked a significant
break with the religious practices of medieval and early modern relics.[7]
Most particularly, relics came to refer to objects touched by or taken
from the bodies of the unsainted, even secular dead. These mementos
were often taken from the body of a loved one whose hair, clothes, or
other possessions were kept and transformed into a portable reminder
of presence turned into absence. The most prominent of these practices
was hairwork. These elaborate creations were made of human hair,
woven, stitched, or braided into arts ranging from buttons to wreaths.
Hairwork was the height of nineteenth-century sentimental material
culture. It served as a literalization of the emotional bonds between
family members or other loved ones on opposite sides of the divide
between life and death.[8]

But reliquary culture suffused more terrestrial technologies as well.
Oliver Wendell Holmes's comments on the new daguerreotypes suggested that they too were containers of a kind of spirit, capable of
spreading "tiny pieces of a person into faraway places."[9] Indeed, the
pervasiveness of relics in the nineteenth century is best illustrated by
what we might call their distributed intimacy. They moved not only
from sacred to secular, but also increasingly from objects that were

---

[7] There is a larger debate about continuity and change in the reliquary cultures of the nineteenth century. Most convincing to me is Teresa Barnett's assertion that the concept of
the relic in the period was substantially divorced from its earlier meanings and was merely
another way in which Americans of the period drew upon an imagined vision of the
past. See Teresa Barnett, *Sacred Relics: Pieces of the Past in Nineteenth-Century America*
(Chicago: University of Chicago Press, 2013). Deborah Lutz notes the particular uses of
relics in Victorian culture and, building on an earlier body of scholarship cited elsewhere
in this chapter, argues for their integration into cultural life and literary portrayals as not
quite sacred objects. The implied continuity between these and earlier reliquary objects
elides many significant historical changes in the ensuing centuries. See Deborah Lutz,
Relics of Death in Victorian Literature and Culture. (New York: Cambridge University
Press, 2015).

[8] Helen Sheumaker, *Love Entwined: The Curious History of Hairwork in America* (Philadelphia: University of Pennsylvania Press, 2011).

[9] Oliver Wendell Holmes, "The Stereoscope and the Stereograph," *Atlantic Monthly*, 3,
no. 20 (1859), www.gutenberg.org/cache/epub/11751/pg11751.html (accessed April 16,
2022).

cherished and familial to things that were both public and more universal. This is most clearly illustrated by the collecting of mementos from
famous (or infamous) bodies.

This new category of relics ranged from the dried heart of Shelley
and other Romantic-era poets to the bones and skulls collected and
venerated by Civil War–era sanitary commissioner Henry Bellows. Relics of Charlotte Cushman or other celebrities were less grisly, though
arguably no less intimate. The ring plucked from her finger and given
to Fanny Seward was particularly valued by its recipient for having
been so recently worn by its gifter. Some trace of its wearer seemed to
remain in the object.[10] These are only the most exceptional examples
of a broader celebrity reliquary practice. Scores of artists famed for
their emotional resonance with their audiences distributed mementos of
themselves, intentionally or not. Not all of this was motivated by profit.
The collecting avidity of the fans of many of these nineteenth-century
luminaries recalls nothing so much as the hordes of memento seekers at
lynchings a few decades later. In part this reflects the fact that not even
these intimate things were protected from burgeoning consumerism. As
Nancy Bercaw notes, the significant home industry in the production
of relics sought to make them "objects of the heart" even as they were
inextricably linked to market demands.[11] This twinned domestication
and commodification of relics seems contradictory in retrospect. But it
followed closely from the logic of the mid to late nineteenth century,
where sensationalism and emotion were not confined to the private
spheres of hearth and home. Indeed, relics were the most prominent
form of a material culture that stemmed from overt display. These cultural shifts were somewhat slower to reach the South. But when they
did, they helped fuel the meaning of racial violence and the public materiality of sensation.

In the social context of the South and of spectacle lynchings, the relic
continued its long evolution. These bodily relics materialized desire and
longing, much as their earlier counterparts had. Their basis was not in
love or affection, but rather in the need to express hatred through possession. The South was not unique in its appetite for violent tales of murder,

---

[10] Nemerov, *Acting in the Night*, 20, 226; Judith Pascoe, *The Hummingbird Cabinet: A Rare and Curious History of Romantic Collectors* (Ithaca, NY: Cornell University Press, 2006), 2–3, 8.

[11] Nancy Dunlap Bercaw, "Solid Objects/Mutable Meanings: Fancywork and the Construction of Bourgeois Culture, 1840–1880," *Winterthur Portfolio* 26, no. 4 (1991): 233.

sex, and mayhem.[12] But without giving into myths of southern exceptionalism and essentialism, we can acknowledge that the region was one particularly obsessed with death and loss as a structuring element of its self-fashioned identity. In the post-Civil War years, retrospective commemoration came to represent the South as much as or more than its drive toward modernity. A region externally motivated by the promise of its future was also obsessed with its imagined past and the preservation of the Lost Cause of the Confederacy.

The earliest examples of Confederate memorialization adhered closely to reliquary material culture then still in vogue. The groups of elite women responsible for the first Lost Cause monuments sought to materialize emotion in much the same way as their contemporaries across the English-speaking world. The first such monuments fit neatly within the funerary traditions of the period (albeit ones where cemeteries were a private if not civic space of leisure and reflection.)[13] For example, Wilmington, North Carolina's first Confederate monument was in the works as early as 1867. The local Ladies' Memorial Association petitioned Wilmington's cemetery board for the donation of a prominent plot in the city's new Oakdale Cemetery. The ensuing years of fundraising and planning led, in 1872, to the erection of a monument nominally dedicated to the several hundred unknown Confederate dead from nearby Fort Fisher. Like other monumental creations, the statue's large inscription – "To the Confederate Dead" – overrides its more specific memorial intent for casual visitors. Certainly, many visitors received it as a more general testament to the dead soldiers allied with the Confederacy. Those curious enough to venture closer and read the statue's inscription found a quintessential evocation of materialized sensation: "SELF DENIAL – WORK – PRAYERS – TEARS – HEARTS BLOOD / ENTERED INTO ITS BUILDING."[14] Here in the quasi-public space of the cemetery was a monument supposedly constructed of the bodily

---

[12] On national and regional cultures of sensation, see Duggan, *Sapphic Slashers*; Trotti, *The Body in the Reservoir*; and David Monod, *The Soul of Pleasure: Sentiment and Sensation in Nineteenth-Century American Mass Entertainment* (Ithaca, NY: Cornell University Press, 2006).

[13] On the evolution of funerary traditions as part of the Lost Cause, see Gaines Foster, *Ghosts of the Confederacy: Defeat, the Lost Cause, and the Emergence of the New South, 1865–1913* (New York: Oxford University Press, 1987).

[14] "Confederate Soldiers Monument, Oakdale Cemetery," Commemorative Landscapes of North Carolina, University of North Carolina Libraries, https://docsouth.unc.edu/commland/monument/291 (accessed April 16, 2022).

materials of the memorial organization. Its granite and bronze composition notwithstanding, this statue was a bodily relic equal to the most
elaborate hairwork locket or wreath.

What began as a newly public version of a formerly private ritual
gradually turned more fully into the civic realm. Early efforts of collective mourning increasingly became an avenue for the articulation of
cultural white supremacy. As implied by the Wilmington merger of the
earlier Ladies' Memorial Association with the United Daughters of the
Confederacy, southern Lost Cause memorialization established itself in
places and expressions more prominent than the gated cemetery. These
early monuments to the Confederate dead evolved both spatially and
conceptually into permanent reminders of the emerging Jim Crow apartheid. Like many other relics, they tried to stop time in its tracks, to not
so much commemorate the past as recall an imagined version of history
that could be applied to the present. An imagined history, with largely
invented significance, became the basis of what were presented as hom-
ages to the past rather than monuments to the present.[15]

The Confederate Memorial of Cabarrus County was dedicated in
May 1892, just steps away from the jail where Johnson and Kizer were
abducted a few years later. The chief orator for the occasion dedicated
the monument to the historical stasis of the Lost Cause and its vision
of an imagined past. William McKendree Robbins was a Confederate
veteran, former politician, and frequent correspondent with the doyenne
of the Lost Cause, Varina Davis.[16] Robbins stepped to the podium amid
a pageantry that included thirteen "beautifully dressed girls ... who represented the original 13 states" to invoke the storied past of the nation's
founding. His version of the past folded the founding of the Confederacy

[15] Barnett, *Sacred Relics*, 27. Though historians have long known that invented tradition
was at the basis of most Confederate memorialization, Adam Domby's recent book suggests how much of this mythology was based on outright falsehood and fabrication. See
Adam Domby, *The False Cause: Fraud, Fabrication, and White Supremacy in Confederate Memory* (Charlottesville: University of Virginia Press, 2020).

[16] "The Dead Confederates of Cabarrus Remembered," *Daily Concord Standard*, May
5, 1892; Brenda Marks Eagles, "William McKendree Robbins," NCPedia, January 1,
1994, www.ncpedia.org/biography/robbins-william-mckendree (accessed April 16,
2022). Robbins's correspondence with Varina Davis can be found in his papers at the
University of North Carolina: William McKendree Robbins Papers, #04070, Southern
Historical Collection, Louis Round Wilson Special Collections Library, University of
North Carolina, Chapel Hill. On the centrality of Varina Davis in Confederate memory,
see Joan Cashin, *First Lady of the Confederacy: Varina Davis's Civil War* (Cambridge,
MA: Belknap Press of Harvard University Press, 2006).

into a long line of descent from the principles of the Classical world. This historical evocation was intended to "vindicate the motives of our fellow soldiers and the Southern people in general." In the context of contemporaneous memorial practice, his speech was unremarkable and filled with the usual obfuscating narratives of states' rights and sectional sovereignty. The indignities that a generalized northern populace inflicted included the sending of "booted satraps and carpet-bag miscreants to insult and rob us." Most gallingly, both government officials and private citizens apparently "exalted our poor ignorant and incompetent servants into rulers over us." The suffering of the southern people was so great, he intoned, "we have envied our happy dead heroes who have found a refuge in the grave." As Robbins viewed it, the defeat of the South was less martial than a problem of perception. Northern writers had "seized the pen of history and are busily engaged in distorting the record and perverting the truth." The solution was to counter that narrative with oratory and, more importantly, material reminders of the region's loss. These more immediate appeals were in keeping with the sensationalist public culture of the day. Monuments like the one being erected that day would be the most permanent counters to the falsities of a defeated South. Defiant in defeat, they would transform their very landscapes into repositories of loss, grief, and overcoming. Those emotions were made material in monuments and extensible through their linkages to white southern identity.[17]

In succeeding years, the Concord monument continued to be both itself a relic and a site for the performance of the reliquary cultures still dominant in white southern society. Just two weeks before Johnson and Kizer's lynching, a local women's book club hosted "an assembly at the monument" for Confederate Memorial Day. They brought flowers to decorate the statue and honor the Confederate dead. It was, said one account, a "celebration of sad but glorious memories, [an] occasion of sad, sweet memory in which we are all equally interested."[18] These memorial practices were different from ones of earlier decades not in their intensity, but in their more public fervency. This reliquary culture was still a domestic one, dominated as it was by women's organizational efforts and gendered practices of mourning and commemoration (like the

[17] "A Big Occasion," *The Concord Times,* May 5, 1892; "Major Robbin's Speech," *The Concord Times,* May 12, 1892.
[18] "Flowers for Our Confederate Dead," *Daily Concord Standard,* May 10, 1898.

laying of flowers in Concord). But it had now moved more fully into both the public and civic spheres. As in hundreds of other counties, the Cabarrus courthouse and court square had now become containers for relics and reliquary practices. This overlap made county seats more than commercial and cultural centers. The larger implications of the dominance of reliquary cultures in the post-Civil War South was to transpose intimate material practices fully into public life, and, indeed, make them the basis for much white public culture. This extended to rituals far outside the conventional realm of commemorative practices.

The embodied intimacy of the monuments – ones symbolically built of women's sweat, tears, blood, and hearts – mirrored a wider concern with white female bodies. Monument dedications may have been dominated by the oratory of men, but the spectacle of ongoing memorial practices relied upon the visibility of white womanhood. In groups, and in the elaborate costume of early twentieth-century formal dress, they held fundraisers, brought flowers, led schoolrooms and Sunday school classes in the rituals of the Lost Cause. Their own bodies – pure, white, delicate – were the backdrop for memorialization efforts. Indeed, as we saw in the early Wilmington monument, it was the apparent mingling of their efforts with the martial exploits of the common solider that gave rise to this peculiar mix of past and present. Like other reliquary cultures, this commingling was intentional in giving Confederate monuments a broader purpose.

White women's bodies were at the forefront of these newly public expressions of reliquary intimacy. White men might revel in the distributed glory that such practices cast on them, but they also felt compelled to acts of patriarchal domination motivated alike by long precedent and the threats of a changing society. Most obviously, this meant the protection of white women's bodies against the imagined threats of public life. The corollary to that concern was a near obsession with the bodies of Black men. As the inverse of white womanhood, Black manhood seemed to represent a systemic threat. Paradoxically, it was asserted dominion over both of these sets of supposedly oppositional but equally commodified bodies that defined the contours of white southern masculinity. White men paid remarkably close attention to the most intimate practices of Black men – the sex they had, the food they ate, the places they walked, the clothes they wore.[19] Reliquary culture helped turn intimate

---

[19] There is a broad range of excellent historical literature on the entanglements of race, gender, and racial violence, particularly as it pertains to this period of the emergence

matters public. Relics, as they evolved to be comprehended in this period, were not just tokens of mourning or sadness. In their memorial practice there was embedded a complex admixture of loss and longing, of grief and triumph. They expressed, materially, not defeat, but defiance. These southern reliquary practices brought the intimate longing of the domestic sphere fully into public space. The clothing of Tom Johnson and Joe Kizer then deserves attention as intimate objects in two senses. In the process of its collection and preservation, the clothing became a reliquary object. But even before that transformation, it was a symbol of the body. At once intimate and public, the clothes of Black people were stand-ins for their bodies in both life and death.[20]

AFRICAN AMERICAN CLOTHING IN SLAVERY AND FREEDOM

In a long and detailed life history interview with Moses Asche, W. E. B. Du Bois recalled the lynching of Sam Hose as a pivotal event of his time in Georgia. In a rare break from his practiced, fluent recitation, Du Bois's voice briefly faltered over the memory of Hose's "fingers and toes being exhibited" in the window of a meat market in downtown Atlanta. The resonances of this display are clear. Not only were the bodies of Black

of Jim Crow. The earliest, and still among the most useful studies of white women's relationships to lynching, is Jacquelyn Dowd Hall, *Revolt against Chivalry: Jesse Daniel Ames and the Women's Campaign against Lynching* (New York: Columbia University Press, 1974). Of particular use on the broader contours of womanhood and Jim Crow is Glenda Elizabeth Gilmore, *Gender and Jim Crow: Women and the Politics of White Supremacy in North Carolina, 1896–1920* (Chapel Hill: University of North Carolina Press, 1996). Excellent recent works building on these earlier examples include Feimster, Southern Horrors, and Kate Côté Gillin, *Shrill Hurrahs: Women, Gender, and Racial Violence in South Carolina, 1865–1900* (Columbia: University of South Carolina Press, 2014). I also found Blain Roberts's work on the twentieth-century evolution of southern beauty ideals particularly useful in thinking about these intersections: Blain Roberts, *Pageants, Parlors, & Pretty Women: Race and Beauty in the Twentieth-Century South* (Chapel Hill: University of North Carolina Press, 2014).

[20] I am building here on a large body of literature on the body, bodily intimacies, and the wearing of clothes. Broadly useful are excellent theorizations from labor history: Ava Baron and Eileen Boris, "'The Body' as a Useful Category for History Working-Class History," *Labor* 4, no. 2 (2007): 23–43, https://doi.org/10.1215/15476715-2006-061); military history: Joanna Bourke, *Dismembering the Male: Men's Bodies, Britain and the Great War* (Chicago: University of Chicago Press, 1996); and fashion history: Joanne Entwistle, *The Fashioned Body: Fashion, Dress, and Social Theory*, 2nd ed. (Cambridge, UK: Polity Press, 2015); Patrizio Calefato, "Fashion and Worldliness: Language and Imagery of the Clothed Body," *Fashion Theory* 1, no. 1 (1997): 69–90, https://doi.org/10.2752/136270497779754534.

lynching victims reduced to commodities, but their constituent parts also became souvenir stand-ins for the whole body. Du Bois never says that these body parts were for sale; rather he emphasizes their public display. Body parts were perhaps the most exaggerated form of artifact taken from lynching sites. They mirrored both earlier and contemporaneous practices of reliquary creation by being imbued with enormous communal power. There was no better demonstration of the material rites of spectacle lynching than the exhibition Du Bois invoked.[21]

To understand the material culture of lynching, we need to look at both the most exaggerated spectacles and fervent participants and at the equally gruesome but more commonplace spectacle lynching like that of Johnson and Kizer. Spectacles serve to exaggerate existing social structures and attitudes. And in spectacle lynchings, the expression of those preexisting attitudes was a fixation on the Black body and all it represented. Though this attention was never exclusively on clothing, it was most often clothing that served as the literal and metaphorical container for white scrutiny of the bodies of Black people. It was easier to make note of clothing and for it to serve as a symbolic substitute. And because they were so close to bodies that were the subject of so much fury and fascination, scraps of clothing were easily transformed into a relic that would preserve some small, essential part of the lynched body and the lynching. In this way, it followed the pattern of other ordinary objects translated into relics. Clothing taken from lynched bodies built upon an existing fascination with Black bodies more generally. To better track that transformation as part of the ritual process of lynching's material meaning making, we can look at a deeper history of Black-worn clothing and white observation in the South.

By the 1890s, Black and white people alike were beginning to gain access to readymade consumer goods from local merchants.[22] These

---

[21] On the performative rituals of the Black body during lynchings, see Young, "The Black Body as Souvenir in American Lynching," 646–648. Young builds upon this argument in his book Embodying Black Experience. See also W. E. B. Du Bois, "A Recorded Autobiography," interview by Moses Asch (Washington, DC: Folkways Records, 1961).

[22] The broader transformations in menswear in the nineteenth century necessitates historical and historiographical contextualization. For the former, Anne Hollander, *Sex and Suits* (New York: Knopf, 1994), is useful as an overview of the changing expectations of male dress. Leora Auslander points out that within the context of historical material culture studies, there has been undue focus on the production of clothing and its implications for gender roles. More attention to wear of clothing, as I am attempting to do here, brings men and their relationship to clothing into further clarity: Auslander, "Deploying Material Culture to Write the History of Gender and Sexuality."

sellers crowed in full-page newspaper ads about the price, variety, and even fashion of their offerings. Rural African American workers like Kizer and Johnson wore some combination of these newer goods and older clothing types, persistent since the days of slavery. They still wore rough, shapeless shirts of tow, pants or bib overalls of denim, and other cheaply made clothing that nonetheless held up to the rigors of manual labor. Black people's relative lack of access to the world of consumer display and purchase visualized, for white observers, a material continuity between slavery and freedom. They perceived the status of many African American people not just as workers, but as holdovers from a previous era of servitude and white ownership. These visual markers of status heightened the already prominent separations of skin color and tone.[23] Deeply embedded in this new system was a logic of appearance that underlay the new structures of spatial segregation. If you looked Black, you were forced into the Black section of the restaurant, park, city. These were intimate appraisals of material worth, undergirded by southerners' growing reputation as race experts.[24] And though these visual markers of division were absolute, they were not without gradation. The enforcement of segregation and the other emergent structures of Jim Crow was practiced by its white citizens through observation and surveillance. Comportment and, especially, clothing emphasized observed racial difference and heightened the ease of its enforcement. In short, the clothes Kizer and Johnson wore illustrated to white observers their class status, their likely occupations, and, when added to their skin color, their perceived guilt in the rape and murder of Emma Hartsell.

The history of this perception was deep rooted. Unsurprisingly, clothing was one of the original markers of unfree status in the early American construction of a visual-racial identity. Since the early modern period in Europe, clothing had denoted social and occupational status with an increasing degree of subtlety.[25] In the context of American slavery, this allowed white observers to classify Black people based on their knowledge of slave clothing. After slavery's transition to an assumed status for all Black people, clothing further came to represent a stand-in for

---

[23] On these visual observations of racial characteristics, and particularly as color, see Matthew Pratt Guterl, *Seeing Race in Modern America* (Chapel Hill: University of North Carolina Press, 2013).

[24] K. Stephen Prince, *Stories of the South: Race and the Reconstruction of Southern Identity, 1865–1915* (Chapel Hill: University of North Carolina Press, 2014), 226–235.

[25] Jones and Stallybrass, *Renaissance Clothing and the Materials of Memory*, 6–8.

enslaved status.[26] Early colonies and then states even constructed entire sections in their Slave Codes about the requirements of dress and the assumption of particular kinds of comportment. These definitional documents, starting with South Carolina's Negro Act of 1735, formalized the linkages between Black bodies and the kind of rough working clothes that would persist for well over a century.[27] But clothing was never only the domain of custom or enforced legislation. The basic elements of dress were sometimes less important than how a Black person carried themselves while wearing that clothing. An official insistence on servile postures – eyes downcast, yielding space in city streets – never overwhelmed either the expressive outfits crafted from little, or the proud comportment of both enslaved and free Black people.[28]

Relatively few accountings of typical slave clothing survive. Even fewer of the objects themselves are extant. Of the reported *observances* of slave dress, many are fixated on the clothes themselves as commodities outside the context of wear. The best evidence of how enslaved people were perceived to wear clothing comes from incidents of expressivity undertaken while costumed in the exaggerated, outlandish garb of Jonkonnu or other exceptional occasions where slave clothing drew notice. In all but the most extraordinary incidences – a person running away, a carnivalesque celebration – slave clothing was characterized in large part by its anonymity. The observational practices of white people viewing Black clothing and comportment vacillated between detailed description of elaborate self-fashioning, and vague descriptors of interchangeable clothed bodies.[29]

In runaway slave ads, perhaps the best source we have for depictions of enslaved people, clothing's centrality accumulated a definitional weight that far surpassed its status as simple garments designed to protect the body

[26] Patricia Campbell Warner and Debra Parker, "Slave Clothing and Textiles in North Carolina, 1775–1835," in *African American Dress and Adornment: A Cultural Perspective*, ed. Barbara Martin Starke, Lillian O. Holloman, and Barbara Nordquist (Dubuque, IA: Kendall/Hunt, 1990), 82–96, p. 88.

[27] Helen Bradley Foster, *New Raiments of Self: African American Clothing in the Antebellum South* (Oxford; New York: Berg, 1997), 134–135.

[28] Monica L. Miller, *Slaves to Fashion: Black Dandyism and the Styling of Black Diasporic Identity* (Durham, NC: Duke University Press, 2009); Shane White and Graham White, *Stylin': African American Expressive Culture from Its Beginnings to the Zoot Suit* (Ithaca, NY: Cornell University Press, 1998), 66.

[29] On this topic, see Van Dyk Lewis, "Dilemmas in African Diaspora Fashion," *Fashion Theory* 7, no. 2 (2003): 164; Cassandra Jackson, *Violence, Visual Culture, and the Black Male Body* (New York; London: Routledge, 2011), 4.

from work and weather. As both a practical necessity and an indication of status, the clothing of Black people marked forms of identity, employment, or personality. Jonathan Prude notes that there was a visual exchange of sorts between observer and observed. Wealthy people, and eventually the majority of white Americans, dictated a set of expectations for seeing the working bodies of enslaved and free Black people, despite a practiced ignorance of their presence in most situations. The standardized uniformity of slave clothing became an excuse to look without seeing, to substitute one generic working body for another. It was only when enslaved people escaped that the lie of that studied indifference was exposed. Advertisements for runaways betrayed an attention to bodily marking and appearance, from detailed representations of skin tone to minute descriptions of scars and their origins. Clothing was even more specific, with both broad categorizations of fabrics used for slave clothing, more localized vernacular names, and much description of special waistcoats or dresses that the freedom seeker had brought with them.[30] What these occasional observations and advertisements revealed is that white people were looking at Black bodies, and the clothes that covered them, with careful scrutiny. More than that, they were projecting their own assumptions, beliefs, and fantasies onto the people who wore this clothing. They might caricature them as loyal and trustworthy, as deceived or duplicitous, but always their clothing and the ways they fashioned it promised a reflection of their character and essential quality. It is too simple to merely suggest that white slaveholders – and eventually their descendants – were conflating two forms of commodity fetishization: bodies and clothing. But in a way, the two had come to stand in for one another. Clothing was a representation of the body made into a commodity.

Materially, the early years of freedom often made little difference in the clothes that Black people wore. After Emancipation, the label of "plantation clothes" lingered for decades. This might seem like an innocuous form of categorization that reflected the most likely use of the clothing in question. Indeed, it had that purpose. It denoted a distinction between readymade, manufactured goods and the more expensive tailored clothing, as an 1866 Alabama store that offered stocks of both "custom made and plantation clothing" suggested.[31] But the label also worked as a form

---

[30] Prude, "'To Look Upon the Lower Sort'"; Foster, *New Raiments of Self*; White and White, *Stylin'*.

[31] "$50,000 Worth of Custom Made and Plantation Clothing!" *The Montgomery Advertiser*, October 23, 1866.

of bodily inscription, linking its wearers to a particular institution of compelled labor, and to particular places. "Plantation clothes" built on the existing presumptive status of Black people as bodies laboring for a master. This new marketing and labeling served to reinforce long connections between one's clothing and one's body as commodified forms that could be controlled and exchanged.

Plantation clothing made these linkages between slavery and freedom visible and material through the practices of advertising, sale, and daily wear. In the absence of many surviving garments from the period, these advertisements are among our best sources for insight into these classifications and their meaning. Indeed, they give us a sense of the categorizations plantation clothing fit into. One New Orleans merchant advertised "fine fashionable clothing, plantation clothing" as two distinct products on offer in his store.[32] This was a dichotomy based not just in perception but in the reality of the cheap, tow, osnaburg, or other sturdy and scratchy fabrics that continued to make up these offerings.[33] Still other stores offered "low price plantation clothing" at postwar rates hovering around "FIVE DOLLARS PER SUIT (sack and pants)." These were sometimes cloaked in the illusion of consumer choice – "for the Freedmen's use" – though undoubtedly few of the formerly enslaved could afford much better two years after the war's end.[34]

The immediate persistence of this grade and label of clothing is hardly surprising. But, perhaps to an even greater extent than the notion of the plantation itself, the idea of plantation clothing persisted for decades after abolition. An 1888 advertisement in upcountry South Carolina noted the "largest stock of ... plantation clothing ever brought to Sumter." As it had been two decades earlier, this stock of clothing was explicitly contrasted in grade and quality from "Business Suits, School Outfits," and other types of menswear "fresh from Northern markets."[35] Partially this was a term of convenient art used to describe the types of rough, durable clothing that one would wear for the numerous tasks of a plantation. But

---

[32] "Fine Fashionable Clothing, Plantation Clothing," *Times-Picayune*, December 10, 1867.

[33] On the composition and comfort of slave clothing, Booker T. Washington remarks that the flax shirt he had to wear as a boy was "the most trying ordeal that I was forced to endure as a slave": Booker T. Washington, *Up from Slavery: An Autobiography* (New York: Doubleday, Page, 1907), 11. On the persistence of these materials and styles after emancipation, see Foster, *New Raiments of Self*, 208–212.

[34] "Great Opening of Fall and Winter Clothing at George Little & Co's," *The Charleston Daily News*, October 29, 1867.

[35] "Clothing! Clothing! Clothing!" *The Manning Times*, December 12, 1888.

it also implied a class and race of wearer for the clothing as well. It came amid an early wave of other cultural productions that simultaneously nostalgized the plantation South and preserved its legacy as a racialized site of meaning.[36]

Other merchants were even more explicit about the connections between race, clothing, and perceived status. Just two years and a couple dozen miles away from the Concord lynching, Charlotte's Belk Brothers store centered its distinctive ad copy around its potential as an outfitter for the wearable necessities of plantation work. Reflecting on the changing nature of fashion, its lengthy description notes that "times change, scenes of boyhood days can scarce be recognized." Belk Brothers, of course, allowed you to change with the fashions and adapt your outfits to the trends of the day. But like more fully articulated cultural productions, it also had a significant nostalgia for the vanished past and its comforts. As a testament to the size of their storeroom, its owners noted that they "fit and furnished one whole plantation in clothing last week." This testimony brought a reminiscent tone to the quintessentially progress-oriented narrative that this and other Belk ads presented. With Black workers clad in plantation clothing, "it really looked like old Dixie times."[37] Even in advertising, then, the plantation and its clothing were salves for the woes of a hurried modern life. This image – of an entire plantation's worth of workers shoved into an uptown department store – embodies the contradictions of the New South and its impressions of Black clothing. The most quintessentially up-to-date capitalist showcase could serve as the vehicle to return Black people back to plantation slavery. Despite the implied rewards of consumerism, it too proscribed status. African American consumers were denied access to certain stores and even categories of goods by both emerging Jim Crow and capitalist structures.[38]

Indeed, rather than representing just a continuity from slavery to freedom, the persistence of "plantation clothing" was one way of materially confining the bodies of Black men to the emasculating, restrictive posture

---

[36] On the persistence of the plantation as a persistent cultural logic, see Jessica Adams, *Wounds of Returning: Race, Memory, and Property on the Postslavery Plantation* (Chapel Hill: University of North Carolina Press, 2007).

[37] "Belk Bros. Cheapest Store on Earth," *Charlotte Observer*, May 6, 1896.

[38] On the segregation of consumer markets in the Jim Crow South, see Grace Elizabeth Hale, "Bounding Consumption," in her *Making Whiteness: The Culture of Segregation in the South, 1890–1940* (New York: Vintage, 1999), 121–196.

of the "ragged slave."[39] This category of restrictive historicity in the clothed body of Black people came amid broader changes in both men's dress globally and in the self-fashioning image of everyday Black men. As the last decades of the nineteenth century saw a global shift in the expectations of male dress, newly freed men tried to adapt to new customs and demonstrably perform their freedom through the clothes they wore. The few accounts of working-class African American men that we have from this era are suggestive of both the difficulties of maintaining clothing, and the lengths they often went to in order to present a neat appearance. Of his time prior to his first teaching job, Booker T. Washington noted that "to wear one suit of clothes continually ... and at the same time keep it clean, was rather a hard problem for me to solve."[40] Early twentieth-century Alabama sharecropper Ned Cobb likewise noted at length the scarcity of clothing in his early years as a child of a formerly enslaved sharecropper, and the value and centrality of clothing in his later, relatively more prosperous years. In one of his first years of independent work around 1900, he "got one suit of clothes out of my labor that year, store-bought Sunday suit of clothes."[41] He remembered this vividly more than a half century later. He did not think this sufficient payment for his work, but clearly his employer did. He recalled in even greater detail the outfit he had on during a stand against county authorities in 1935 Alabama. His clothing was his winter kit for the year: "a pair of Big-8 overalls, brand new ... a white cowboy hat and my jumper ... and a pair of Red Wing boots about knee high."[42] Undoubtedly the vividness of this memory stemmed from the importance of the occasion. But Cobb also marked time, season, and event through his clothing. Clothes mattered to him as tools that would guard him against the elements and aid his work. But clothes were also symbols of a degree of family prosperity. For Washington, clothes were likewise a mode of self-fashioning in keeping with his rhetoric of self-sufficiency and respectability. The cliché – clothes make the man – seemed to apply here in ways that were vital and literal. Clothes may not have afforded Black men more respect from white observers, but they could forestall scrutiny and the inevitable problems that could come with it.

[39] Sarah Jones Weicksel, "To Look like Men of War: Visual Transformation Narratives of African American Union Soldiers," *Clio. Women, Gender, History*, no. 40 (2015): 127.
[40] Washington, Up from Slavery, 60.
[41] Theodore Rosengarten, *All God's Dangers: The Life of Nate Shaw* (New York: Vintage Books, 1984), 39.
[42] Rosengarten, *All God's Dangers*, 327.

KIZER'S AND JOHNSON'S CLOTHING

Relics represented the elision of self and object. The intense observation of Black people that came to characterize public life represented its seeming opposite: a rejection of Black people and Black identity. But the commonalities between reliquary and surveillance cultures are instructive. Each was about display, observation, and objectification. Black men in particular could not avoid this scrutiny. Their every move was subjected to a surveillance culture linked to assumptions about blackness and criminality. When Emma Hartsell's body was discovered, people immediately turned their attention to Johnson, Kizer, and the clothing they wore. Their clothing, the material traces of events left on it or excluded from it, and the way they wore it stood in for the men themselves. In the absence of sure knowledge about their character or backgrounds, their pants, shirts, suspenders, and caps told the story people needed to justify their lynching.

Frank Pharr, a wealthy white landowner who employed Joe Kizer as a tenant farmer, eagerly volunteered his descriptions of the clothes Kizer wore on the last day of his life. Pharr's account focused primarily on Kizer's dress and its role in his daily routines and customary practices. He noted that "he saw Kizer at 11 o'clock Sunday morning and that he had his overalls on then and also a dirty shirt." His apparently close scrutiny of his employee continued later in the day. When Pharr returned from church "about 5 o'clock he saw Kizer washing himself in the rear of his home."[43] Likely this was part of Kizer's usual Sunday ritual, though his employer assigned it retrospective significance. For other rural African Americans, it was a weekly fact of life. Booker T. Washington noted that in rural areas, there was rarely "any place provided in the cabin where one could bathe even the face and hands, but usually some provision was made for this outside the house, in the yard."[44] For people with little free time and few material resources, this semi-public bathing was an important ritual of cleanliness and self-care. Indeed, Washington noted this repeatedly in *Up From Slavery*, as he recounted the centrality of cleanliness and comportment in his lessons to students at schools in Virginia, West Virginia, and Alabama. Ever the brilliant reader of white expectations, Washington knew that these details of bodily attention could

[43] "A Horrible Crime!" *The Concord Times*, June 2, 1898.
[44] Washington, *Up from Slavery*, 112, 175. Though observation of African Americans in the late nineteenth- and early twentieth-century South was certainly systematic, few

modify perception enough to make a Black person seem a less conspicu-
ous threat to distrustful eyes.[45]

Pharr continued his detailing of the mundane events in his tenant's
cabin. In another event he assigned significance to later, Pharr noted that
a bit after 5:00 p.m., he "saw a big smoke coming from Kizer's chimney
and thought he could detect the smell of burning clothes." Apparently
familiar with the habits of his tenant, he knew this could not be his dinner as "they ate only twice a day and had already eaten dinner about the
middle of the afternoon."[46]

Pharr's comments deserve a bit more analysis. On the one hand, they
reveal the casual surveillance of Black life that characterized the existence
of sharecroppers and tenant farmers. Tom Johnson's employer similarly
"easily recognized" a pair of the man's pants "because he had been working for [him]."[47] Both men were subject to constant scrutiny, made easier
by the built environment of sharecropping, which entailed both proximity
to the landowner and an expectation of his (generally unwanted) comments and intervention. Kizer's house was apparently close to the rear of
his employer's, allowing for even casual glances to be routine and frequent.
In this case, as in many others, it was combined with general assumptions
about African American habits, customs, and comportment. Pharr clearly
expected "his" Black workers to wash themselves and their clothes a certain amount, to eat a certain amount and at regular times, and to otherwise
act and dress in a manner that met his understanding of their behavior. In
all likelihood, his understanding was a product of his upbringing. His was
among the wealthiest families in the county. Around the time of the son's
tenth birthday, Pharr's father claimed ownership to seventeen enslaved
people and hundreds of acres of personal property.[48] The structure Kizer
lived in was almost certainly a repurposed slave cabin on the land Pharr
inherited. The white son of a plantation owner, Pharr grew up amid the

---

people undertook these observations with the intention of academic study. The few who
did do somewhat infrequently mention the bathing and other sanitary practices of Afri-
can American people. See for instance "Madge" in Johnson's *Growing Up in the Black
Belt,* who reports twice weekly baths: Charles S. Johnson, *Growing Up in the Black
Belt: Negro Youth in the Rural South* (New York: Schocken Books [American Youth
Commission of the American Council on Education, 1941], 1967), 33.

[45] Washington, *Up from Slavery,* 75, 87, 126.

[46] "A Horrible Crime!" *The Concord Times.*

[47] "Johnson's Pants Found," *The Standard,* June 9, 1898.

[48] 1860 US Census, Cabarrus County, North Carolina, slave schedule, Western section,
p. 4, Samuel Pharr, enslaver, digital image, Ancestry.com; 1860 US Census, Western
section, p. 6 s.v. "Samuel Pharr," digital image, Ancestry.com.

plantation landscape learning what he undoubtedly perceived as a kind of visual intimacy with Black people, and which read for them as a form of close surveillance. This landscape became the model for the postbellum tenant plantation and the larger culture of surveillance that sought to preserve the structures of control and inequality of the era.[49]

Pharr's account suggests either a supreme level of focus on mundane aspects of the lives of African Americans, or a significant degree of exaggeration. Likely, it was both. Those reading the accounts did not need to believe that Pharr literally smelled burning clothes, for instance. They knew that his close observation and study of Black habits throughout his life were sufficient to believe what was undoubtedly a retrospective assessment. This level of detail was accepted as believable by his contemporaries. They too – rural people and town dwellers alike – would have had practice in carefully observing details of Black dress and comportment. The emerging Jim Crow order was made up of many of these moments of both seeing intently and performatively ignoring Black people. The segregated spatial order emerging in Cabarrus County and across the South at the time was one based on frequent contact and interaction across the color line, but only in particular situations and with an eye toward white enforcement of de jure and de facto rules alike.[50] This kind of surveillance was a part of everyday life for Kizer and Johnson, and it only intensified in the immediate aftermath of Hartsell's murder, when every Black man in the county could be presumed a suspect.

[49] Though frequent attention has been paid to the politics of space on the antebellum plantation, significantly less work has been done on the continuities and changes in the postbellum period. The available work suggests a continued or even renewed scrutiny of Black employees on the postbellum plantation. That observation is borne out by the logic of these landscapes and the testimony of many who endured the period. On the antebellum plantation landscape, see Stephanie M.H. Camp, *Closer to Freedom: Enslaved Women and Everyday Resistance in the Plantation South* (Chapel Hill: University of North Carolina Press, 2004); *Cabin, Quarter, Plantation: Architecture and Landscapes of North American Slavery*, ed. Clifton Ellis and Rebecca Ginsburg (New Haven: Yale University Press, 2010). Particularly insightful in the latter volume is a reprinting of Dell Upton's "White and Black Landscapes in Eighteenth Century Virginia." Among the best of the few studies on the postbellum plantation is Charles E. Orser, *The Material Basis of the Postbellum Tenant Plantation: Historical Archaeology in the South Carolina Piedmont* (Athens: University of Georgia Press, 1988).

[50] Stephen Berrey, *The Jim Crow Routine: Everyday Performances of Race, Civil Rights, and Segregation in Mississippi* (Chapel Hill: University of North Carolina Press, 2016); Simone Browne, *Dark Matters: On the Surveillance of Blackness* (Durham, NC: Duke University Press, 2015).

J. S. Hill, the jailer for the county, was sent out by the sheriff to detain likely suspects after Hartsell's body was discovered. Before Johnson and Kizer were even suspected, Hill zeroed in on the latter because of his appearance. When he approached him around 6:00 p.m., "his pants and shirt were perfectly clean."[51] To readers today, this might appear to be a complete absence of evidence. To Hill, Kizer's cleanliness meant he had just changed clothes and was thus suspect. He remarked that "there was not a spot on his shirt, and though the day was very warm, there was no perspiration on it anywhere."[52] This absence of evidence, material or otherwise, Hill took as positive proof. His assumptions, like Pharr's, relied upon his own beliefs about Black people and the way they presented themselves. Both clothing and the way it was worn were indications of nefarious actions.

Most striking is that it was absence that Hill took as an indicator of guilt. There was a particular irony in his assumption of Kizer's guilt. Apparently Kizer came to town with Pharr's children, as they and other locals gathered at news of the lynching.[53] So it is entirely possible that his reported bathing, change of clothes, and lack of perspiration were due to a concerted effort to present his best appearance before facing what he surely knew would be a crowd of people more suspicious than usual of any Black man. For him and Johnson both, clothing was expensive and difficult to obtain. A material indicator of his complicity in the crime – blood, sweat, dirt – might have been equally damning, but even this lack of evidence was observed as proof. Material absence was apparently an indicator of a guilty conscience. With this telling absence of material proof, Hill arrested Kizer and took him to jail. He and Johnson were abducted and hanged within a few hours.

MAKING RELICS

After Kizer and Johnson were lynched, their mutilated bodies were left to the crowds. The mobs that visited the site in the two days after the lynching took "souvenirs of different kinds," including "parts of the clothing and etc."[54] Closer insight into and further detail of this practice came from a *Charlotte Observer* report after the coroner had taken the bodies down. It revealed that "Johnson had a brand new pair of suspenders on

[51] "A Horrible Crime," *The Maxton Scottish Chief*, June 9, 1898.
[52] "A Horrible Crime," *The Maxton Scottish Chief*.
[53] "A Horrible Crime," *The Maxton Scottish Chief*.
[54] "A Day of Tragedy," *Daily Concord Standard*, May 30, 1898.

when he was hanged." When his body was cut down, "not more than six inches of them were on him, they having been utilized as souvenirs."[55] This suggests the crowd's deep intimacy with the bodies, for them little more than "gruesome looking objects."[56]

Some – more it seems than an intrepid few given the state of Johnson's suspenders – were not content to break off a stick or even scrap of clothing from the man's hem. They came close to the body, touching his breast, chest, or back to snip off their own souvenirs. This bodily proximity resembled nothing so much as the beginning of the rites of burial. And yet this was a clear inversion of that practice, a grab for keepsakes centered on the collectors' desire and intended as sacrilege rather than sacrament. Again, the distinction between souvenirs, trophies, or other categories of collectible and relics becomes apparent here: these pieces of clothing were valued for their proximity not just to the event, but to the bodies of Johnson and Kizer.

Up to this point, I have emphasized the fluid definition of reliquary objects in the nineteenth century, alternating between the personally crafted memento of a loved one and the jealously claimed piece of a famous person. What holds these definitions together is a desire for ownership and possession of the person they were derived from. In another world, the bodies of two dead men might have gone to their families. In an inversion of the process of the lynching's aftermath, the nearly two days that the men hung on the tree would have been spent preparing their bodies for burial. Perhaps their family members would have taken small tokens of remembrance from their bodies, to hold memories of their loved ones close to them. Pieces of their overalls might have become family heirlooms. They could have been lovingly passed down as permanent, intimate relics. I invoke these contingencies because the reality of the situation is almost the precise opposite, a ghastly inversion of the rituals performed on a dead body afforded respect. Instead, collectors rushed to grab every piece of the men they could.

Once these mementos were exhausted, relic hunters' attention turned to the articles of clothing the men had worn during their alleged crime. Before he died, Kizer had protested his innocence, noting that "his overalls were in Mecklenburg County."[57] The matter of the missing overalls and the role of clothing as evidence took on greater prominence as further speculation and collecting continued. Articles in the days after the

---

[55] "The Lynched Negroes Buried," *The Charlotte Observer*, June 1, 1898.
[56] "Judge Lynch at Cabarrus," *The Lexington Dispatch*, June 1, 1898.
[57] "The Lynched Negroes Buried," *The Charlotte Observer*.

lynching detailed the search for these garments, with the implied hope that their discovery would set to rest any lingering doubts and prove, again, all of the assumptions that people made about the victims and their guilt. The lingering, manufactured question about Joe Kizer's clothing was settled by the discovery of the purported overalls a few days after his death. The paper of record in nearby Charlotte got in on the speculation and interest, noting on June 5 that "since that horrible affair Kizer's overalls have been found in a pool of water."[58] This was newsworthy enough to deserve an entire headline and article. Another of the more local papers went into greater depth, detailing the discovery of the overalls by Whit Pharr, son of the farmer Frank on whose land Joe Kizer was a tenant. Their discovery was far from accidental. Frank Pharr and his son had "raked the ashes in Kizer's house to see if any buttons or buckles could be found." Not having any luck, Frank Pharr sent his son to search a nearby watering hole, where he found the pants. This discovery secured a better class of relic for the family than a mere button, buckle, or scrap. They possessed the whole thing.[59] Seemingly motivated by a similar collecting mania, Johnson's employer also searched his property for a memento of the lynched man. Johnson's pants were subsequently "found in a wood pile," allegedly stained with blood in the same place as the top pants he had been wearing when he was killed. As with Kizer, the line between this clothing as evidence of guilt and purely a memento was beginning to blur. With the men's guilt already decided and defended, people still sought out their clothing and other remainders of their bodies and lives.[60]

What use people made of these mementos or what value they held is another matter altogether. Of no economic value as an article of clothing, these scraps nonetheless bore close resemblance to other relics from a slightly earlier period. It is not difficult to see the parallels. The collection of the suspenders or a cap mirrored both the rites of burial and

---

[58] "Kizer's Overalls Found," *The Charlotte Observer*, June 5, 1898.

[59] "Joe Kizer's Overalls and Tom Johnson's Pants Found," *The Concord Times*, June 9, 1898.

[60] "The Lynching Was Just," *The Concord Times*, June 16, 1898. Evidenced in part by there being at least four articles written in multiple newspapers detailing the search for and discovery of various items of their clothing. These are notable too in that each article, while brief, does not appear to be a simple reprint of earlier ones. This demonstrates a particular attention to and interest in the specific matter of their clothing: "Johnson's Pants Found," *The Standard*, June 9, 1898; "The Trousers Found," *The Charlotte Observer*, June 7, 1898; "Joe Kizer's Overalls and Tom Johnson's Pants Found," *The Concord Times*, June 9, 1898, 3; "Kizer's Overalls Found," *The Charlotte Observer*, June 5, 1898.

the commemoration of the dead afterward. Reliquary practices derived much of their power from those overlaps. A piece of clothing or a lock of hair evoked the last bodily rituals, those of the body being prepared for burial. But they were also reminders of other bodily intimacies. Relics might be derived from death, but they evoked the practices of life: a shirt stained by the sweat of work, the remains of a meal, a final, fatal wound. The process of making a collected object into a relic was one of imbuing it with these memories and associations. Those who made relics of the remains taken from Kizer's and Johnson's bodies were not motivated by love or affection, but they surely felt the passion of other reliquary collectors. These objects were invested with the significance of the event and suffused most thoroughly with the men who had once possessed them. Their bearers now could be people associated with a significant historical event, who owned a piece of what newspapers were already calling the most significant day in the county's history.[61] Undoubtedly the objects went into the collections of people who had keepsakes of loved ones who had passed on, even if these lynching relics were held in a very different kind of regard. Joe Kizer and Tom Johnson were quickly erased from the events as people, if the mob had ever even recognized them as such to begin with. But as objects, as material traces, their memory persisted, and their legend grew.

Pharr and his son eagerly sought out Joe Kizer's clothing. It is hard to imagine them giving up their sought-after relic easily. Whitt Phar lived until 1971, never straying far from his hometown. Perhaps he kept the clothes he had collected as a boy with him all his life, using them as a means to assert his place in an important local story.[62] Other people probably did the same thing, passing along their length of suspender or piece of shirt to the next generation. More likely though these prized relics, subject to so much fervor in their collection and creation, eventually lost their magic. My speculation about what happened to these things is more than idle. Without the accompanying firsthand

[61] Barnett, *Sacred Relics.*

[62] US Federal Census, 1900, Cabarrus County, North Carolina, #12 Township, June 9, 1900 s.v. "Whitt Pharr," digital image, Ancestry.com; US Federal Census, 1920, Cabarrus County, North Carolina, #11 Township, June 14, 1920, s.v. "Whitt Pharr," digital image, Ancestry.com. 1930 US Federal Census, Cabarrus County, North Carolina, No. 11 Township, s.v. "F. Whitt Pharr," digital image, Ancestry.com. Certificate of Death, Frank Whitt Pharr, October 28, 1971, North Carolina State Board of Health, Office of Vital Statistics, digital image, Ancestry.com.

experience or secondhand stories, it would be easy for these things to become mere objects again, scraps of cloth buried in a pile of rags or pieces saved for a quilt. The irony of this likelihood lies in how much value was placed on these everyday objects in the first place. When value could no longer be attached to relics of lynched bodies, they had little of the efficacy of *things* and likely vanished from memory, perhaps into the literal dustbin.

As for the possibilities of any burial rites, we know even less. Johnson and Kizer were buried, but at least officially they were not the recipients of any of the niceties of African American burial rites.[63] There are traces of family members – a wife in Lincoln County, a girlfriend near Concord – but no mention of any of them attending to the men's remains or accompanying their bodies at burial.[64] If no family was there to dress and prepare them, they were likely confined to the ground in the scraps of clothing that the mobs had left them. Their other items of clothing taken by Frank Pharr and Larkin Bonds probably represented the majority of their remaining wardrobes and a significant part of their material possessions. Perhaps they had a winter coat or spare shirt left behind with their survivors. If so, these would have been some of the few tangible reminders of their lives and bodies, both. As Peter Stallybrass notes, clothes hold the imprints of their lost wearer. This left-behind cloth "receives our smells, our sweat, our shape even." The clothes of dead people "hang there, holding their gestures, both reassuring and terrifying, touching the living with the dead."[65] The clothing of the dead, more than other mementos, even others turned into relics, haunts its owners. Certainly, it exceeds the abilities of history to speculate on the metaphysical properties of even these most potent things. But perhaps these relics, the last and closest remnants of two murdered men, made their new owners uncomfortable. Maybe Pharr and Bonds were kept awake by the shadow of the pants they had sought out, now hanging in their closets. Or they were chilled by a glimpse of the blood stains on a pair of pants tucked away into a bureau drawer. Maybe these collectors were haunted by the relics they secured.

[63] My thinking on the particularities of these rituals and their overlaps with these more violent actions has been particularly influenced by Karla Holloway's work on African American mourning: Karla F. C. Holloway, *Passed On: African American Mourning Stories* (Durham, NC: Duke University Press, 2002).

[64] "The Lynched Negroes Buried," *The Charlotte Observer*; "A Horrible Crime!" *The Concord Times*.

[65] Stallybrass, "Worn Worlds," 28.

One other collector who seemed to have been alive to the particular possibilities of the men's clothing as reliquaries was Zeb Walter, a resident of the rural township just north of Concord. He came to the lynching site and for his troubles left with "one cap, a piece of rope, and a rag of the garments." Given the apparent value of such a prized haul, Walter was likely either part of the lynch mob, or one of the very earliest relic hunters to arrive on the scene. The article that details his haul is conspicuously silent on the matter, likely not wanting to implicate him any further. The reporter did detail more of Walter's curatorial practice with his newfound relics. He secured "the garments from the two darkeys" in the corn granary on his farm. Apparently this same building had been broken into "and his corn stolen some time ago ... by some colored people (so he says)." He might have suspected Johnson and Kizer. After their deaths, they were accused of a variety of petty crimes in the area, scapegoats for minor thefts and disruptions in the community.[66] Taking their newly prized clothes then was an act of general revenge, either against them specifically or against the generalized "colored people" who allegedly stole Walter's grain. They could be at once mementos of the specific event and relics representing a general anti-Blackness. This was how reliquary culture operated, its meaning built on the power of individual objects within a larger system of belief. For Walter and other lynching relic collectors, that structuring system of belief was an unwavering perception of Black criminality and guilt. Their use of these objects could only reinforce those beliefs, allowing the objects to become part of a kind of ritual practice. What did it mean for Walter, Pharr, Bonds, and the other collectors to inhabit a place that also held these intimate markers of a stolen life? Clearly they valued these clothes for something more than their monetary worth, and either displayed them or kept them under lock and key, each a ritual practice of valuation. Like with relics of an earlier period, they took the materials of everyday life and transformed them into things of great power. Unlike those relics of an earlier period, though, these could easily lose the context of their specialness. Time distanced the intimacy of their connection to the lynching and rendered them again everyday objects. And with the increasing access to a consumer culture built in part on reproducibility and replaceability, it was ever more difficult to project such power onto an individual object that did not immediately

[66] See for instance the claim that they cut cows in the neighborhood with a razor: "A Horrible Crime!" *The Concord Times.*

bear the signs of its importance.[67] Maybe Johnson's and Kizer's clothes got repurposed into scraps for rags or quilts, sold to the rag man or donated to a charitable resale store. Maybe they were just packed away somewhere along with the other accumulated objects of a lifetime.[68] Their clothes were haunting and haunted reminders of the men and their bodies, but the "terror of the material trace" requires some recognition for its enduring power.[69] These specific objects are lost to us now and have been for a long time. Even if they still existed as objects, they would not exist as *things*, as relics of the men they were taken from.

CONCLUSION

The past, and historians' reconstruction of it, proceeds from the assembly of scraps and pieces. I stitched together parts of the stories of Frank Pharr, Zeb Walter, and Larkin Bonds because they reveal much about the lynching and its aftermath. But they also function as a reminder of the absences at the center of this story. Tom Johnson and Joe Kizer became, to these men and the hundreds of other people who viewed their bodies, took souvenirs, and preserved the narrative of their assumed and inherent guilt, objects. The relics made of their clothing were substitutes for the bodies, but never for the men themselves. Kizer and Johnson were denied a complete story, even to the extent of the quilted patchwork we can piece together for these other historical actors. But we can still see them in traces. Befitting the metaphor of the material culture considered here, we can reconstruct by patchwork, relying not on the false certitudes of the written word, but rather on the mysteries and counterfactuals contained in objects.

In thinking about Johnson's and Kizer's clothing, I was drawn to other relics made up of old clothing taken from the bodies of Black men. I found a profound counterpoint to the reliquary grabs of the mob in the britchy quilts of the Alabama artist Catherine Somerville. Her *Log Cabin (Pig Pen Variation/Checkerboard)* brings to mind the possibilities of memorializing and honoring body, clothes, and person alike. A striking, intimate thing, it

[67] I am thinking here of Walter Benjamin's theorizations, both "The Work of Art in the Age of Mechanical Reproduction," in *Illuminations*, ed. Hannah Arendt, trans. Harry Zohn (New York: Schocken Books, 1969), 1–26, and the unfinished *Arcades Project*, which deal extensively with the practices of collecting and historical knowledge: Walter Benjamin, *The Arcades Project*, trans. Howard Eiland (Cambridge, MA: Harvard University Press, 2002).

[68] On the early history of charitable clothing resale, see Jennifer Le Zotte, "'Not Charity, But a Chance': Philanthropic Capitalism and the Rise of American Thrift Stores," *New England Quarterly* 86, no. 2 (2013): 169–195.

[69] Stallybrass, "Worn Worlds."

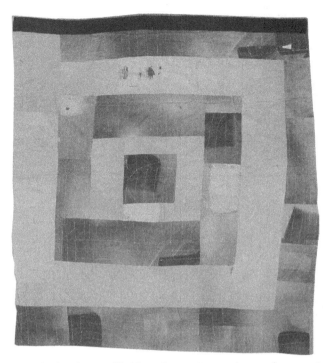

FIGURE 3.1 Catherine Somerville (American, 1870–active to about 1960), Log Cabin (Pig Pen Variation)/Checkerboard, about 1950–1960, cotton, cotton/ polyester blend, and polyester, 76 1/2 x 70 inches, Montgomery Museum of Fine Arts, Montgomery, Alabama, Association Purchase, 2004.21.19

is pieced together from the remnants of turn-of-the-century work clothes of the type worn by Johnson, Kizer, and many succeeding generations of working-class Black men. The quilt shows both marks – trademarks, brand names – and wear – stains, scrapes, patches upon scraps. In the anonymity of each of its parts there is a collective sense of memory preserved. These are clearly clothes that had been worn to their breaking point (Figures 3.1 and 3.2). Like Johnson's and Kizer's clothes, these bits of denim, duck, and canvas were taken from garments made for work, in this case from men in Somerville's family around Aliceville, Alabama. There is no explanation or exact date of origin for the quilt, but from the many different patterns of wear and types of cloth, it was likely made from clothing worn, patched, and discarded over years in the early to mid-twentieth century. It is a relic of sorts, too. Like Jim Crow–era Confederate memorials or other mourning relics, it builds intimacy through an invocation of loss, and makes the domestic practices of marking and mourning that loss public. The quilt invokes that domesticity

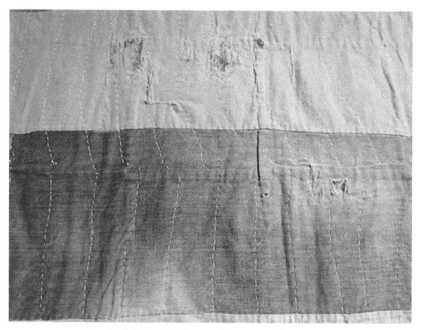

FIGURE 3.2 Detail of Catherine Somerville, *Log Cabin (Pig Pen Variation)*,
showing clothing wear and repair, c. 1950–1960

through its forms (literally a house shape) and the quotidian nature of its
materials. It is a collective commemoration that, like the Confederate monuments, bears its intimacy outwardly. Even as an ostensibly private object it
is clearly made for display with its double-sided pattern, whorled stitching,
and eye-catching details.

But it functions as a commemoration not of abstract honor or heroism, but of the ravages of the passage of time. It is a testament to bodies
and the work they did, not the more sentimental and less specific veneration of other bodily relics. Each individual piece marks not one task
or event, but many hundreds of them. As a whole, it is a testament to
the poetics of working people and the utility of working clothes. It is
also a haunted thing. It is difficult not to read the traces of bodies on it
and the supposed threats that they represented. Like Kizer and Johnson,
the men whose clothes figure into this quilt were Black, working men.
Undoubtedly they too faced the same threats of Jim Crow violence. Their
home in Pickens County was a particularly violent place. Seventeen Black
men were lynched there between 1886 and 1917 alone.[70] The last two

---

[70] "Pickens County, Alabama," *A Red Record.*

lynching victims in the county – Sam Meeks and Poe Hibbler – were contemporaries of Somerville and the men whose clothes made up her quilt If she and her family did not know the victims, they certainly knew about the lynching. Catherine Somerville made this work in the broad context of Jim Crow and its threatened violence against the kind of Black people whose clothes she worked into her quilt. And it is easy to imagine her reflecting on the long legacy and many acts of violence she had witnessed during her lifetime in Pickens County.[71]

But Somerville's work also clearly speaks to the even more immediate racial terror lynchings of its day. The museum that holds this quilt estimates its date of completion at sometime between 1950 and 1960. This puts Somerville working on it during the early phases of the Civil Rights Movement era.[72] In this context, the quilt invokes Emmett Till and the strenuous preparations of respectability that he, his body, and his clothes underwent in the wake of his 1955 lynching. His mother famously insisted that his mutilated body be publicly displayed. More prominent than those images though were of the respectable young man with a natty hat, point-collar shirt, and two-tone tie.[73] Even in death, this image of a smiling, nonthreatening boy was meant to challenge the unfounded assumptions of him as another lynched Black brute. Clothes carried weight. But they hardly mattered enough. For many hundreds of years, Black people learned to dress and act a certain way to either avoid notice or avoid the wrong kind of notice. And yet white people continued to observe, to notice, and to act, commodifying Black people into Black bodies first economically, and then ritually.

---

[71] 1940 US Census, Pickens County Alabama, s.v. "Catherine Somerville," digital image, Ancestry.com. Though the Somerville or Sommerville name was somewhat commonplace in Pickens County, I can only find one Catherine among them during the first four decades of the twentieth century. This Catherine was born in 1910, making her a young child during the 1916 and 1917 lynchings in the county and in her twenties when she began what the International Quilting Museum identifies as her active period of work. See "Britchy Quilt," International Quilt Museum, www.internationalquiltmuseum.org/quilt/20000040116 (accessed May 2020). On the lynching of Sam Meeks, see "Short Paragraphs over the State," *The Cullman Tribune*, July 6, 1916. On Poe Hibbler's lynching, see "3 Alabama Negroes Lynched in 2 Days," *The Shreveport Journal*, July 25, 1917 and "Alabamans Lynch Negro," *Daily Arkansas Gazette*, July 26, 1917.

[72] I capitalize this here to distinguish the 1950s and 1960s era from the "long civil rights movement" as outlined by Jacquelyn Dowd Hall, "The Long Civil Rights Movement and the Political Uses of the Past," *Journal of American History* 91, no. 4 (2005): 1233–1263.

[73] Elliott Gorn notes that the images of Till's body in his coffin were not widely circulated outside Black publications until their use in documentaries in the 1980s. See Elliott J. Gorn, *Let the People See: The Story of Emmett Till* (New York: Oxford University Press, 2018), 235–288.

4

The Tree

Observations of the tree used to lynch Joe Kizer and Tom Johnson read like a botanical journal or nursery catalog. "The tree was small, not over 8 inches in diameter" and so thin that it could hardly bear the weight of the two men. After their deaths, they were left suspended "twelve or fourteen inches above the ground." They were wrapped around the tree "within eighteen inches of each other. If it were not for the trunk of the tree, their elbows would touch." These recitations of size and specimen focused on the tree as much as the men whose bodies were hanged from it.[1]

That held true when people started taking souvenirs from the site of the lynching. Other keepsakes might have been more prized, but the tree was the most plentiful supplier of mementos. People took limbs and sticks in the first couple of days. Within a year, the whole tree was cut down. We do not know whether the strain of souvenir takers caused its death, or if a more enterprising soul sought to industrialize the practice by using the whole tree. But "several persons [took] limbs ... and one man contemplate[d] making some walking canes out of the body of the tree." The canes may never have materialized, but almost three-quarters of a century later, at least one of the limbs was still prized as a souvenir. It had been passed down as an heirloom by a local white family.[2]

This chapter is about the process of collecting the landscapes of lynching. As the broader story of this book – and particularly of this section – shows,

[1] "A Horrible Affair!" *Concord Times,* June 2, 1898; "Horrible Affair!" *The Messenger and Intelligencer,* June 2, 1898.
[2] "A Day of Tragedy," *Daily Concord Standard,* May 30, 1898; "[The Dogwood Tree]," *Chatham Citizen,* March 8, 1899; Ned Cline, "Even Negroes Took Part in Last Cabarrus Lynching Play," *Salisbury Post,* November 29, 1964.

lynching was made comprehensible and its memory preserved through cultures of collecting. Collecting is an act rooted in observation and extraction. The dogwood tree on which the men were hanged was both an expedient choice of makeshift gallows, and a potent symbol of the intersections of belief, tradition, race, and region. Hanging Johnson and Kizer from a dogwood tree was an evocation of these many meanings. If the mob's intentions in this selection are illusory and irrecoverable, the constellations of meanings that the tree evoked are far less obscure. The dogwood was a stand-in for the meanings derived from collecting the places of the South.

In this chapter, I use the landscape of lynching as both a metaphorical entity and a material reality. My focus here is primarily on the structures of feeling around the lynching, as participants and observers sought to make and preserve meaning with the collected remains of the dogwood tree.[3] I contextualize this acquisitive and narrative impulse within the larger collecting practices of explorers, academics, and tourists of the southern landscape. Natural history, folklore, and sociological documentary projects sought to capture and portray versions of the South through its physical environment. Tourist economies constructed a southern landscape of beauty and plenty, far apart from both its primitive origins and its pathological structures. Each of these movements turned on shallow knowledges taken from and substituted for the places themselves. They envisioned a landscape that might stand in for many of the nation's problems and stand outside and apart from its changes. Landscape souvenirs of lynching demonstrated this tension. The dogwood became symbolic of both a generic landscape romanticism, and the performance of the most vicious enactments of white supremacy and racist violence. These object worlds were mutual and overlapping, and they suggest the complexities of collecting the landscape of a region. As objects collected from lynching sites began to be commercialized, they entered into tourist economies as souvenirs. Lynching souvenirs were meant to commodify the experience of witness and invoke the scene of the lynching many months and years later. In this way, the meanings of lynching were both embedded in and extracted from the southern landscape.

---

[3] I am invoking here "structures of feeling" as Raymond Williams formulated the concept. Though a wide range of scholars have expanded upon his insights into effect and historical understanding, his notion of cultural structures still in sometimes unconscious formation undeniably remains useful. See Raymond Williams, *Marxism and Literature* (Oxford; New York: Oxford University Press, 1977), 128–135.

DOCUMENTING AND COLLECTING THE SOUTHERN LANDSCAPE

Landscape had long stood in for the southern region in the imagination of those documenting it. The eighteenth-century naturalist and explorer William Bartram carefully observed each swamp and settlement, working toward a portrait of the places he visited that was at once particular and comprehensive. The world of his South was one frozen in a prelapsarian stasis, its flora and indigenous people all a part of a rich naturalism. He did not inaugurate the practice of naturalizing indigenous peoples into the landscape, but arguably built the most durable example of that practice in the emergent "South."[4] Later naturalist historians, like John James Audubon, were fully immersed in the cosmopolitan, Atlantic South, but nonetheless detailed the beauties of the southern wilderness as representative of the region. Audubon helped further the notion of the South as untrammeled wilderness, full of grand New World specimens.[5]

[4] There is a wide literature on William Bartram, particularly as it pertains to his role in the creation of an American natural history that was rooted in perceptions of a southern wilderness. In particular see *Fields of Vision: Essays on the Travels of William Bartram*, ed. Kathryn E. Holland Braund and Charlotte M. Porter (Tuscaloosa: University of Alabama Press, 2010) and Michael P. Branch, "Indexing American Possibilities: The Natural History Writing of Bartram, Wilson, and Audubon," in *The Ecocriticism Reader: Landmarks in Literary Ecology*, ed. Cheryll Glotfelty and Harold Fromm (Athens: University of Georgia Press, 1996), 282–302. My hesitant use of "the South" here is a recognition of the realities of southern regional identity, which was both very much still in formulation and indebted more to a settler colonial vision of regionality than an indigenous one. On this "South before the South," see Eric Gary Anderson, "On Native Ground: Indigenous Presences and Countercolonial Strategies in Southern Narratives of Captivity, Removal, and Repossession," *Southern Spaces* August 2007, https://southernspaces.org/2007/native-ground-indigenous-presences-and-countercolonial-strategies-southern-narratives-captivity-removal-and-repossession. Other recent work in Native American studies likewise looks at the specifics of place formation and identity within a larger framework of a reclaimed indigenous South: Justin Mack, "The Chickasaws' Place-World: The Mississippi River in Chickasaw History and Geography," *Native South* 11 (2018): 1–28; Melanie Benson Taylor, "Indian Givers: Reterritorializing the South in Contemporary Native American Literature," *Mississippi Quarterly* 60.1 (2007): 101–128. It is also worth noting that this trend of the naturalized Indian and the essentialized landscape goes back much further and arguably to the earliest European attempts at documenting contact and region. The quasi-ethnographic drawings of John White are perhaps the best example of this: John White, *America, 1585: The Complete Drawings of John White*, ed. Paul Hulton (Chapel Hill and London: University of North Carolina Press; British Museum Publications, 1984).

[5] Of course, Audubon and Bartram were only part of a much larger world of natural history description and belief in early America. Thomas Jefferson's *Notes on the State of Virginia* is the most famous among its peers for its outlandish claims about the flora and fauna of the "New World": Lee Alan Dugatkin, *Mr. Jefferson and the Giant Moose: Natural History in Early America* (Chicago: University of Chicago Press, 2009); Thomas

In Audubon's later mammalian studies, the branches and flowers of his earlier work gave way to landscapes in miniature, including the working rice fields of the low-country South in his rendering of the cheerful cotton rat.[6] My point here is not merely that southern landscapes, even those of plantation slavery, were aestheticized. Rather, images and other remainders of these landscapes came to stand in for the complexities of the place itself, including the people living there. If Bartram, Audubon, and these other earlier nature writers anticipated the birth of anthropology in the nineteenth century, they helped define it within the scope of the natural world. Their nature was one defined not just by flora and fauna, but by all of its human and nonhuman inhabitants, neatly rendered as part of the landscape. That trend began with Native Americans affixed to the landscape, but settler colonial fantasies of removal eventually saw them eclipsed by African Americans. In both cases, the picturesque landscapes were defined, reciprocally, by the people who were made a part of them. Defining the southern landscape went hand in hand with naturalizing its inhabitants as both heirs of and impediments to its supposedly natural fecundity.[7]

Jefferson, *Notes on the State of Virginia*, ed. William Peden, 3rd ed., Published for the Omohundro Institute of Early American History and Culture, Williamsburg, Virginia (Chapel Hill: Omohundro Institute and University of North Carolina Press, 2006); Pamela Regis, *Describing Early America: Bartram, Jefferson, Crevecoeur, and the Rhetoric of Natural History* (DeKalb: Northern Illinois University Press, 1992).

[6] John James Audubon is the subject of many biographies and histories, many of which note his southern sojourns largely in passing. Some recent work has tended more closely to his time in the South. See for instance Michael K. Steinberg, "Audubon Landscapes in the South," *Mississippi Quarterly* 63, no. 1–2 (2010): 313–329. Steinberg is particularly important in documenting how Audubon adopted a southern plantation identity as a means of furthering his presentation of rugged authenticity. Similarly, his linkages to plantation culture in the low country particularly are well documented in Debra Lindsay, *Maria Martin's World: Art and Science, Faith and Family in Audubon's America* (Tuscaloosa: University of Alabama Press, 2018). Outside of scarce early folios, Audubon's later documentation of mammals and other quadrupeds is less well known. A recent exhibition and catalog helpfully collect and contextualize many of these images. The landscapes here are particularly well realized and serve as far more than backdrop: John James Audubon, *Audubon's Last Wilderness Journey: The Viviparous Quadrupeds of North America*, ed. Tom Butler (London; Auburn, AL: Jule Collins Smith Museum of Fine Art in association with D. Giles Limited, 2018).

[7] On Bartram as a precursor to nineteenth-century anthropological practice, see Mark Sturges, "A Deep Map of the South: Natural History, Cultural History, and William Bartram's *Travels*," *South Atlantic Review* 79, no. 1–2 (2014): 46. On the naturalization of Indians to the landscape, see also Shepard Krech, *The Ecological Indian: Myth and History* (New York: W. W. Norton, 1999).

This was a tradition that persisted in the latter half of the nineteenth century with the growth of southern travel accounts. Long a genre that helped to create the region as a world apart, writing about travel to the South was arguably more commonplace throughout most of the antebellum period than was traveling there. In this way, the South was a landscape imagined as much as it was experienced.[8] Travelers depicted a benighted region with economic possibilities embedded in the landscape and climate. By the late 1840s, hot springs and other salubrious elements of the southern landscape were positioned as the new cure-alls for northern ailments. The wildness and wilderness of the South could seemingly be harnessed for the good of the country as a whole.[9]

Certainly, this idea extended to one of the most comprehensive chroniclers of the antebellum southern landscape: the young farmer and later pioneer of landscape architecture, Frederick Law Olmsted. Some scholars have linked Olmsted's later practice as a designer and transformer of the built environment to these travels in the 1850s, but it was primarily his early-life vocation as a farmer that colored his serialized accounts of southern journeys.[10] Amid a deepening sectional crisis, Olmsted painted

---

[8] This imagined South has a very long history in popular writing. John Cox reconstructs this period in early America, where the South served as an internal other in the process of nation building: John D. Cox, *Traveling South: Travel Narratives and the Construction of American Identity* (Athens: University of Georgia Press, 2005). Also useful in this regard, particularly as it pertains to the exoticized imagination of the South, is Matthew Pratt Guterl, *American Mediterranean: Southern Slaveholders in the Age of Emancipation* (Cambridge, MA: Harvard University Press, 2013). Finally, Karen Cox reconstructs the ways in which the South was imagined through the lens of popular culture from the late nineteenth century to World War II: Karen Cox, *Dreaming of Dixie: How the South Was Imagined in Popular Culture* (Chapel Hill: University of North Carolina Press, 2011).

[9] The early origins of tourism in the South are well documented in Rebecca Cawood McIntyre, *Souvenirs of the Old South: Northern Tourism and Southern Mythology* (Gainesville: University Press of Florida, 2011), esp. 11–39. Among the most intensively developed tourist economies beginning in the antebellum period and intensifying in the latter half of the nineteenth century was the North Carolina mountains and particularly the tourist town of Asheville. This growth is well developed in Richard D. Starnes, *Creating the Land of the Sky: Tourism and Society in Western North Carolina* (Tuscaloosa: University of Alabama Press, 2005).

[10] Though Olmsted's southern journeys are often referred to in historical studies, most scholars and biographers have focused primarily on his more justifiably famous work as one of the primary minds behind American landscape architecture and design. Beveridge does more than most biographers to make this early background an important part of Olmsted's professional practice: Charles E. Beveridge, Paul Rocheleau, and David Larkin, *Frederick Law Olmsted: Designing the American Landscape* (New York: Rizzoli, 1995). Perhaps the most comprehensive work on Olmsted's multiple sojourns to the

for his largely northern readers a portrait of fertile farmland poorly managed. He excoriated the inefficiencies of enslaved labor. For him, the South was a place of great potential whose residents polluted it with their corrupted system of labor and lack of industry. In his assessments of the land, if not the cultural landscape, there is more than a hint of a colonizing desire on behalf of fellow land poor northerners. This was land that could and should be seized, collected, and used by those outside of the region who might put it to better use. Its Black inhabitants were to be both pitied and condemned, mere fixtures on the landscape and obstacles to progress than active agents of cultivation.

Postwar accountings were even more nakedly desirous of the war-wrecked land. Edward King, another serial traveler, roamed perhaps even farther through the region than his predecessor of two decades prior. His missives for *Scribner's* sometimes read like an advertisement for northern capitalist investment.[11] More crucial than King's words though are the accompanying illustrations, most of them by J. Wells Champney. Champney's portraits were often conventional landscape illustrations of the type one would expect in a rebuilding society: physical infrastructure like bridges, natural resources like rivers and ports, tools of commerce like steamboats and rail lines. His final illustrations in the book of collected accounts published in 1875 are of what he calls "Southern Types." True to their labeling, these are broadly drawn figures immersed in commercial, plantation, and urban scenes of the South. They lack the specificity of location of earlier illustrations, which were documentary reflections of the author's and illustrator's travels through Reconstruction-era southern landscapes. These "types" are largely African American. Like the other

South comes from a volume of essays on the topic. See *Olmsted South, Old South Critic, New South Planner*, ed. Dana F. White and Victor A. Kramer, Contributions in American Studies 43 (Westport, CN: Greenwood Press, 1979). Most recently the journalist Tony Horwitz followed Olmsted's path through the region. Though his book does not function as a work of scholarship on Olmsted, he nonetheless has keen insights on the relationship between these two, seeming disparate, identities: Tony Horwitz, *Spying on the South: An Odyssey across the American Divide* (New York: Penguin Press, 2019).
[11] Though much of the focus on the postbellum New South is on urban development in particular, there is a growing literature on the other than specifically rural built environments: Reiko Hillyer, *Designing Dixie: Tourism, Memory, and Urban Space in the New South* (Charlottesville: University of Virginia Press, 2015); Jack Temple Kirby, *Mockingbird Song: Ecological Landscapes of the South* (Chapel Hill: University of North Carolina Press, 2006); Erin Stewart Mauldin, *Unredeemed Land: An Environmental History of Civil War and Emancipation in the Cotton South* (New York; Oxford: Oxford University Press, 2018).

Southern Types—Negro Shoeblacks.

FIGURE 4.1 An image of Wells and Champney's postbellum South in context. North Carolina Collection, University of North Carolina Library at Chapel Hill

illustrations in the book, and other southern landscape chroniclers before him, these characters are figured as part of their surroundings. A typical image is of four "Negro Shoeblacks." They are Black boys ranging from about five to twelve years old, arrayed around the gates of an unnamed city. The nominal focus of the picture, they are less finely rendered than the donkey cart, docked ships, steam-powered factory, and other signs of progress in the port surrounding them (Figure 4.1). Other drawings in this series rely more heavily on caricature and racist assumption, like the documenting of "A Little Unpleasantness" in what appear to be former slave quarters (Figure 4.2). Here, *Scribner's* viewers saw their own perceptions of the South reflected back to them: a plantation landscape with African American people more inclined to petty disagreements and leisurely enjoyment than hard work. These documentary illustrations were responsive to a growing demand for narrative and visual accountings of the South. Moonlight and magnolias mingled with similarly romantic dreams of the money to be made from extracting the region's rich

FIGURE 4.2 Champney's stereotyped illustration of postbellum Black Southern life. North Carolina Collection, University of North Carolina Library at Chapel Hill

environmental resources.[12] King and Champney's work also represented a continued evolution in the linkages between southern land and (some) southern people. Poor and elite white people were given significant character sketches. King detailed the oddities and problems of poor white people in particular, unwinding long descriptions that were both sympathetic and a little mocking. Black people though were fixed entities for King and for Champney. They seemed a part of the landscape, an inexhaustible resource to be pictured and extracted like any other. This marked a long transition from Native people's inextricability from the landscape to a naturalization of African descended peoples. Visual removal of Indians paved the way for the ubiquitous portrayal of Black people in, on, and as part of the southern landscape.

By the last years of the nineteenth century, then, there was a well-established journalistic and artistic documentary tradition around the landscapes of the South. Though there was certainly intraregional variation in this practice, there was also a growing consensus that there was something essential contained in the physical localities of the South itself. The earliest portraits of southern wilderness had portrayed a place populated by exotic flora and fauna and peopled with indigenous inhabitants

---

[12] Much southern cultural history has focused intently on the relationship between the South as a real place and as a constructed identity. See in particular Cox, *Dreaming of Dixie*; Prince, *Stories of the South*; Nina Silber, *The Romance of Reunion: Northerners and the South, 1865–1900 Civil War America* (Chapel Hill: University of North Carolina Press, 1993). Hilyer's *Designing Dixie* focuses particularly on the intersections between this romantic vision of the region and the more economically focused one that sought to extract and re-form the southern built environment.

little separated from the land. This had gradually given way to both literal and symbolic removal of Native people and lifeways. In this evolving narrative, the earlier fecundity of the land under supposed neglect had given way to astonishing productivity. And the natural Native had been replaced by the toiling slave. Emancipation and its aftereffects brought further changes, with the freed slave continuing to be a fixture in the places of the changing South. The examples I have offered above are representative of an even longer and broader tradition of attempting to define, document, and capture the landscapes of the South. By naturalizing Blackness to the southern landscape, these documentary efforts helped to build up a South at once pathologized and full of premodern places and people. In a significant sense, regional identity was formed through these documentary and definitional efforts. Landscape became a container for regional identity. And the South became a region set outside both the country and modernity. These earlier studies laid the groundwork for early twentieth-century academic regional studies. Like their predecessors, these folklorists and sociologists sought to collect the remnants of a supposedly pure premodern world.[13]

---

[13] The national perception of the South in the late nineteenth and early twentieth centuries was marked by both romantic notions of the region and a tendency toward pathologizing. The tension between these two Souths, both imagined, was aided by a range of cultural productions and resulted in significant philanthropic, legislative, and regulatory apparatuses. Indeed, Natalie Ring links intervention in the South during this period to the rise of the liberal state: Natalie J. Ring, *The Problem South: Region, Empire, and the New Liberal State, 1880–1930* (Athens: University of Georgia Press, 2012). On the tensions inherent in this work of documentation and intervention in the South, see Scott L. Matthews, *Capturing the South: Imagining America's Most Documented Region* (Chapel Hill: University of North Carolina Press, 2018). The early decades of the twentieth century saw a significant national discussion on the cultural backwardness of the South that in many ways proceeded from the entanglements of its created mythos. Perhaps most prominent of these critics was H. L. Mencken, whose "Sahara of the Bozart," published in 1917 (in *The American Scene*, ed. Mencken (New York: Knopf, 1977), 157–168), was marked by both longing for an imagined antebellum intellectual culture and condemnation of its perceived provincial attitudes in the early twentieth century. A whole generation of white writers and academics adapted his retrograde stance, furthering in many ways a different mythos of the antebellum South based less on its romanticism and more on its intellectual and political ideologies. These movements are well covered in many of the excellent intellectual histories of the South. See Paul Murphy, *The Rebuke of History: The Southern Agrarians and American Conservative Thought* (Chapel Hill: University of North Carolina Press, 2001); Michael O'Brien, *Rethinking the South: Essays in Intellectual History* (Baltimore: Johns Hopkins University Press, 1988); Daniel Joseph Singal, *The War Within: From Victorian to Modernist Thought in the South, 1919–1945* (Chapel Hill: University of North Carolina Press, 1982).

THE LEGENDS OF THE DOGWOOD

The most comprehensive of these early twentieth-century chroniclers of the South were regional folklorists. Beginning around the turn of the century, professionals and hobbyists scoured the holdouts of "primitive" culture to locate survivals of society's past glories. In this way rural and working-class people came to be seen as repositories of otherwise vanished knowledge. These studies were balanced, if often uneasily, between valorization and casual dismissal. Framing aside, these projects grant unparalleled access to the traditions and customs of a wide range of southern landscape and life.

The seven volumes of what came to be called the *Frank C. Brown Collection of North Carolina Folklore* represented the comprehensive collecting impulse of early American folklorists. The early practice of folklore in the United States sought out the remains of earlier eras of Anglo-derived folk culture. The "survivals" they looked for were the objects, traditions, songs, and customs (what later came to be called folkways) of a kind of American folk nationalism. It's unsurprising then that the first of these collecting groups appeared in the South.[14] They built on the same assumptions as the intellectual strain of collecting practiced by Bartram and Audubon, King and Champney, and furthered by their contemporaneous, regional sociologists. These collectors viewed the "backward South" of other academics not as a liability for a developing region, but as a premodernity to be promoted, preserved, and collected. The *Frank C. Brown Collection* aspired to be comprehensive, the definitive

---

[14] The first professional folklore society in the United States was founded in Texas in 1909: www.texasfolkloresociety.org/our-society/history (accessed April 16, 2022). North Carolina's followed a few years later in 1913: Theodore Barry Buermann, "*A History of the North Carolina Folklore Society*," MA thesis, University of North Carolina, 1963. The fieldwork approach in American folklore studies was really pioneered in such state organizations who empowered collectors a few decades before similar approaches were formally institutionalized in academic departments of folklore in the following four decades. This institutional history is well-covered in a recent edited volume: *Folklore in the United States and Canada: An Institutional History*, ed. Patricia Sawin and Rosemary Levy Zumwalt (Bloomington: Indiana University Press, 2020). On the history of folklore as a professional field of study, see Regina Bendix, *In Search of Authenticity: The Formation of Folklore Studies* (Madison: University of Wisconsin Press, 1997); Simon J. Bronner, *American Folklore Studies: An Intellectual History* (Lawrence: University Press of Kansas, 1986). For Bendix, the entire field in both America and Germany was premised on the search for authenticity, lodged first in notions of the premodern or unspoiled and eventually evolving toward other forms of perceived authentic culture.

catalog of the "body of knowledge and of material things possessed by the simple illiterate people."[15]

Dogwood was among the most prominent symbols that these early North Carolina folklore collectors found. In the published volumes of the project, the tree mentioned many dozens of times and manifested in verbal, material, and customary genres of ritual. Though the collectors did not interpret it this way, their cumulative efforts found a material system of belief around and about the dogwood. In North Carolina, every bit of the dogwood tree from root to bloom was part of this wide-ranging system of folk beliefs and customs. It both predicted the weather – its berries falling off augured a hard winter and its earliest blooms announced an inevitable storm – and reflected social responses to it. A popular rhyme statewide had it that "when the dogwood is white/fish begin to bite," and its blooming was likewise the indicator that it was time to plant cotton or corn. But it was not merely a harbinger of changes in the weather or season. A full catalog of the dogwood's folkloric properties would exhaust several pages: It could reveal true love, predict marriage, and cure coughs, chills, Bright's disease, pneumonia, malaria, and bad skin. As both symbol and instrument, the dogwood's bark, blossoms, and wood were rich with meaning and purpose for North Carolinians and for southerners more generally. The dogwood had a power that stemmed in part from its ubiquity, a plant whose trunks and blooms populated roadsides and forests and the imaginations of people across the region. It was at once an entirely ordinary category of object and one that illustrated for southerners the potent possibility of things in the natural world to impact human affairs.[16]

Of the dozens of mentions of dogwood trees, bark, and blossoms over the several thousand pages of the *Frank C. Brown Collection*, there's only a single documented instance of the most enduring dogwood myth. And crucially, it is a mention by comparative omission. An unnamed source claims that it was "the willow, not the dogwood which was cursed by Jesus."[17] This comparison suggests that the myth of the dogwood as

---

[15] Frank C. Brown et al., *The Frank C. Brown Collection of North Carolina Folklore: Popular Beliefs and Superstitions from North Carolina*, 1st ed, vol. 1, 7 vols. (Durham, NC: Duke University Press, 1952), 7.

[16] Brown et al., *The Frank C. Brown Collection of North Carolina Folklore*, 176, 348, 476, 512, 523.

[17] Brown et al., *The Frank C. Brown Collection of North Carolina Folklore*, 500.

a religious symbol was so well known as to be unworthy of recording. But "The Legend of the Dogwood" (as it is most often called) is both the most persistent piece of dogwood folklore and emblematic of the meanings made from and imposed on the southern landscape.

The legend, as recounted in 1930s Virginia, tells of an angry yet merciful Jesus. Having been crucified on a cross of dogwood and "sensing their [the tree's] regret for his great suffering," he curses it to never again be large enough to be made into a cross.[18] That curse is recounted in detail through the words of Jesus in the Virginia version. He vows to make the tree "slender, bent, and twisted," with blossoms "in the form of a cross, two long and two short petals and in the center of the outer edge of each petal there shall be nail prints, brown with rust and stained by blood" and with a crown of thorns in the center.[19] The "old and beautiful legend" was certainly circulating by the 1880s, and likely much earlier if that description is any indication.[20] It had the effect of making a routine part of southern life into a piece of religious symbolism. In this way, a ubiquitous fixture on the landscape was transmuted into an expression of vernacular religion, and an example of the materiality of popular religious expression that was coming to dominate southern culture in these transformational years.

The dogwood was certainly not alone in serving as an expression of popular religion that merged the sacred world with everyday ritual and experience. Folklorists looked to a premodern past for the origins of southern belief, but it was the transitional period in the years after Emancipation that saw the birth and growth of a white civic religion that mingled the intertwined strains of folk and religious belief. Paradoxically, the omission in the Brown Collection only serves to highlight the ubiquity of this story. Whether or not North Carolinians and southerners believed in its literal truth, the "Legend of the Dogwood" revealed how religious life, folk belief, and racist ideology were deeply embedded in the southern landscape.

This extension of biblical parable to the dogwood seems particularly suited to its apparent origins in the post-Emancipation South. It brings Christ into the cosmological landscape of the region, a place "Christ-haunted" by the grotesqueries of Jesus's death and the recognition of

---

[18] "The Legend of the Dogwood Tree," in *Virginia Folk Legends*, ed. Thomas E. Barden, Publications of the American Folklore Society (Charlottesville: University Press of Virginia, 1991), 61–62.

[19] "Legend of the Dogwood Tree," 61–62.

[20] "A Legend of the Dogwood Blossom," *The Times-Democrat*. February 10, 1889.

southern Christianity as a bloody, visceral, religious practice.[21] The dogwood, like the cross, was an emblem of this violent system of belief. The world inhabited by turn-of-the-century southerners seemed to invoke the omnipresence of their materialized religious practices. Indeed, anti-lynching advocates routinely made linkages between lynching and Christ's crucifixion. Du Bois referred to Sam Hose's mob murder as a crucifixion, and the Virginia minister Edwin Taliaferro Wellford published an entire book comparing Jesus's death to a lynching. Intended to rouse the consciences of southern Christians, Wellford's is a bizarre, quasi-legal analysis that invokes alike the Lost Cause and other forms of southern material religion. Early on Wellford notes that "the populace has tasted blood ... they are conscious of their physical power." He goes on, in thundering proclamations, to claim "it was Jesus at the stake! Lynched by the insatiate passion of a misguided multitude!" In Wellford's analogy, not only was Jesus a lynching victim, but everyday reminders of human sacrifice could both recall to viewers his martyrdom and spur southern Christians to follow his example. Wellford ends the book with a (likely fictionalized) account of encountering a stranger weeping over the grave of a fallen Confederate soldier at Chickamauga. Despite not knowing the soldier, the man had erected a headstone that noted "He Died for Me" as a reminder of the common sacrifice of the Confederate dead. Wellford intended this a reminder of the magnanimity of white southern Christianity, which might not forgive accused criminals but would at least allow them to die from legal execution, what he termed "the sword of justice." The southern world he created in these pages is one where the moral absolutes of biblical parables were constantly being enacted.[22]

In this way, the South became a biblical landscape whose every aspect was implicated in the material expression of religion. The sense worlds of

---

[21] Flannery O'Connor, "Some Aspects of the Grotesque in Southern Fiction," *PEN America: A Journal for Writers and Readers* 1, no. 2 (2001 [1960]): 145–152. More recent works have examined the material religious practices of the South and their overlaps with public and civic life. See Anderson Blanton, *Hittin' the Prayer Bones: Materiality of Spirit in the Pentecostal South* (Chapel Hill: University of North Carolina Press, 2016); Chad E. Seales, *The Secular Spectacle: Performing Religion in a Southern Town* (New York: Oxford University Press, 2014).

[22] Edwin Taliaferro (E. T.) Wellford, *The Lynching of Jesus: A Review of the Legal Aspects of the Trial of Christ* (Newport News, VA: Franklin Printing Company, 1905), 12:104–105, 9. On Du Bois's comments, see Donald G. Matthews, *At the Altar of Lynching: Burning Sam Hose in the American South* (New York: Cambridge University Press, 2018), 11. More recently, a work of popular theology has also made these linkages: James H. Cone, *The Cross and the Lynching Tree* (New York: Orbis, 2013).

the South were strong ones: The smell of the magnolia called to mind a picture of romance and fading grandeur, the sight of the dogwood bloom a reminder of a tortuous execution. In this world the dogwood was both everyday object and potent religious symbol, imbued with significance and spiritual meaning. As Charles Reagan Wilson suggests, it is this spirit that "needs to be placed at the center of efforts to understand what made southerners invest so much meaning in their social identity." The dogwood was among the most visible markers of this system of material meaning. The mob who chose this particular tree to hang Johnson and Kizer, from amid a forest of others, likely had its complex symbolism in mind. They lived in a world full of reliquary objects and imagined themselves in an environment laden with symbols and signs, what Du Bois memorably called "the soul life of the land."[23] Theirs was not a premodern or primitive world, but one built on abiding and present systems of belief and alive to the power of objects.

The connections between lynching and religion are clear. Despite Wellford's attempts to invert the practice of lynching into an expression of religious forgiveness, most southerners still viewed it in the context of sanctifying ritualism. As religious historian Donald Matthews points out, southern lynch mob members imagined themselves as partaking in a ritualistic practice "far more complex and meaningful than an execution." Lynching was a central rite in the secular religion of white supremacy, part of a growing religiosity that marked the post-Emancipation South. The 1880s and 1890s saw an explosion in churchgoing.[24] But the period also saw the formation and rapid growth of new *civic* religions. The Lost Cause of the Confederacy, born out of commemorative cultures, saw its symbols and objects increasingly made sacred in the early twentieth century. Civil war scholar Lloyd Hunter conceives of this as a material process of sacralization, in which the "Stars and Bars, 'Dixie', and the army's gray jacket became religious emblems ... Lee and Davis emerged as Christ figures, the common soldier attained sainthood."[25] Monuments

---

[23] Both the Du Bois quotation and the notion of southern spirit come from Charles Reagan Wilson. Though he expounds upon the notion of spirit (and religion) in much of his work, I take both these quotes from his introduction to his edited volume of essays on the topic: Charles Reagan Wilson, "Introduction: 'The Soul Life of the Land': Meanings of the Spirit in the U.S. South," in his *Flashes of a Southern Spirit: Meanings of the Spirit in the U.S. South* (Athens: University of Georgia Press, 2011), 4.

[24] Matthews, *At the Altar of Lynching*, 9, 41.

[25] Lloyd Hunter, "The Immortal Confederacy: Another Look at Lost Cause Religion," in *The Myth of the Lost Cause and Civil War History*, ed. Gary W. Gallagher and Alan

served as shrines and temples to this state and cultural religion. But the Lost Cause was part of a more expansive religiosity.[26] This was made manifest in the numerical increases of churchgoing or religious adherence, but also in the fervor with which white southerners embraced the contours of expanding cultural and political doctrines of white supremacy. And as Matthews points out, it was lynched men who served as sacrifices at the altars of the new state religion. In a complex ritual, their bloodshed was a sanctifying act, their god some version of the avaricious Old Testament deity reconfigured as the "transcendent meaning of whiteness."[27] This was a world enriched by the objects of the new cosmic order. White southernness took on the fervor of religion, and everyday objects were transformed into reliquaries for the practice of civic religion. The beliefs and stories related to the dogwood tree are a clear expression of the materiality of this system of belief. Indeed, these deeply rooted beliefs were transformed into an explicitly white supremacist originary myth. Like nearly all other facets of southern belief, the dogwood was transformed into a symbol of white supremacy.

True to this formula, the implicitly white southern epic of the "Legend of the Dogwood" had a shadow, explicitly white supremacist twin. As with the more popular dogwood mythos, we can only recover the history of the dogwood as an "emblem of white supremacy" in small pieces.

T. Nolan (Bloomington: Indiana University Press, 2000), 286. Hunter builds from earlier analyses of the Lost Cause as a civic religion in southern life, particularly those of Charles Reagan Wilson. See Charles Reagan Wilson, *Baptized in Blood: The Religion of the Lost Cause, 1865–1920* (Athens: University of Georgia Press, 1980). There is a rich literature on Lost Cause monuments, cited at length elsewhere in this book, but relatively little writing explicitly from a material culture perspective that deals with cultures of collecting. One recent exception is Nicole Maurantonio, *Confederate Exceptionalism: Civil War Myth and Memory in the Twenty-First Century* (Lawrence: University Press of Kansas, 2019), which deals with the collection and preservation of relics related to one of the most venerated saints of Lost Cause religion, Thomas "Stonewall" Jackson.

[26] Historians have begun to expand on Charles Reagan Wilson's notion of the Lost Cause as a civic religion by looking at other modes of public interaction that we might likewise think of as constituting a religious, if not spiritual practice. The overlaps with varieties of white Christian religious expression are unavoidable, given their inextricability from one another. The South's characteristic and assumed religiosity was still nascent in this period, and just as much influenced by these civic religions as the now more prominent Christian ones. See Arthur Remillard . *Southern Civil Religions: Imagining the Good Society in the Post-Reconstruction Era*, The New Southern Studies (Athens: University of Georgia Press, 2011); *Religion and Public Life in the South: In the Evangelical Mode*, ed. Charles Reagan Wilson and Mark Silk, Religion by Region (Walnut Creek: AltaMira Press, 2005).

[27] Matthews, *At the Altar of Lynching*, 93.

The most thorough explication of this myth comes from the objects surrounding a lynching in Sabine County, Texas. There in 1908, nine men were killed in a brutal few days of spectacle lynchings. Afterward, a postcard was printed in at least two local stores (a printer's and a drugstore). In pictorial content it differed little from many hundreds of other such images. On the postcards, a photograph of five of the victims was abstracted enough through the poor quality of its focus and reproduction that they were discernible as little more than anonymous bodies. National and local headlines trumpeted the "9 Negroes Lynched by Texas Mob." Like so many others, the lynching was understood through the abstraction of numerical ordering (nine people lynched, hundreds in the mob) more than the specifics of the event. Even now, only six of the men murdered – Will Manuel, Cleveland Williams, Moses Spellman, Will Johnson, Jerry Evans, and Frank Williams – have been identified. This collectivized absence refocused the vantage point of the postcard away from its photographic content and toward its written words. Accompanying the image on both versions of the postcard was a poem linking lynching and the dogwood tree.

Departing from the usual vague messages of terror and warning, each postcard was printed with this fully articulated white supremacist myth, titled, simply, "The Dogwood Tree." It centers the dogwood bloom as the "emblem of white supremacy." In this postcard, text and image worked together to convey meaning. The anonymization of the men in the photograph was key to this interpretive process. Carefully objectified and rendered as nothing more than anonymous victims of an anonymous mob, the men's bodies became a legitimating peritext for the poem that carried equal weight in the object's reception. Its recipients were familiar, likely intimately so, with the casual distribution of similar images of violence. This justifying poetics then only deepened their associational understanding by linking it to the dogwoods so prevalent in their symbolic and material worlds.[28]

The postcard produced in the wake of the lynching sought to commodify the experience of witness. Its production and circulation were convoluted, themselves almost mythic.

---

[28] On peritext, epitext, and other paratextual formulations, see Genette, Paratexts. I am also relying here, again, on Robert St. George's formulation of the referential interdependence of word, deed, symbol, and object: Robert St. George, *Conversing by Signs: Poetics of Implication in Colonial New England Culture* (Chapel Hill: University of North Carolina Press, 1998).

According to one newspaper account, the poem printed on the postcard had initially appeared pinned to the jacket of one of the lynching victims.[29] Its composition is uncertain. Did the mob choose a dogwood tree because it already had these associational ties to white supremacy? Or was the poet inspired by the choice of implement of torture to expand the expressive culture already surrounding the tree type? From its supposed origins, the text apparently made its way to at least one newspaper and two printers. Perhaps the text was mediated, reprinted from the newspaper articles. Or maybe one or both of the printers kept it for themselves. Like other lynching postcards, this was clearly designed as a memento at least as much as a mode of communication. It was intended primarily to recall or re-create a visit to the site of the lynching. Like any other good touristic souvenir, it was both specific and general all at once, rooted in a particular place and event but abstracted enough to have broad appeal. This souvenir differed from the relics discussed in the previous chapter by being reproducible, distributable, shared. Unlike other postcards, it laid bare in text what was typically carried by the visuality of violence in the reproduction of dead bodies. It generated an excess amid a system already overdetermined in its symbolism and beliefs.

The photograph, enlarged to the point where each of its elements is little more than a nonspecific stand-in, takes up roughly two-thirds of the front of the postcard. The rest is given over to "The Dogwood Tree." The text is short, just two stanzas:

> This is the only branch of a Dogwood tree;
> An emblem of WHITE SUPREMACY
> A lesson once taught in the Pioneer's school,
> That this is a land of WHITE MAN'S RULE
> The Red Man once in an early day,
> Was told by the Whites to mend his way.
> The negro now, by eternal grace
> Must learn to stay in the negro's place
> In the Sunny South, the Land of the Free
> Let the WHITE SUPREME forever be.
> Let this a warning to all negroes be,
> Or they'll suffer the fate of the DOGWOOD TREE.

They stick out on the page primarily for the irregular capitalization that draws the viewer's eye, negating in many ways the written structure of the poem. Read as a kind of acrostic, these words emphasize the crude, simplistic message of the poem: WHITE SUPREMACY, WHITE MAN'S

[29] "The Fruit of the Dogwood Tree," *Times-Leader*, July 13, 1908.

RULE, WHITE SUPREME, DOGWOOD TREE. The visual function of the poem serves much the same purpose as the other image on the postcard's front. It distills the rhetorical message of the words into a shorthand, mimicking the impact of the photograph's widened focus.

The text of the poem is a white supremacist epic in miniature. In two short stanzas, it outlines a detailed story of settler colonial governance in North America as a precursor to the white supremacist political ideology of the early twentieth century. Like earlier renderings of the southern landscape, it saw both Native Americans and African Americans as paradoxically inextricable from the landscape and inevitably removable from it. We are told that the emblematic white supremacy of the dogwood tree was "once taught in the Pioneer's school" to Native peoples directed to "mend [their] way." A clear invocation of Manifest Destiny, it links the fate of lynching victims to a broader project of conquest and holds up "the Sunny South" as the enduring heir of that imperial American legacy. Even more directly, it links lynching directly to the landscape and symbols of it. There is a complexity in the crude message of the poem. The dogwood is at once a conquering symbol of whiteness, and a reminder of the delicate beauty of the place. The poem lays a claim for the dogwood as a native symbol of southern whiteness, actively recounting the process of it coming to stand in for white nationalism. But it is also clearly building upon these other widely understood meanings of the tree and bloom, like the one outlined in "The Legend of the Dogwood." Instead of giving it specific historical references, this twin of that original legend puts the dogwood even more firmly into the realm of mythic whiteness, inventing yet another deep past for it that supersedes any of its other histories.

This was the mythic historical logic that got applied to the dogwood in the Sabine lynching. The seemingly harmless traditions of the dogwood were repurposed as both justification and explanation. Whether or not the poem originally appeared on the clothing of one of the victims, it and the dogwood helped turn the lynching into a naturalized spectacle of white dominance over the southern landscape. Its admonition that "the negro now, by eternal grace/Must learn to stay in the negro's place/In the Sunny South the land of the free" seems to be both warning about outmigration and against any form of progress or protest. A part of the South, Black people have to "Let the WHITE SUPREME forever be." The ending couplet – "Let this a warning to all negroes be/Or they'll suffer the fate of the DOGWOOD TREE" – both continues the intentional, aggressive capitalization and offers a confusing coda to the rest of the poem. Clearly "the fate of the dogwood tree" is an open threat of violence to any Black people who would dare step out of "the negro's place" reserved for them. Less clear is whether that is a fate *of* or *from* the tree. That is, how entangled in the larger mythology of the dogwood is this white supremacist symbolism? Is this threat suggesting that the dogwood is an instrument of white supremacist violence? Or does it imply a similar cursed status for Black people in the South, akin to the tree's own as alternately accursed and embraced?[30]

That a ubiquitous tree with prominent white blooms would be a stand-in for whiteness seems obvious. But it is also impossible to divorce this symbolism from its larger meaning and purpose in the South. Seeing it within its own discursive visual and material context allows us to at least begin to explicate a world governed by the chaos of white supremacist thought. The dogwood seems like an innocuous symbolic object. But as the entanglement of these various legends suggests, its presence on the landscape was the marker of deep wellsprings of belief. It stood as part of a long line of perceptions about the landscape and what it might represent in terms of southern identity. As I have suggested, this was a process that began before the South was even defined. It continued as those regional particularities were documented, studied, and interpreted by a variety of experts and through the lenses of the many paradoxes of its landscapes.

In the twentieth century, that intensive collecting was mediated through the rise of a new consumer culture and commercial world. Scholarly study intersected with touristic interest, and the landscape represented both physical locality and regional identity. Collecting became a commercial practice, even more than it had been before. Things collected from lynching – and particularly these dogwood objects – sit at these intersections. They represent the liminal representational space between the sentimental reliquary culture of the nineteenth century and the commodified touristic objects of the twentieth. The meanings of the dogwood as an object and a symbol overlapped and accumulated throughout the course of the twentieth century. Relics sometimes became souvenirs. And the potent, quasi-religious systems of tradition and belief were transformed into little more than regional oddities. This was particularly the case with material and visual representations of the landscape, like the dogwood. It might circulate as a touristic souvenir of the romanticized South, but that meaning was never far removed from its religious or white supremacist origins.

---

[30] Sabine County (Tex.) Lynching Postcard, 1908, #05694-z, Southern Historical Collection, Louis Round Wilson Special Collections Library UNC Chapel Hill.

CIRCULATING DOGWOOD SOUVENIRS

Lynching keepsakes occupy significant conceptual space in the realm of southern objects. But the quasi-religious mythology of the dogwood also fits into a larger culture of mass consumption and tourism. The intensive collecting and theorizing about dogwoods and the southern landscape were a part of souvenir collecting practices that emerged more prominently in the years after the Civil War. Dogwoods and other landscape souvenirs indexed the complex meanings of the southern landscape into handheld things. They contained a surplus of meaning beyond the commercial aspects of their collecting, marketing, and sale.

Landscape, and especially tree, keepsakes have a long tradition in American history and memory. As early as the seventeenth century, they were rendered symbolic of the freedom offered by the American landscape. Even as they served as a utilitarian economic resource, the stands of hardwoods still present in this New World piqued the imaginations of early settler colonists. At the dedication of Rhode Island's Liberty Tree, one speaker noted that it was representative of "'that Liberty which our Forefathers sought out and found under Trees, and in the wilderness.'" The supposedly untrammeled wilds of the continent represented a release from the unfreedoms of the old world, even as these new settlers remained immersed in many of its folkways and customary practices. American trees were at once unprecedented specimens and the basis for material goods, stories and legends, and other expressive cultures of tradition.[31]

This early American veneration transitioned into the sentimental reliquary practices of the nineteenth century. Trees were still a fixation of these collectors, but only a single element of the sublime landscape that one

---

[31] This fixation on both the symbolism of trees and the reliquary culture of objects made from them is well covered: Arthur M. Schlesinger, "Liberty Tree: A Genealogy," *New England Quarterly* 25, no. 4 (1952): 435–458, 444 (first quote), 446; Laura Turner Igoe, "'The Limb in My Fathers Arms': The Environmental and Material Creation of a Treaty Elm Relic," *Commonplace* 17, no. 1 (2016), http://commonplace.online/article/the-limb-in-my-fathers-arms. These are both excellent examples of the density of symbolic meaning that Robert Blair St. George invokes in his notion of the poetics of implication in early America. Expressive life was rich with material symbols like the ones discussed in Schlesinger and Igoe, and these relics marked those multiple ties to the originary myth of the American wilderness. The myth of America's wilderness and wildness was just that, as William Cronon notes. But it nonetheless structured interaction with and perception of the built and "natural" worlds from the founding years of what became America until the present. See William Cronon, "The Trouble with Wilderness or, Getting Back to the Wrong Nature," *Environmental History* 1, no. 1 (1996): 7–28.

could observe, extract, and collect. Tourists to sites of important national identity – Liberty Trees, presidential homes – took souvenirs from the landscape, breaking off twigs, tearing leaves, pocketing a handful of pebbles or dirt. They might rework these into more useful and recognizable objects or keep them as small tokens of a moment where they brushed against tangible remnants of the nation's glorious past. As Teresa Barnett argues, this was the inauguration of a new relationship of the individual to that past, "a specifically historical mode of collecting that came into being in concert with a new sense of the past as an entity in its own right." These landscape keepsakes were representative of the broader practices of the day. Reliquary objects could render the sublime into the handheld and allow tourists closer access to the important people and places of the past. What began as an extractive process from the most monumental landscapes turned more mundane with the rise of southern tourist economies in the late antebellum period. There people increasingly took "small items picked up or snipped from the natural landscape of a particularly impressive southern scene."[32] This further blurred the lines between the relic and the souvenir. People might be attempting to commune with the deep natural histories of the landscape or, increasingly, with the stereotyped vision of the picturesque southern place. Souvenirs might masquerade as reliquary objects or, by virtue of a particular association or attachment, be transformed into one. The distinction between these two object categories was never a neat one. And souvenirs always had the potential to become something more than a reminder of an event past or a place visited. They could be markers of one's brush with the greatness of the past, just as easily as they could be discarded or forgotten.

Keepsake objects like these stood in for the larger span of the southern landscape. Already laden with meaning, the romantic and economic investment in ideas of this place only deepened in the last years of the nineteenth century. Mass consumer objects depicting "the ease of southern life" were omnipresent throughout the country.[33] As in the travel and booster narratives from this period, the landscape was the most enduring marker of that supposed ease. Both visits to the region and projected

[32] Barnett, *Sacred Relics*, 22–28; Eric W. Plaag, "'There is an Abundance of Those Which are Genuine': Northern Travelers and Souvenirs of the Antebellum South," in *Dixie Emporium: Tourism, Foodways, and Consumer Culture in the American South*, ed. Anthony J. Stanonis (Athens: University of Georgia Press), 29–31.
[33] Karen L. Cox, "Branding Dixie: The Selling of the American South, 1890–1930," in *Dixie Emporium: Tourism, Foodways, and Consumer Culture in the American South*, ed. Anthony J. Stanonis (Athens: University of Georgia Press), 51.

FIGURE 4.3 Tag for a cotton souvenir from Newnan, Georgia, early twentieth century. Courtesy Karen Sieber.

fantasies of it borrowed keepsakes from the landscape. Nina Silber notes that New York society women viewing the 1891 plantation melodrama *Alabama* were each gifted a cotton boll "courtesy of the 'ladies of Talladega.'"[34] Early twentieth-century visitors likewise continued to pluck specimens from the landscape. Canny southerners commercialized this process, as with the early twentieth-century souvenir cotton tags from Newnan, Georgia, that elided the distinction between agricultural product and regional keepsake. The visitor might not take home a cotton boll picked amid a picturesque field of laborers, but they could possess a marker and encapsulation of that process. Land and people were both absent but suggested. The tag, like other souvenirs, was less a representation of a specific place or person than a container for the memory of an experience (Figure 4.3). This abstraction represented the shift toward a souvenir culture, one where the South and the southern landscape were objectified as a series of supposedly harmless stereotypes and myths.

But the primary vehicle of this growing commercial souvenir culture was the postcard. By the middle of the 1890s, the mass-produced picture postcard could visually represent the landscape scenes that earlier illustrations and mementos sought to capture.[35] The photorealism of some of the earliest North Carolina postcards, like 1902's "Below the Narrows, Green River," allowed the receivers or holders of the card to project themselves into the scenic landscape (Figure 4.4). Tourists could thus re-create their experiences, or allow their loved ones a glimpse into vistas their words failed to convey.

[34] Silber, *The Romance of Reunion*, 94.
[35] Dorothy B. Ryan, *Picture Postcards in the United States, 1893–1918*, 2nd ed. (New York: Clarkson N. Potter, 1982).

FIGURE 4.4 An early North Carolina postcard showing the tourist landscape. North Carolina Collection, University of North Carolina Library at Chapel Hill

Yet from the first, these souvenirs also capitalized on the exotic possibilities and inhabitants of the places they depicted. Often, that exoticism was created through visual difference with little or no textual explanation. Scenes of everyday life in the South were different enough from the everyday experiences of the national consumer to be circulated as regional oddities. Take for instance a 1901 postcard produced by the Brooklyn-based Albertype Company. It depicted "The Charcoal Burner" and his children in the stunted piney woods of southeastern North Carolina. They sit perched atop an oxcart in a pine forest marked by subtle signs of human industry. Like Champney's earlier illustrations, the titular subject was a stock figure whose presence helped characterize the landscape. This was all the more the case for the particular locational context of this postcard. Produced in Brooklyn for a national audience, it depicted the growing tourist mecca of Pinehurst. Pinehurst's salubrious climate and well-manicured golf courses were its primary stated draws, but the local color of its African American residents was a significant part of its appeal as well.[36] Resorts sponsored cake walks and other contests to put Black customs and Black people on display. Perhaps the most egregious of those was a "best baby" contest, which served as "'the first opportunity many of our guests have had to inspect little pickaninnies at close range.'"[37] In this sense, it was not just the supposedly primitive or exotic customs of Black people that were a tourist draw. Simply by existing, Black people themselves were an attraction to curious northerners who could observe, inspect, and study, as so many of their predecessors had. Postcards like the one of the charcoal burner allowed them to do that at a distance, either as a reminder of or substitute for a visit to the place itself. Like a 1905 postcard from Concord, the image depicted working landscapes and working people. This helped to paint those quotidian sites of labor as exotic, by calling attention to the oddities of workers far removed from the everyday life of the postcards' consumers. Landscape was still and always associated with people, and even the most mundane tasks were worthy of depicting and collecting for outsiders primed to see the South as a mixture of economic potential and leisurely consumption (Figures 4.5 and 4.6).

Just as often, the mundane workings of people and landscape were exaggerated through a lens of racialized humor. Black people in the South were depicted as characters of enormous appetite and rustic simplicity. Old myths about the bounty of a landscape where little work was required were replayed in these tourist images of simple, playful Black people.[38] Many others of the earliest North Carolina postcards relied on racist tropes supposedly captured on its landscape. A postcard from New Bern, circa 1900, depicted a young Black boy eating an oversized slice of watermelon in front of an abundantly fruited fig tree (Figure 4.7). Both the landscape and its people were meant to be excessive, ridiculous. The boy seems to be thrilled at the prospect of the bounty

[36] On the history of Pinehurst as a tourist, resort community, see Michael Winslow. "Cultivating Leisure: Tourism, Progressive Agriculture, and Technologies of Landscape at Pinehurst, North Carolina, 1895–1935," *Agricultural History* 94, no. 1 (2020): 61–83, https://doi.org/10.3098/ah.2020.094.1.061; Orin Starn, "Caddying for the Dalai Lama: Golf, Heritage Tourism, and the Pinehurst Resort," *South Atlantic Quarterly* 105, no. 2 (2006): 447–463.
[37] Quoted in Winslow, "Cultivating Leisure," 66.
[38] The most useful work on the visual culture of the traffic in racist trade cards as part of late nineteenth- and early twentieth-century consumerism comes from Kyla Wazana Tompkins. In her book *Racial Indigestion* she draws from a wide collection of trade cards that rely upon racist tropes of Black life to sell products, north and south. See Kyla Wazana Tompkins, "'What's De Use Talking 'Bout Dem 'Mendments?' Trade Cards and Consumer Citizenship at the End of the Nineteenth Century," in her *Racial Indigestion: Eating Bodies in the 19th Century* (New York: NYU Press, 2012), 145–182.

FIGURE 4.5 Postcard of "The Charcoal Burner" in Pinehurst, 1901. North Carolina Collection, University of North Carolina Library at Chapel Hill

FIGURE 4.6 An industrial tourist postcard from turn-of-the-century Concord, 1905. North Carolina Collection, University of North Carolina Library at Chapel Hill

FIGURE 4.7 An early twentieth-century postcard of racist caricature from North Carolina. North Carolina Collection, University of North Carolina Library at Chapel Hill

around him, with the overturned barrel repurposed as a seat serving as yet another nod to the leisure and pleasure of Black life in the southern landscape. Even more overt racialized landscape caricatures evolved in the first two decades of commercial postcard production in the South. "A Fruitful Long Leaf Pine," from around 1915, was produced just up the road from Pinehurst as tourism in that area intensified. The verisimilitude of the earlier postcard was gone, replaced with an uncommonly bright illustrated style in sharp contrast to the documentary realism of the charcoal burner photograph. This later image depicted a fearful Black man high up in a longleaf pine, grasping at a possum perched on the limb. He is clearly meant to be "picking" the fruit of the tree, allowing for the consumer to laugh at the absurdity of both the Black man's belief and his fear. The title is a mocking inside joke that the image itself only furthers (Figure 4.8).

A Fruitful Long-Leaf Pine
Southern Pines, N. C.

FIGURE 4.8 A postcard combining several racist caricatures, 1915. North Carolina Collection, University of North Carolina Library at Chapel Hill

This postcard clearly built on the omnipresent stereotypes of the voracious appetite of African American people – a burlesque commonplace in advertising, musical, and other popular cultural expressions of the era. Possums in particular were supposed to be evidence of this uncommon appetite, as animals that were not deemed edible by any other than the poorest people.[39] But these bodily characterizations also exaggerated tropes of the southern landscape. We can see this as a clear analog to the "strange fruit" of the lynching tree, a term of art made popular by the Abel Meerpol–penned Billie Holliday song, but used frequently in earlier characterizations of lynching.[40] In this configuration, the southern landscape was a place of exceeding wonder. The fruitful pine, the strange fruit of the lynching tree, and other such fantastical elements represented a different kind of unreality from consumer fantasies of moonlight and

[39] The folklorist Stephen Winnick offers an excellent overview of the opossum and its culinary applications in his blog post for the American Folklife Center at the Library of Congress. In particular, he draws attention to the popular dialect song "Carve Dat Possum," which was another reflection of the common associations of the animal as food for Black people alone: "A Possum Crisp and Brown: The Opossum and American Foodways," *Folklife Today*, August 15, 2019, https://blogs.loc.gov/folklife/2019/08/a-possum-crisp-and-brown-the-opossum-and-american-foodways (accessed April 19, 2022).
[40] David Margolick, *Strange Fruit: The Biography of a Song* (New York: Ecco Press, 2001).

magnolias. Both Souths were near-mythic places. But that mythology was less a reflection of real beliefs than a commodification of perceived difference. These exaggerated portraits of place turned the South (its beliefs, its problems) into something not actual and thus ignorable, even laughable. In this way postcards were reductive portraits of the southern landscape and the people rendered natural to it. In evoking these miniature worlds, postcards built on both a long tradition and many enduring symbols. True to that form, if the viewer looked in the background of "A Fruitful Long Leaf Pine" they would see that most enduring symbol of the mythic South: dogwood trees in full bloom.

Indeed, the dogwood bloom was an increasingly popular feature of southern souvenir postcards. It came to stand in not just for the South, but for particular states within the region. Their blooms were signifiers of a state and region in the throes of spring (though their range extends outside the traditional boundaries of the southern states). Most often these dogwood postcards included some variation of the dogwood myth that had seemingly always been a mixture of genuine belief and Christian allegory. By the 1930s and 1940s, the "Legend of the Dogwood" became the basis for many mass-produced postcards and other tourist souvenirs. The dogwood became even more an outsize signifier of southern distinctiveness and the mythic landscape. Through a contemporary lens, it is hard not to read these keepsakes as anything other than tourist kitsch. But even the implied judgment of that label does not undermine the importance of tourist souvenirs as invocations of place and markers of authenticity. Tourist objects like dogwood postcards recalled both the deeper symbolic worlds of belief around the dogwood, and the longstanding patterns of collecting and interpreting the southern landscape.[41]

My own collection of "Legend of the Dogwood" souvenirs ranges from the 1930s to the 1990s with consistent wording and imagery. Only rarely is the legend featured alongside any other or overt Christian symbols, though a circa 1980s plaque from West Virginia features a gold plastic crucifix transposed over the bloody nail prints on the edge of each petal. The Christ figure was almost never directly transported into the southern landscape on these postcards and other souvenirs. Instead, most featured generic photographs of blooming dogwoods. More often the flower was combined with other symbols of particular southern states (the cardinal,

[41] On kitsch and tourism, see Kaori O'Connor, "Kitsch, Tourist Art, and the Little Grass Shack in Hawaii," *Home Cultures* 3, no. 3 (2006): 251–271, https://doi.org/10.2752/174063106779090749.

for instance) that might allow tourists to bring a keepsake home from their sojourn south. Nearly every state in the former Confederacy seems to have adopted the dogwood legend as a tourist souvenir at some point. In states like Virginia and North Carolina where the dogwood blossom was already the state flower, that made sense. But the hanging wooden plaque from West Virginia or the tropical dogwood scene from Florida is more curious. These objects adapt the legend to particular places and local particularities without actually modifying its text or meaning. The legend came to be associated at once with no place and every place.[42] The objects are stand-ins for a generic, mythic South. The intertwining strains of the landscape-collecting impulse converged here in manufactured objects designed for tourists and stripped of all but the vaguest references to either the land or the legends from which they derived.

This then is indeed tourist kitsch. Kitsch of this sort is reductive but not ridiculous. It is viscerally sentimental, a distillation of the emotional background that informs it. It is intended most often as an object of personal remembrance and the collective origins of its symbols are largely irrelevant. Kitsch is a process of dehistoricization. In a reversal of the reliquary object's individual embrace of the past, the object of kitsch intentionally negates the complexities of an object's pastness.[43] It comes to stand in for personal and particular experience, and any broader historicity is merely implicit. Differing from relics, souvenirs are markers not of a longer or deeper history, but of personal experience of a place or event alone.

Both these attachments to objects explain the cultures of collecting, why people might keep and attach themselves to things. This was perhaps especially true for the objects taken from lynching sites. They might rotate through cycles of meaning, moving from relic to souvenir and back again. The first person to take an object from the lynching site might have an intense attachment to it. That attachment was linked to their experience of the lynching and its aftermaths, their impression of its justice, or any

---

[42] "Dogwood Legend, West Virginia," plastic crucifix on cedar placard, date unknown, personal collection of the author. "Legend of the Dogwood in Florida," postcard, Curteich-Chicago circa 1952, personal collection of the author. There are dozens, likely hundreds, of dogwood legend postcards. My own collection of two dozen objects (postcards, mugs, plaques) suggests a near-universal emplacement in the South and a fairly typical usage of the legend as a marker of both regional and state identity.

[43] My understanding of kitsch here builds on Judy Attfield's exploration of the aesthetic and particularly her nuanced discussion of its affective potential for the consumer: Judy Attfield, "Redefining Kitsch: The Politics of Design," *Home Cultures* 3, no. 3 (2006): 201–212. On the pastness of nineteenth-century relic culture, see Barnett, *Sacred Relics*, particularly 29–75.

number of other complex emotional and cultural attitudes. Subsequent generations in possession of the object were necessarily a step removed from that fervor and intensity. They inherit both the object and a ready-made meaning of its significance derived from transmission, not firsthand experience. This process might go on and on until the object is rendered meaningless, or its original worth nearly forgotten. Except, that is, in the case of objects like the dogwood and its associated ephemera. It might be easy for a scrap of cloth to slip unnoticed into a pile of similarly anonymous things. Not so for a postcard showing men hanging from a dogwood tree, or for an entire limb stored away and preserved. These are things that have some meaning owing to the broader cultural associations of the dogwood, but that are always overlain with the specificity of their extraction and collection. Of course, this process of circulation was never quite as neat as the categorization into relic and souvenir, kitsch and keepsake suggests. These were objects that slipped into and out of various frames of meaning, changing with time and occasion. Lynching was, in several senses, part of a culture of collecting. By way of striving to understand the complexity of these objects, we can look at familial inheritance and the traces of Johnson and Kizer's lynching left behind. The overlaps with reliquary and souvenir cultures hint at the inheritances of meaning kept in lynching's material culture.

CIRCULATING LYNCHING SOUVENIRS AND RELICS

As I note with some frequency in this book, the archive of lynching is largely a personal one. Collectors might jealously guard mementos of lynchings, especially those extracted from the site itself, against the desires of others. Over subsequent generations, once-venerated objects might become illegible, odd remnants of no worth other than residual sentimental value. This inheritance of collected objects by its very nature negates the *collection*, since objects that are not immediately visibly apprehensible may well disappear into the detritus of accumulated, purposeless objects.[44] But these things were also sometimes passed down as family heirlooms. Like other objects of memory, their original intention and meaning were sometimes preserved, sometimes transmuted into

---

[44] On the notion of the collection as possessed (indeed, possessive), I am thinking of Baudrillard and his distinction both between accumulation and collection and between possession and utilization. For him, collecting is intentional and built on having a thing, rather than utilizing it. It also recalls a kind of cultural valuation and intentionality.

an expression of mute remembrance. It is not difficult to imagine the souvenirs taken and created from Johnson and Kizer's lynching tucked away into a photo album or stored away in a shed. Like any other souvenir, they might be kept less for any lingering attachment to the objects themselves than for the initial emotions they might have provoked. Like other objects of memory, lynching souvenirs were reminders not necessarily of the event itself, but of the initial revelation of its impact, the feeling the souvenir taker got when the object first came into their hands.[45]

If we look at the scarce records around the lynching of Tom Johnson and Joe Kizer, we can see traces of the dogwood that remained prized and prominent multigenerational objects. In 1964 Jack Foil of Mt. Pleasant "still [had] a limb off the tree, believed to be the limb on which one of the victims was hanged." According to an account, "the limb was given to his father by a witness of the lynching, and has been kept through the years." More likely, Foil's father had been one of the "citizens from all sections of the county [who] came to the site and chopped the tree apart, each getting a limb or branch as a souvenir." The writer reporting on Mr. Foil's inheritance goes on to call it one of the many "prized trophies" collected and kept by people throughout the county.[46] This seems the much more typical model for the collection and preservation of lynching mementos, particularly for obtrusive and disruptive objects like a tree limb. It might be easy to conceal a postcard, an object easily hidden away or quickly justified given its ubiquity. Limbs eluded the easy justification of the everyday object. They came from the quotidian world of material symbols. But once separated from it, they were

---

Objects, even individual ones, do not become collected (part of a collection) by accident. So whether or not these lynching souvenir hunters had other lynching objects, they most certainly fit them in with other objects of cultural significance (be it other dogwood memorabilia or other white supremacist tokens). In this way, objects became part of a collection and more comprehensible: Jean Baudrillard, "The System of Collecting," in *The Cultures of Collecting*, ed. John Elsner and Roger Cardinal (Cambridge, MA: Harvard University Press, 1994), 7–24. I also take up the notion of the object removed from its collection in Chapter 3 of this book in conceptualizing clothing as a reliquary object.

45 This understanding of memory is based on Michel-Rolph Trouillot's formulation. He notes that memory comes to us from the force of revelation, not necessarily the actual recollection of an event's occurring: "It is at least possible that events otherwise significant to the life trajectory were not known to the individual at the time of occurrence and cannot be told as remembered experiences. The individual can only remember the revelation, not the event itself"; Trouillot, *Silencing the Past*, 15.

46 Ned Cline, "Even Negroes Took Part in Last Cabarrus Lynching," *The Post*, November 29, 1964.

incongruous objects, whether stored away in a shed or proudly displayed on the mantle. In Judy Attfield's term, they were wild things, ones whose originary point in the environment was overlain with the romanticization of the southern landscape and the omnipresent ideologies of white supremacy.[47] Whatever Jack Foil did with the limb, or wherever he got it, it is clear that he sought to preserve some of its original meaning as a souvenir. His recitation of its origins seemed like nothing so much as an authenticating measure, a way of proving provenance for the skeptical newspaper man. His proximity to this historic object made him important merely through its possession.

This romanticization of the landscape and proximity to the event were perhaps even more embedded in photographs and postcards made of the lynching. More numerous and reproducible than tree limbs or sticks, they too were preserved and passed through the generations. The tree is decidedly not the main subject of the photograph that is designed to showcase the dead bodies of Johnson and Kizer.[48] But the dogwood at the very center of the frame is far from incidental to the meaning the postcard conveyed. Unlike other lynching scenes, this one pictured the men in an almost wilderness with no visible crowds, houses, buildings, or other markings of human habitation. Seeming to anticipate "The Dogwood Tree" poem of Sabine County, it places dogwoods and nature both at the service of a structuring white supremacist violence. Lynching is naturalized to this landscape. It becomes a marker of it in the same way that dogwood earlier had, these two symbols of southern nature and place overlapping.

It is hard not to juxtapose these lynching dogwood mementos with the tourist souvenirs that gained increasing popularity throughout the first several decades of the twentieth century. For one thing, it seems likely that they were part of the same collection in individuals' homes. Dogwood postcards were ubiquitous. And photographs commemorating Johnson's and Kizer's deaths were likewise commonplace and passed down. The musician J. E. Mainer had and reproduced such an image in the early 1960s. In the 1970s, a Stanly County textile mill worker named Laton Burris likewise had a small collection relating to the lynching:

---

[47] Attfield, Wild Things.
[48] As I explain elsewhere, I have opted not to include the full images of lynchings and particularly lynched bodies, out of concern that they both reify the original intentions of such images and unnecessarily create traumas of encounter. The image referred to here is the only surviving one of the Kizer and Johnson lynching. I detail one narrative of its circulation in a later chapter, but it was likely reproduced in postcard form locally.

a copy of the photograph, and a clipping of a 1934 newspaper article recounting the murders. He clearly recognized the historical value of these keepsakes: he let a local museum copy them in 1979, but declined to donate them to its collection. A decade later, "Mrs. Ira Dayvault," born Grace Heglar in Concord in 1926, likewise loaned her postcard to a researcher writing a school paper. She does not recount how she came to take possession of the postcard, but it seems certain that it was something she inherited. Her family was rooted in Concord, and their having this remembrance of an important event that took place in the past of the place they lived in was a reminder of local identity. That she still had the postcard and could loan it out ninety years after it was made suggests that she kept ready access to both the object and the stories attached to it over generations. Perhaps she did not value this postcard or the stories connected with it. Shame, guilt, or other complex mixtures of emotion are also a part of material memorial practices. Maybe her purpose in loaning the postcard for a school project was to help historicize it and make the lynching into an event of the collective past, rather than merely family memory. Or maybe she was proud to share the story for a generation that was beginning to forget. These inheritances of material objects often came with memories and points of view already attached to them.[49]

Some others kept or acquired a photograph or postcard without sure knowledge of its origins. But for anyone who came to possess it, it seemed to clearly tell an obvious story of a lynching in the wilderness. Its visual clarity and lack of framing interference did even more to efface the stories of the men at its center and imply a kind of justice being rendered. In 1994, Steven Keefer "obtained" a copy of the Kizer and Johnson lynching photograph from "the estate of Lydia Reith." Born in Winston-Salem to a furniture-making family, Reith lived most of her ninety-two years in Indiana. When she died in 1992, apparently some of her possessions went to Keefer, a relative living nearby. He called and wrote the Cabarrus County library seeking information about the photograph that had come into his possession from the estate, using the curious word "obtained": not quite bought, not quite inherited. He sought to place the object in his

[49] "Hartsell Lynching Scrapbook," photocopied, September 24, 1979, Eastern Cabarrus Historical Society, Mount Pleasant North Carolina, copy in possession of the author; Rebecca Jones, "The Murder of Emma Hartsell," February 9, 1989, Emma Hartsell Vertical File, Local History Reading Room, Cabarrus County Libraries, Cannon Memorial Branch; Grace Heglar and Marvine Ira Dayvault Certificate of Marriage, July 26, 1947, Cabarrus County, North Carolina, digital image, Ancestry.com.

family's history, no doubt puzzling at the incongruity of multiple generations of Indianans holding on to the visual keepsake of a North Carolina
lynching from a century earlier. Still, he did not surrender the photograph to a library either, despite inquiring after its historical significance.
Maybe he kept it as a small souvenir of his family's past and their ties to
North Carolina and its landscapes. He had inherited the postcard, but
not the explanatory apparatus that would come from living in a place,
among its traditions. For all that it might have once been, it was now
even less than a souvenir, only a memento removed from all but its most
immediate, violent context. Maybe he sought to restore some of its personal history, to reconstruct what the lynched men and the place where
they were murdered might have been to the distant ancestors that had
originally acquired it. Souvenirs like this one were made for the market,
but passed into different modes of valuation and possession.

This was always the case from the moment of their first transition to
things that straddled the line between relic and souvenir. But it became
all the more so as they entered into the realm of memory objects, their
inherited, intergenerational meanings overlapping with conscious erasure
and moves toward forgetfulness. The dogwood remainders were particularly paradoxical objects. On the one hand, they were part of a culture
of souvenirs that consisted of shallow symbols and a reductive vision of
southern landscape. But they also marked the complexities of remembering and forgetting. Deep and abiding beliefs were rendered into objects
made mute either by the denial of their power as mere kitsch or through
the active processes of familial concealment and denial. Collected things
could do and be both: things of extraordinary individual meaning and
a passing attachment. The work that they did in the world vacillated
between these two poles, the relic and the souvenir. But the material
worlds of lynching objects were not just those collected and preserved.
They were also characterized by the processes of remembering and forgetting, of imagining and becoming. It is to the processes of those object
worlds that we now turn.

5

The Hammer and Chisel

Amid the excitement generated by the lynching of Tom Johnson and Joe Kizer, it was easy to miss the small notice buried in the weekly newspaper: "All tools that were left upstairs in the jail will be advertised free of charge in THE STANDARD. None have been given to us yet."[1] In their haste, the mob had abandoned their tools. The mob used the tools they had at hand, multipurposed things whose utility for work lay not in their specificity of design and use, but in their adaptability. Likely the tools discarded there were the ones extraneous to the work of the moment, things ill-adapted to an unsuited task. Most accounts emphasized only the work of the hammer, or hammer and chisel. These were the tools that accomplished the task of breaking the lock and gave the men of the mob unfettered access to Tom Johnson and Joe Kizer. Perhaps these too were among the collection of orphaned tools, left behind either in haste or out of an inability to lug heavy implements the quick miles their users would travel to a lynching site. With their work accomplished, they too became temporarily useless.

Most people might miss the notice because, even amid the ferocious desire for details of the lynching, such minor signifiers of everyday work seemed inconsequential. Likely only the men who needed them for work on Monday were even looking for the misplaced tools. The sabbath and the night of the lynching brought some distraction, an extension of the weekly respite from working life. But Monday saw a return to routine, even among the immediate disruptions of the lynching and the broader changes in their working lives.

[1] "It's All Over," *Daily Concord Standard*, May 31, 1898.

In that world, these repurposed tools had a deeper significance. They allowed insight into the debates and theories about work and labor: what tasks counted as work, where work took place, who was allowed to work, how work determined identity. As objects, they give us insight into the evolving beliefs about the nature and history in the turn-of-the-twentieth-century South. This perception was one that struggled to reconcile the working past as white people understood it, with the complicated, evolving present. Tools like the hammer and chisel could accomplish the ordinary tasks of farm and shop or serve as instruments in the commission of a lynching. But they also represented the dangers of evolving work in the South: Black men armed with heavy tools, new forms of industrial labor, a seemingly tenuous existence for the working-class white man. These tools then were representative of a larger construction of working memory.

The phrase "working memory" represents two particular means of understanding the material culture of this lynching and its intersections with working culture. On the one hand, it refers to the construction of a particular and evolving vision of work and labor in southern communities. This usable past relied upon widely held and often ahistorical beliefs about the places of white and Black men in the working order of the South. "Working memory" also refers to the enactments of this vision of historical conditions.[2] Even more than other objects, tools function only in combination with people, in this case with the bodily effort required to turn them from inert objects into discrete tasks, and from tasks to work. Work is both verb and noun, action and object. These tools – used and unused, taken or left behind in the jail cell – open up larger questions about the changing nature of work in the turn-of-the-century South. The linkages of work to race, age, and status were all being questioned. Work was confused, the places, people, and things that performed it disordered and subject to extraordinary shifts from long-held practices.

Cabarrus County was one of the epicenters of the new "public work." These new institutions were transforming life by employing the whole family, not on the farm or at home, but in the close confines and strict hours of the industrial world. That world was made of the brick and

---

[2] In thinking about the turn-of-the-century contestations over memory and work, I am particularly reliant on Scott Nelson's work on John Henry. See Scott Reynolds Nelson, *Steel Drivin' Man: John Henry, the Untold Story of an American Legend* (New York: Oxford University Press, 2006).

steel of factories, but also of the post and stick of workers' shacks, and of the cycles of laboring people from the countryside fields to the burgeoning cities. It was also a white world, except, briefly, in Cabarrus County. Concord was home to the first Black-owned and -operated textile mill. Warren C. Coleman's operation was just up the road from the site of the lynching and established at the very same time. This new mill, opening amid the other monumental changes in working life, became a site for contemporaries to reflect on the nature of work, the people who were fit to do labor as they understood it, and the spectacle of Black laboring bodies and people. These tools then are central to our understanding of Tom Johnson and Joe Kizer's lynching. Left behind in both fact and narrative, they open up our understanding of the complexities of evolving work and its linkages to the contemporaneous eruption of racial violence. This chapter examines how these forms of work connected to lynching and other forms of racialized violence both in the moment, and in the memory of the next several decades.

The overlap between the rise of lynching and the changes in southern working life are more than incidental. As far back as Ida B. Wells, scholars have understood the economic motives that underpinned so much of the racial violence in the turn-of-the-century South.[3] But these tools and their use invite us to further, more specific understanding of those complexities. Black people represented not just a generalized economic threat, but a particular challenge to white people's notions of themselves as working bodies, heads of families, and the dominant force in their own social and material worlds. The tools that the mob used in their abduction revealed the shifting ground of work as a site of a reconstructed vision of everyday life. In this world where race was made increasingly central, even (and especially) work became a way to segregate and assert dominance. For white people, participation in a lynch mob exaggerated those everyday violences. For African American people, work became yet another of the structures of life that they were allowed limited or no participation in. Work was central not only to the symbolic functions of community, but to the actual task of living in it. The tools used in the lynching of Joe Kizer and Tom Johnson embodied the centrality and importance of work, even as it illustrated its confused (and confusing) adaptability to the structures of a remade object world. In fact and in memory, the tools of work became central components of a white supremacist racial order.

[3] Ida B. Wells, *Southern Horrors: Lynch Law in All Its Phases* (New York: New York Age Print, 1892).

MAKING WORK PUBLIC

The late nineteenth-century South saw the rise of so-called public work. In the wake of Emancipation's compelled shift to wage labor, the underlying assumptions of an agrarian working order centered around the plantation and the enslaved laborer was undone.

The rise of sharecropping preserved and reproduced many of the conditions of the former system. But even that attempt to cling to tradition came amid a concerted wave of industrialization. New or reinvigorated models of industrial work came to dominate the South discursively, if not yet in actuality. This new work was both a problem and a solution, the imagined resolution to sustained economic woes and a call for many thousands of trained workers who did not yet exist. The urbanizing, industrializing forces of the much-discussed "New South"[4] manifested in more localized ways as well. But these new kinds of work were only part of the transformation of working life in the period. Public work also required a new *public* to people its reconfigured tasks. The places of work changed, but so too did the notion of the work and the people allowed to do it. This new work was imagined as a salve to poor white people, and as a continuation of the subordination of Black workers. Tensions arose when memory and imagination failed to meet the realities of a rapacious capitalism built on exploitation and only secondarily concerned with the preservation of the racial order.[5]

In Cabarrus and much of the surrounding Piedmont, industrial work was synonymous with the new textile mills. Cabarrus was one of the hotbeds of this movement, with around fifteen mills operational by 1900 (and a dozen more in the next two decades).[6] One local Cabarrus

---

[4] Though the New South has entered into historical and popular usage as a broad term for the post-Reconstruction South, its origins in the words of Atlanta booster Henry Grady had a specific meaning for the centrality of work to life and region. For more on Grady and the specificity of the phrase and of the New South, see Edward L. Ayers, *The Promise of the New South: Life after Reconstruction* (New York: Oxford University Press, 1992), 20–33.

[5] There is a rich literature on many aspects of the contradictory labor, economic, and social transformations in the post-Emancipation South. On the changes in landscape and environment particularly, see Charles Aiken, *The Cotton Plantation South since the Civil War* (Baltimore: Johns Hopkins University Press, 1998) and Mauldin, Unredeemed Land. On the broader evolutions in southern labor, see *Reconsidering Southern Labor History: Race, Class, and Power*, ed. Matthew Hild and Keri Leigh Merritt (Gainesville: University Press of Florida, 2018). One of the important contributions of this recent volume is an expansion of the typical timelines and geographic foci of much previous work on southern labor. Though much of my writing here is focused on one of those traditional areas of interest for southern labor historians (textile mills), it shares with Hild and Merritt's volume an interest in the broader, transhistorical transformations in southern labor and our understanding of it.

[6] Kathryn L. Bridges, "Cabarrus County, NC Textile Mills, 1839–2000," Local History Room, Charles A. Cannon Memorial Library, Cabarrus County Public Libraries, 2000.

historian of the period consciously linked then present-day transformations with those of an earlier era, pointing to the site "out on the Beattie's
Ford road, near town" where the first attempts at a cotton mill had been
made in 1840.[7] Another of her group wrote about the years in between
and the changes to the county. For "Miss Mary King," writing in 1908,
"the reconstruction period was not so horrible here in Cabarrus as in
other places" because they had "some few bands of the Ku Klux Klan"
to keep order.[8] Her accounting of recent local history is full of wistful
nostalgia for both a bygone era and the last gasps of the old system. She
and the other members of the Concord "Study Club" were attempting
to write histories of the county that fell into line with other turn-of-the-
century memorial work that saw white heritage and the southern past as
synonymous.[9] She maintained that the county was still largely agricultural and "some few live on their ancestral acres [while] most do not."[10]
Her comments on ownership were true – the end of slavery and rise of
tenancy had deprived all but the most wealthy Cabarrus planters of their
large holdings. But in the years immediately after the lynching, when this
Study Group were seeking to establish an agrarian past as a blueprint for
the future, it was no longer an agricultural county. By 1900, Cabarrus
was at the very heart of the industrial Piedmont.

   This change happened quickly. In 1880, Concord had 1,260 inhabitants. Adjoining Kannapolis, eventually an important center of the
textile industry, was virtually nonexistent. By 1900, Concord was the
eighth largest city in the state and one of its hubs for cotton production
and shipping.[11] Growth in industrial labor deepened existing economic
gaps. Farm tenancy in Cabarrus County outpaced the state average by nearly ten points into the 1930s.[12] But the simple rural–urban,

[7] Mrs. D. L. [Catherine] Bost, "Historical Sketches of the Foundation of Cabarrus," writ-
     ten date unknown, Historical Sketch of the City of Concord, Concord, NC Study Club:
     1926, North Carolina Collection, Louis Round Wilson Special Collections Library, Uni-
     versity of North Carolina at Chapel Hill.
[8] Mary King, "The Early History of Cabarrus County, April 9, 1908, *Historical Sketch of
     the City of Concord*, Concord, NC Study Club: 1926, North Carolina Collection, Louis
     Round Wilson Special Collections Library, University of North Carolina at Chapel Hill.
[9] Brundage, *The Southern Past*, 2.
[10] King, "The Early History of Cabarrus County."
[11] Peter Kaplan, *The Historic Architecture of Cabarrus County, North Carolina* (Concord,
     NC: Historic Cabarrus, 1981), xi, 24.
[12] Olaf Wakefield, Charles Horace Hamilton, Eugenia Thomas, J. Banks Young, and
     Dan H. Jones. *Survey of the Rural Relief Situation, Cabarrus County, North Carolina*
     (Raleigh: North Carolina State University, 1934), 22, North Carolina Collection, Louis
     Round Wilson Special Collections Library, University of North Carolina at Chapel Hill.

agricultural–industrial dichotomies of the era did not capture the fluidity of movement and identity between these two polls of the county. An early 1930s report on the relief efforts in Cabarrus captured the complexities of conforming to the changed working order. The predominant "class of families" was one that "cannot ... be termed either rural-nonfarm, rural-farm, or urban." In this hybridized system, "one member of the family will labor on the farm ... while other members of the family will obtain employment in industry."[13] This was the reality of public work for many white workers, who might move between mills and between mill labor and farm life with relative ease. For African American workers, this led to an exaggerated casualization of their already undervalued labor. Barred from the segregated floors of the lily-white mills, they constituted both a majority of Cabarrus's sharecroppers and, by 1930, "about 70 percent of the common laborers."[14]

In short, public work remade the laboring class, and forced people to reimagine the contours of work. The same people might work in a broad array of jobs, spanning the seasons and the landscapes of the county. This instability of opportunity was a stand-in for and exaggeration of larger changes across the region. The broadening labor model also brought with it dramatic changes to the landscape and the way that people used it for work. These were transformations marked materially with the proliferation of new cities and new, larger types of buildings. The scarce examples of grand, spatially dominant plantation mansions were replaced in prominence by the new brick factories. These buildings anchored their own suburban developments, and themselves sometimes borrowed lightly from the neoclassical orders that equated white dominance with antiquity.[15] These grand industrial palaces were, at least in

---

[13] Wakefield et al., Survey *of the Rural Relief Situation*, 22.

[14] Wakefield et al., *Survey of the Rural Relief Situation*, 32. On the eventual and industry-wide integration of textile mills, see Timothy Minchin, *Hiring the Black Worker: The Racial Integration of the Southern Textile Industry, 1960–1980* (Chapel Hill: University of North Carolina Press, 1999). Prior to this late twentieth-century integration, most textile mills were not racially integrated on the production floor, with the few Black workers employed working as common laborers or cleaners at lower wages. I discuss earlier attempts to run southern textile mills with enslaved Black labor later in this chapter.

[15] On the late nineteenth-century neoclassical revival in North Carolina as an extension of the era's white supremacist ideology, see Bishir, "Landmarks of Power." Though mills were not generally as transparently neoclassical as either antebellum mansions or late nineteenth-century suburban homes, they included small details of form and ornamentation that set them apart from the brick edifices of the other prevailing textile regions in the United States. On these distinctions and representative examples of "the monolithic power of factory architecture," see Bishir, North Carolina Architecture, 432.

the new southern textile mill world, surrounded by "villages" of modest frame houses, designed to hold families of workers. They became sites of both work and social life, an all-encompassing place that historians rightly labeled "a southern cotton mill world" for the scope of its reach.[16] Visually, the landscape of the countryside was less dramatically altered. The continuity of the rural architectural vernacular where "requirements for outbuildings remained largely unchanged after 1865," promised a kind of stability amid this growth.[17] Workplaces there were also increasingly a site of community and gathering. This was certainly true of the new mills and worker villages, like the one in nearby Kannapolis that became among the largest in the South in the first years of the twentieth century. But the postbellum transition away from enslaved labor also necessitated the growth of community cotton gins and other shared, commercial means of agricultural production.[18] Places of work were public in a way that they had not been before.

These new jobs, tasks, and locations were hardly the steadying constant that work once had been. There were material transformations to the landscape of work, but also of the ways people did work *with* and *in* places. Work was unsteady and confused, a jumble of new jobs and old tasks that held only little promise for a better economic situation. This new public white worker was a more prominently visible laboring class whose needs were central in a public discourse around the changing of work and labor. Amid these transformations was one constant: the sublimation of Black labor to white needs. White workers could be variously and confusingly defined, but they also had the ready assumption of work that accounted for them, that sought to solve the problems of employment in their favor. Black workers were largely an afterthought, an assumed constant whose labor underpinned the entire system of life in the region. The abstraction of this labor, and the lives of the people being categorized, was central to the redefinition of work at the dawn of the twentieth-century South.

This symbolic transformation and reimagination of the working landscape also extended to smaller material objects. Newly available tools, like the complex machinery of the factory, represented an unfamiliar material

[16] On the origins of the mill village model in the 1880s, see Allen Tullos, *Habits of Industry: White Culture and the Transformation of the Carolina Piedmont* (Chapel Hill: University of North Carolina Press, 1989), 21–25; Jacquelyn Dowd Hall, James Leloudis, Robert Korstad, Lu Ann Jones, and Christopher B. Daly, *Like A Family: The Making of a Southern Cotton Mill World* (Chapel Hill: University of North Carolina Press, 1987).
[17] Kaplan, *Historic Architecture of Cabarrus County*, 20.
[18] Kaplan, *Historic Architecture of Cabarrus County*, 15.

world. In this advanced technology, white men no longer had the advantage of superior strength or working knowledge. The period saw many admonitions to white men to counteract "the growing scarcity and inefficiency of labor" with "the best and most modern tools for labor" and to insist on the value of their work. In this formulation, white men were the best users of tools for their ability to maintain and use them properly.[19] But underlying this pride in work was a constant and growing form of racial superiority that maintained the white man's higher calling. An 1891 mock "Indian Legend" exemplified this strain of thought. Evoking deep historical roots, it told the story of how race was made through the selecting of tools proffered by a "Great Spirit." The Indian received a bow and arrow, the Black man "shovels and other implements of labor," and the white man pen, ink, and other "fine tools." This invented past, rooted in deep time, represented an excuse for white replacement in acts of manual labor and for Black dependence on that same work.[20] Though this was only one strain of a much wider discourse, it became one excuse to confine all Black workers to the most difficult manual labor, and elevate all white men to the work of the mind. Traditional tools then increasingly became a central piece of these imagined shifts in the world of labor. As white men saw the value of their own labor undermined, they worked to redefine it. This meant in part an appeal to the past and to the supposedly natural state of Black workers. These imagined histories became even more crucial with a series of pressing questions around labor.

THE PROBLEMS OF INDUSTRIAL LABOR

The years around the turn of the twentieth century saw a series of animated public conversations around the future of industrial work. These centered on the nature of the new industrial workforce, the central problem of what otherwise might be the South's economic salvation. Though these self-styled labor crises – of age, of gender, of race – are often considered separately by historians, in reality they were symptomatic of larger anxieties. Work was the most visible form of public life, and the ability

---

[19] "Farm Machines," *The Enterprise*, October 24, 1901; "Some Sound Advice," *The Asheville Weekly Citizen*, December 21, 1893 (quote 2). On the value of white male labor, see for instance "The Labor Question," *The Gastonia Gazette*, May 20, 1904; "Another Prosperity Wave," *The Caucasian*, October 20, 1898; "Machine Made Tools," *The Wilson Advance*, February 3, 1904.

[20] "An Indian Legend of the Creation," *Fayetteville Weekly Observer*, January 15, 1891; "An Indian Legend," *The Roanoke News*, January 29, 1891.

to participate fully in it marked a broader form of sociality. For observers then pondering the extensibility and limitations of citizenship for freed people and women, the affordances offered by work seemed like a further step toward a limited equality. For African American people, being stripped of their newfound human rights first slowly, then in eruptions of violence, industrial work seemed like another in a long line of tenuous promises to gain a foothold in society.[21]

Perhaps the most famous of these discussions had Cabarrus County as one of its principal sites. In 1912, documentary photographer and anti–child labor activist Lewis Hine visited some of the county's larger "show mills" as part of his duties with the National Child Labor Committee (NCLC). This was his second visit to the mills of the North Carolina Piedmont.[22] He sought to expose their reliance on child labor, and thereby link the suffering of southern children to the broader inhumanities of industrial capitalism. But Hine was only a small part of a much larger movement rooted alike in child welfare and racial protectionism. Perhaps most representative of this labor racism was the political figurehead of the anti-child labor movement, Indiana's Albert Beveridge. During a 1907 filibuster he "emphasized bitterly that the victims of the nation's current labor laws were '*white* children, 6 and 7 years of age.'"[23] Beveridge's advocacy failed in seeing a child protection bill passed, but the NCLC remained an important force. Indeed, despite the huge number of studies and social welfare reforms directed at the South, the NCLC was originally formed as a collaboration between Alabama and New York child protection organizations.[24] Child labor posed even more pressing

[21] On the topic of labor transformations in the wake of the Civil War, particularly as it pertains to hardening divisions of race and class, see Rosanne Currarino, *The Labor Question in America: Economic Democracy in the Gilded Age* (Urbana: University of Illinois Press, 2011); Mark Lause, *Free Labor: The Civil War and the Making of an American Working Class* (Urbana: University of Illinois Press, 2015); David Montgomery, *Citizen Worker: The Experience of Workers in the United States with Democracy and the Free Market during the Nineteenth Century* (Cambridge, UK; New York: Cambridge University Press, 1994); Heather Cox Richardson, *The Death of Reconstruction: Race, Labor, and Politics in the post-Civil War North, 1865–1901* (Cambridge, MA: Harvard University Press, 2001).

[22] A detailed itinerary of Hine's many trips through the industrial South in this period can be found in Lewis Wicke Hine, *Lewis Hine: Photographs of Child Labor in the New South*, ed. John R. Kemp (Jackson: University Press of Mississippi, 1986).

[23] Alexander Nemerov, *Soulmaker: The Times of Lewis Hine* (Princeton: Princeton University Press, 2016), 14.

[24] On reformist movements directed at the South, see Ring, *The Problem South*. Beveridge's role in the larger ecosystem of child welfare laws as well as the founding of the NCLC are

problems for southerners. Their region was, increasingly, the main source of the child labor problem and the place most resistant to any solutions. Alexander Jeffrey McKelway, Hine's colleague as the southern secretary of the NCLC, was particularly strident in his demand for action.[25] For him, the issue of child labor was not one based on pity or the simplistic moral uplift of the mill owners. Instead, it was an explicit and central piece of the project of white supremacy:

We are brought face to face with the fact that the depreciation of our racial stock has already begun, that we have a cotton mill type that can be recognized, that the percentage of illiteracy in the mill village surpasses even that of the mountain counties of some of our states, and that there is already beginning, in a few factory centers, a moral collapse of which I hardly dare speak.[26]

That unspoken moral collapse, the omnipresent specter of miscegenation, was one that structured McKelway's whole argument and his prodigious career as a reformer.[27] Other commenters on the southern industrial world likewise spoke about this "darkest of all phases of the race question."[28] For McKelway, William Garrott Brown, and others, industrial work was also a way to demonstrate and preserve definitive white racial superiority. Brown called whiteness "the true reserve force of the South."[29] McKelway too considered it through a lens of eugenic breeding. He called for the maintenance of the segregated workplace out of "the necessity of preserving with its wonted vigor the racial stock of the South".[30] McKelway increasingly directed his advocacy toward universal white education. He felt that the schoolroom helped to forestall racial mixture in ways that the mill or workshop never could. Barring the civilizing influence of education, even the farm, with its isolation from the corrupting influences of the

---

covered in John Braeman, "Albert J. Beveridge and the First National Child Labor Bill," *Indiana Magazine of History* LX (1964): 10–11.

[25] William S. Powell, "McElway, Alexander Jeffrey," *NCPedia*, 1991, www.ncpedia.org/biography/mckelway-alexander (accessed April 19, 2022).

[26] A. J. McKelway, "The Awakening of the South against Child Labor," in *Child Labor and the Republic* (New York: National Child Labor Committee, 1907), 16.

[27] On the political obsession with miscegenation, see Martha Hodes, "The Sexualization of Reconstruction Politics: White Women and Black Men in the South after the Civil War," *Journal of the History of Sexuality* 3, no. 3 (1993): 402–417. For a detailed accounting of McKelway's career, see Herbert J. Doherty, "Alexander J. McKelway: Preacher to Progressive," *Journal of Southern History*, 24, no. 2 (1958): 177–190.

[28] William Garrott Brown, *The South at Work: Observations from 1904*, ed. Bruce E. Baker, Southern Classics Series (Columbia: University of South Carolina Press), 2014.

[29] Brown, *The South at Work*.

[30] McKelway, "The Awakening of the South," 14.

city or mill town, might suffice.[31] Here, Hine and McKelway agreed. On later visits to North Carolina, the photographer took images of families "Happy and Content on the Farm," while McKelway extolled "the homely virtues of the soil."[32] These depictions were rooted in an agrarian imaginary, where agricultural labor was a wholesome and sustaining basis of white familial life. The omissions of such a world are obvious. They imagine white workers and a white world, isolated from modernity or the subordinate labor of Black people.

But, contrary to McKelway's opinion or Hine's prescriptions, these children and their families were no longer only farmers. They were mill workers. These mill villagers inhabited a liminal geography between the locational poles of town and country, farm and industry. The dangers of public work for them were physical – the long hours, the ventilation systems that favored cotton's preservation over people's health, the fast machines that could easily take a finger. But amid those very real dangers were also other forms of material, bodily worry that did not necessarily manifest physically. This was McKelway's "cotton mill type," an imagined white person whose characteristics were degraded by the confinements and repetitive movements of their work. This was an antiquated though persistent fear. As Bryant Simon notes, "industrialization triggered an almost universal crisis of male identity."[33] This first-generation worker, still often seasonally peripatetic, "feared that the move from farm to factory threatened to emasculate them, reducing them to the status of dependents."[34] That sublimated status was not one that white men, even the poor and disenfranchised ones, were content to cope with as they compared themselves and their accomplishments to the first and second generations of freed people. Labor in the mills required a partial surrender of patriarchal power. Employment there required the acquiescence of not just themselves, but their entire families to the direction of the boss.[35] The surrender of public work was not absolute, but it did bring in the substitute of foreman, manager, or mill owner as patriarch to

[31] McKelway, "The Awakening of the South," 14.
[32] Lewis Wickes Hine, "The Britt Family Happy and Content on the Farm. See Report of Lewis W. Hine on North Carolina, April 1915. Location: Evergreen, North Carolina," April 1915, www.loc.gov/item/2018673967 (accessed April 19, 2022); McKelway, "The Awakening of the South," 17.
[33] Bryant Simon, *A Fabric of Defeat: The Politics of South Carolina Millhands, 1910–1948* (Chapel Hill: University of North Carolina Press, 1998), 29.
[34] Simon, *A Fabric of Defeat*, 22.
[35] Simon, *A Fabric of Defeat*, 39.

the family hierarchy. That frustrating lack of power might be expressed through a lynching – mill workers were likely amid the participants in the lynching of Johnson and Kizer.[36] But on a daily basis, it might manifest in less overtly violent ways like the sharp correction of a family member or the casual assertion of racial superiority to a Black person passing on the sidewalk. White masculinity under threat took refuge in performative expressions of authority.

But it seems clear even from the paucity of firsthand testimony that white workers in particular were making similar linkages between Black labor and the problems of their everyday working and social lives. These issues were never separable. Just as any lynching could never be confined to a single cause or impact, white men in particular clearly associated the potential of African American work with the perceived failures of patriarchal control in the white industrial working class.

Perhaps the best evidence of this from the lynching of Johnson and Kizer came in a profile of Sam Hartsell. The father of the murdered Emma, Hartsell's story and his quest for fuller vengeance were the subject of much of the outrage around the death of the girl and the subsequent lynching of Joe Kizer and Tom Johnson (as is more fully outlined in Chapter 2).

Hartsell remained a subject of interest long after his daughter's death. One widely reprinted profile of him focused on the perceived threats to his role as father, patriarch, and man. Yet another defense of the lynching, this portrait defined Hartsell as an emblem of embattled white masculinity. In at least one instance, it appeared next to news and commentary on the North Carolina textile industry. Juxtaposed with industrial magnate Lawrence Holt's views and prospects, this placement suggested the close dialectic ties between the topics. The article on Hartsell was typically called "Keenly Touching," as it was titled when it appeared alongside the Holt piece in the *Lenoir Topic* of March 29, 1899. The entire, short article serves as a spiritual reflection on Hartsell's manhood and familial role in the wake of the lynching and in the broader context of societal challenges to southern white masculinity. Typical of

---

[36] Bryant Simon writes about the participation of textile mill workers in a 1912 lynching in Cherokee County, South Carolina; see Simon, *Fabric of Defeat*, 14–16. W. Fitzhugh Brundage more fully details the range of mob participation. See Brundage, *Lynching in the New South*, especially 17–48. The relative anonymity of lynch mob participants likely precludes a fuller accounting of the types of people that constituted these mobs, though in counties where textile and other industrial working-class men predominated or were a significant minority, it seems logical that they were participants. Certainly the collection of lynching souvenirs was a working-class diversion, as detailed in J. E. Mainer's possession of a photograph of Johnson and Kizer's lynching (Chapter 6).

commentary about both Black and white working-class men, Hartsell himself never actually appears in the text as anything but an index of frustrated masculinity. "The face of his young wife and daughter" were windows into the father for the reporter, who knew Hartsell "was the type of man his neighbors had described." The here-unnamed wife (Lula) testifies to her husband's deepened and renewed faith after his daughter's death.[37] When the reporter, a northerner covering the South, leaves, he is converted to the southern way of thinking by these simple, secondhand expressions of faith and fatherhood: "I felt for the last time I had condemned these Southern communities for administering justice according to the elemental feelings of manhood."[38]

This resolution excused lynching on the basis of its positive impacts on white masculinity. Each reprinting added comments focused on the the perceived threats of Black violence to white women and the responsibilities of white patriarchs in guarding against it. The *Monroe Enquirer* recalled the religious fervor of the lynching, "when the manhood of North Carolina ... was saying 'amen' to that righteous execution."[39] Building on the original author's point, these commentaries noted the communicative function of "the men of Cabarrus who told to the world ... that home, virtue, and womanhood shall be protected."[40] For these authors, lynching was as much about reinvigorating masculinity through violence and the reclaiming of control as it was about punishment. In an article full of religious language, the original author repents of his assumptions about the inhumanity of the acts and instead sees murder and torture as fundamental protections for fatherhood and a traditional familial structure as much as it was for womanhood. This was part of the dual threat of Black masculinity, which might also see Black men replacing white labor.[41] Plantation fields and African American people's places in it were

---

[37] This name, as well as the Hartsell family genealogy more generally, relies upon an unpublished manuscript of newspaper clippings, genealogical research, and family comments centered on the lynching of Emma Hartsell: "Hartsell Lynching Scrapbook," photocopied, September 24, 1979, Eastern Cabarrus Historical Society, Mount Pleasant North Carolina, copy in possession of the author.

[38] "Keenly Touching," *Lenoir Topic*, March 29, 1899.

[39] "Keenly Touching," *Monroe Enquirer*, March 23, 1899.

[40] "Keenly Touching," *Henderson Gold Leaf*, March 23, 1899.

[41] A good overview of women's roles in the industrializing New South comes from Georgina Hickey's case study of Atlanta: Georgina Hickey, *Hope and Danger in the New South City: Working Class Women and Urban Development in Atlanta, 1890–1940.* (Athens: University of Georgia Press, 2003).

well established and seemingly unquestioned. But new sites of labor were still in flux and indeterminate. Industrial sites might represent possibility for wage labor, but also undermine personal and familial autonomy and patriarchal authority. They might hew toward whiteness and the perceived virtues of white work, but the structuring fears of replacement and displacement were omnipresent. Amid these uncertainties, hammer, chisel, and other familiar tools were anchors to memories of a less complicated world of labor. They continued to represent the possibilities of elemental white male labor working without the complexities of powered machinery or supervision of bosses.

The problem of textile mill and other industrial labor stemmed in part from this uncertainty around who would perform the work, and how they would go about it. Though child labor arguably got more national attention, contemporaries were fixated on the question of African American industrial labor for the better part of a century.[42] As William Garrott Brown complained in the early twentieth century, "the Negro occupies too much of the foreground ... for one who visits or studies the South."[43] He and other writers imagined a world where Black people no longer existed, or at least worked for and kept to themselves. The encouragement of stable employment for white working men might bring about his "most desired" scenario where African Americans "become so few relative to the whites that in this respect we shall approximate the status of the North."[44] Brown's eugenicist vision for racial purity betrayed significant anxieties not only about replacement, but about the superiority of the Black male working body. Black working bodies were loved and

---

[42] Arguably this conversation about Black industrial labor in textile mills began in the 1820s with the downturn in agricultural commodity prices. For an example of the discourse around enslaved mill laborers, see "Manufacture of Cotton in the Southern States," *American Farmer* 9, no. 30 (1827): 235.

Southern legislatures eager to see the profits of their cotton kept in state produced a series of reports on the possibilities of textile production. The legislatures of North Carolina, South Carolina, and Georgia all authorized studies on textile industrialization in their respective states, with the use of slave labor a major focus of each.

Experiments with slave labor in the nascent Southern cotton mill industry were fairly widespread, though few were long-lived. The racialized discourse though carried over into the postbellum period, as the debate became increasingly about the ability and capacity of various classes of laborers to do textile work. For an overview of antebellum experiments in slave-run cotton mills, see Norris W. Preyer, "The Historian, the Slave, and the Ante-Bellum Textile Industry," *Journal of Negro History*, 46, no. 2 (1961): 67–82.

[43] Brown, *The South at Work*.

[44] Brown, *The South at Work*.

loathed, considered sites of potential for their supposed predispositions to difficult labor, but feared for their ability to outman their white competitors in strength, speed, and ability. Brown's prescriptions would see a South largely rid of Black people, or at least one where they were confined to menial tasks at the direction of white men. In this world, there would be plenty of work, and a transformation of all white men into bosses. In this evolving labor memory, hammer, chisel, and other tools began to stand for the intersections of white mastery and Black work. Stereotypes of the "natural" state of the races worked to alleviate white men's fears of replacement.[45]

Unsurprisingly, much of the conversation around the possibility of Black-operated textile mills trafficked in the vicious stereotypes common to the end-of-the-century working world. The most sustained treatment of the idea, the sociologist Jerome Dowd's "Colored Men as Cotton Manufacturers," opens with the reporting of a long-held belief: "The opinion used to prevail in the South that the negroes could never be worked in a factory for the reason that the hum of the machinery would put them to sleep."[46] This maxim had been repeated so often that it appeared as truth to white southerners. In questioning the potential of Black workers, observers turned to both imagined histories and racialized characteristics, like one author who despaired of efficient labor from people "who had always been used to sing and whistle at his work in the open fields."[47] This comparison was ubiquitous. The work of African Americans was never considered except that it was equated to the labor of the plantation. And each speculation about the potential Black-run textile mills was accompanied by theories as to how workers might be adapted to this new labor by

---

[45] Brown is clearly invoking the eugenics movement omnipresent at the time. It suffused nearly all Progressive movements in the South and beyond. Still, there has yet to be a full-scale study of eugenics and what we might call the southern body, those people categorized as other to the implied white, southern, male ideal. Particularly useful in this regard is Anna Krome-Lukens, "The Reform Imagination: Gender, Eugenics, and the Welfare State in North Carolina, 1900–1940," PhD dissertation, University of North Carolina, 2014. On eugenics in other parts of the South, see Gregory Michael Dorr, *Segregation's Science: Eugenics and Society in Virginia* (Charlottesville: University of Virginia Press, 2008). On fears and anxieties over Black working bodies, see Nelson, *Steel Drivin' Man*, 107, and Hazel V. Carby, *Race Men* (Cambridge, MA: Harvard University Press, 1998).

[46] Jerome Dowd, "Colored Men as Cotton Manufacturers," *Gunton's Magazine*, 1902, North Carolina Collection, Louis Round Wilson Library Special Collections Library, University of North Carolina at Chapel Hill.

[47] "Negro Object Lesson: Warren C. Coleman Is Proving to the World That the Negro Can Compete in the Manufacturing World," *New York Tribune*, May 3, 1903.

merging it with the old. Newspapers often noted that Coleman intended to "[locate] his mill in a cotton field," and quoted a formerly enslaved person who "said that he did not see any difference in working there from feeding the old time gin owned by his master."[48] For white commenters, the possibilities of Black textile work were always dictated by its adaptability to Black people's supposedly natural skills as agricultural workers.

Other supposed limitations to Black industrial work came from equally facile observations of Black, post-Emancipation social worlds. Dowd's scholarly observation was little more than personal opinion, with him claiming "it is a notorious fact" that Black workers cannot labor near running water. He referred to the much-celebrated failure of the Vesta Cotton Mill in Charleston, South Carolina. Using that precedent, Dowd claimed that "where the supply of fish is abundant [and] there are too many street parades, camp-meetings, excursions, festivals, and cheap theatrics," no Black workers are likely to stick to the tasks of the mill.[49] Other would-be experts, like Lawrence Holt of the wealthy Burlington, North Carolina, textile family, had similar opinions. Commenting on the occasion of Coleman's mill opening in Concord, he contradicted the existence of the new mill (or at least its success) by claiming that "the time will never come when colored labor will be employed in the cotton factories of the South." Like Dowd, he attributed this to the many distractions of life after Emancipation: "The negro wants to go to a funeral, or a baptizing" or is otherwise distracted by the demands of family life.[50]

Perhaps this was an extension of the disinclination of owners like Holt to build housing for African American workers and thus be able to assert control over their living conditions. But it also clearly stems from prevalent stereotypes about Black workers. In the discursive realm of regional and national commentary, this was the precise reaction to be expected. In the abstract, African American workers seemed to represent little more than a fanciful idea. The linkages of whiteness and industrial work in the South were still tenuous. Even still, the forward-thinking futurity of the industrial world seemed to increasingly represent the preservation of the white race. Black workers might stay at "the most menial work" of the mill, or even have their "labor used on coarser goods," but an equality of opportunity would

---

[48] "A Negro Mill," *The Brooklyn Daily Eagle*, July 9, 1899; "Negro Object Lesson," *New York Tribune*, May 3, 1903.

[49] Dowd, "Colored Men," 254.

[50] "The North Carolina Mills," *Washington Post*, March 18, 1899.

undermine white supremacy and the future of the white race.[51] These were
the rhetorical stakes that Warren C. Coleman faced as he worked to launch
the first Black-owned and -operated mill in the South. When his mill opened
in Concord in the months proximate to the Johnson and Kizer lynching, it
was with decades of negative speculation about the ability of Black workers, the heavy weight of racial expectation, and the localized, specific dread
of racial terrorism.

White workers and their rhetorical champions were seeking to redefine the face and race of the southern industrial worker. Resistant to even
hints of Black industrial work, they sought to make textile work the sole
domain of white workers. This required a cross-class bargain between
owners, managers, and working people. What they produced, increasingly, was an idea of textile work that was too difficult for the primitive
minds of Black workers. Whereas the hammer and chisel had once represented the hard work of the white man, they were evolving throughout
the years of the early twentieth century to stand in for an outmoded
way of work that belonged in the past. Unsurprisingly, the past that
they sought to reimplement in the present was one of the Black agrarian
worker. Hammer, chisel, hoe, and other rudimentary implements were
being reenvisioned as the natural tools of the Black worker.

WARREN C. COLEMAN AND BLACK INDUSTRIAL WORK

Warren C. Coleman's public life posed a challenge to those delimited
possibilities for African American southerners. Coleman is little known
now, but in his lifetime he was spoken of in the same breath as other
Black luminaries of the late nineteenth century. He shared a stage and top
billing with W. E. B. Du Bois at the 1899 National Afro-American Council in Chicago and was widely regarded as "the richest colored man in the
South."[52] When he died in 1904, it was with one of the largest collections
of real estate of any of the new Piedmont industrialists, Black or white.
The centerpiece of his holdings was a textile mill named in his honor and
run by African American operatives. Long a dream of race promoters,
the African American textile mill was intended to be Coleman's signature
achievement. His was an attempt to resituate Black workers outside of

---

[51] A. F. Eshelman, "Letter from Charlotte, North Carolina," *Lebanon Courier and Semi-
Weekly Report*, January 12, 1898

[52] "The National Afro-American Council," *The Broad Ax*, July 29, 1899; ["Coleman"],
The Ocala Evening Star, July 29, 1899, 4. This small news article – just two sentences –
was reprinted widely throughout the country as an item of interest.

the historical, subordinate conditions constructed for them in the working memory of the late nineteenth century.

After the mill opened and shortly before his death, Coleman commented on the meaning of his industrial experiment. Far more than mere economic success, he believed the mill "will be a great thing for the negro race. I have believed in it from the first and have neglected family, State, and my other business for its sake."[53] Though comparisons to the most famous of his contemporaries – like Booker T. Washington and W. E. B. Du Bois – is inevitable, Coleman's influence relied on the astonishing accumulation of capital that served as a racialized recasting of contemporaneous prosperity myths.[54] This single-mindedness made him a figurehead of a certain kind of race progress that earnestly stressed hard work and success as salves for racial injustice and a first crucial step toward racial independence.[55] Coleman became emblematic of the potential of Black people, and particularly of Black industrial labor, to solve the perceived problems of African American life after Emancipation. Deeply tied to the simultaneous crisis of white male identity, the potential of Black people as factory workers was largely hypothetical for many years, but still the source of both rampant excitement and a deep and abiding resentment. Coleman and his factory came to embody each of these competing feelings. His national prominence brought many profiles of the mill, but acclaim also brought with it further attention and entanglement with the abiding forces of white resentment around Black work.

As an historical figure, Coleman is somewhat inscrutable. No collection of his personal papers survives in institutional archives, and the few

---

[53] "Negro Object Lesson," *New York Tribune*.

[54] On the prosperity myth of Horatio Alger and others in the political context of the late nineteenth century, see Carol Nackenoff, *Fictional Republic: Horatio Alger and American Political Discourse*, (Oxford; New York: Oxford University Press, 1994).

[55] Though the transcripts of few of Coleman's public addresses survive, both interviews and some personal letters attest to the complexities of his views on racial progress and industrial work. In one profile he is quoted as saying: "I am of the opinion that progress in industrial pursuits of the colored race must be made by that race itself. our white brethren have helped the colored people in all undertakings since we were given our freedom. and the time has come that we must strike out for ourselves"; "A Negro Mill," *The Brooklyn Daily Eagle*. He depended on investments and patronage from prominent white capitalists, but even in his own letters to them seemed hesitant to commit too much to their support. This hesitancy was proven correct when, after his death, first the Dukes and then the Cannons bought his mill to add to their growing empires. One of the largest collections of correspondence from Coleman is in the Washington Duke Papers at Duke University. He and Duke were frequent correspondents, though Coleman is largely well-mannered and business-like in his letters; Correspondence Series, 1863–1976, Washington Duke Papers, David M. Rubenstein Rare Book & Manuscript Library, Duke University.

pieces of correspondence in other people's collections largely recapitulate the carefully crafted biographical details that were frequently repeated throughout his lifetime. The persona of Warren C. Coleman was one designed to posit relentless hard work as the antidote to race prejudice and structural inequities. In his own words, and in the profiles of him, he was crafted as a figurehead for Black industrial progress. Every aspect of his biography as reported seemed calculated to express this symbolism. Coleman was born in 1849 on the William Coleman plantation in Cabarrus County.[56] His mother was enslaved, a fact that became part of his biography principally as a way to mark his progression from "the log cabin in which he was born." The symbolic annihilation of his origins came when he tore down that cabin to make way for the growth of additional rental properties.[57] Though sources speculated about his father, the man was never named as anything other than a prominent local enslaver. Available evidence suggests that Coleman was the son of Confederate General Rufus Clay Barringer. This seemed widely known or assumed in his lifetime, though he never commented on his parentage and only minimally on his upbringing.[58]

If Coleman was not obsessed with his own upbringing and biography, both African American and white writers were. Even before his death, Coleman was made the subject of hagiographies that marked him as a symbol of Black progress and uplift. One contemporary commenter dubbed him "a Negro Star of the first magnitude."[59] Others rhapsodized even further. A biographer compared him favorably to the greatest hero of nineteenth-century African American communities: "He will rank with Abraham Lincoln as their practical friend and benefactor. One gave them freedom – the other will give them an industrial position."[60] In their telling, he was a person forging an African American history not through

---

[56] Allen Burgess, "Tar Heel Blacks and the New South Dream: The Coleman Manufacturing Company, 1896–1904," PhD dissertation, Duke University, 1977, 94, North Carolina Collection, Louis Round Wilson Special Collections Library, University of North Carolina at Chapel Hill.

[57] "Negro Object Lesson," *New York Tribune*.

[58] Marvin Krieger, "Warren Clay Coleman," *NcPedia*, 1979, www.ncpedia.org/biography/coleman-warren-clay.

[59] W. H. Quick, *Negro Stars in All Ages of the World* (Henderson, NC: D. E. Aycock, 1890), 120.

[60] G. F. Richings, *Evidences of Progress among Colored People* (Philadelphia: George S. Ferguson, 1902), Documenting the American South, University Library, University of North Carolina at Chapel Hill, 2000, https://docsouth.unc.edu/church/richings/richings.html (accessed April 19, 2022).

formal education but in offering evidence that through "'grit and girth' and 'pith and worth' one can become one of the great men of the age."[61] This originary story of hard work and an untutored genius predominated, but even Howard University, which Coleman briefly attended in 1873–1874, proudly claimed his time there as a major influence on his life.[62] Coleman came to embody the various aspirations and various methods of achievement of African American people in this period. In this created public persona was a figure somewhere between the Du Boisian "talented tenth" and Booker T. Washington's ethic of self-sufficient industrialism.[63]

These accountings of Coleman's life's work were not nuanced. Few depictions of his life were intimate or personal, and even his own speeches tended toward grand proclamations rather than specific observations. White depictions of Coleman only emphasized the exaggerated humanity of his public persona. The *Brooklyn Eagle*, for instance, noted that Coleman had a "natural capacity for business."[64] An observer of the textile industry, A. F. Eshelman had it that Coleman was "quite a sharp, hustling business man."[65] These white characterizations of Coleman built on other forms of racial stereotyping rampant in depictions of Black masculinity. In contrast to the Black brute, Coleman was sharp, perhaps even conniving. His innate characteristics were not savagery or brutality, but a kind of shrewdness and sense for how best to profit in a situation. In contrast to African American depictions of Coleman, white-authored profiles tended to emphasize nature and inherent qualities, rather than work or achievement. For these writers, Coleman was an exception to Black male laziness, simplicity, and brutal licentiousness, but his actions were still motivated by racialized characteristics that owed more to birth than to development. These depictions differed from other white depictions of Black men at the time, though they still reduced his success to mere biological determinism. The *New York Tribune* had it that he "was a bright mulatto with the pronounced features of the white type" and inherited both his looks "and his ability to make and accumulate money" from his father.[66]

---

[61] Quick, *Negro Stars*, 115.
[62] "Influences of Howard," *The Colored American*, March 9, 1901.
[63] Allen Burgess notes this confluence of ideas in his dissertation on Coleman: Burgess, "Tar Heel Blacks and the New South Dream."
[64] "A Negro Mill," *The Brooklyn Daily Eagle*.
[65] Eshelman, "Letter from Charlotte."
[66] "Negro Object Lesson," *New York Tribune*.

These white characterizations of Coleman and of his work as an indus-
trialist were typically put forth with an air of condescension. For journalists and other observers, his success was limited by the capacities of his
race. When he was successful, it could be attributed to his white inheritance. When setbacks arose, even manmade ones, it was more likely to be
the result of his African American ancestry. After an 1885 fire resulted in a
massive loss of property for Coleman, a local white man in Concord wrote
to one of the state's main Black newspapers asking for help to aid in his
recovery. While stressing that he "differ[ed] from him in race and politics,"
Paul Means emphasized that Coleman was "a zealous, faithful and liberal
promoter of all the best and proper interests of his and your race."[67]

That qualified, race-specific praise only intensified as Coleman moved
to open his mill in the late 1890s. Commentaries noted that "white people of North Carolina are much interested in the success of the experiment."[68] More than a little doubt accompanied that interest, which was
often qualified by reference to the recent failure of the Black-run Vesta
cotton mill. After the incorporation of Coleman's mill in early 1897,
national reporters made repeated sojourns to Cabarrus County throughout the following years. There they talked with local white people, and
with little other evidence speculated on the innate capacities of Black
workers. One reporter summarized local white opinion: "some think it
will work all right; others who also know thoroughly the negro in all his
elements have great misgivings as to his capacity to be useful in the cotton mill."[69] Downplaying the factory as little more than an "experiment"
and underplaying the capabilities and potential of Black workers were
ways of qualifying its success to a kind of segregated potentiality. The
mill might succeed, but only within the limited confines of Black excellence. This white scrutiny was akin to the exoticizing gaze of audiences
regarding pedagogical exhibitions at the fair or museum. Indeed, at least
one newspaper took Coleman's involvement in the North Carolina Negro
Fair in order to view him as its seeming chief exhibition. They called him
"the best lesson to be drawn from the fair" and claimed that his person
represented "a fair illustration of what they may and can do."[70] Publicly,

---

[67] Paul B. Means, "Letter from Concord," *North Carolina Gazette*, September 26, 1885.
[68] "Owned by Negroes," *The Boston Globe*, December 26, 1898.
[69] Eshelman, "Letter from Charlotte."
[70] "The Colored Fair," *The Anson Times*, December 22, 1881. For a nuanced characteriza-
     tion of African American depictions and self-determination in such fairs and exhibitions,
     see Mabel O. Wilson, *Negro Building: Black Americans in the World of Fairs and Muse-
     ums* (Berkeley: University of California Press, 2012).

both local and national voices endorsed Coleman's success, even if they did not believe it would hold or could be extended to the greater challenge of running a mill. In these accountings, both his potential and his limitations were based on a crude racial capacity, and the ability to achieve only within the confines of a limited potential.

Lost in this commentary was any context of the lynching or of the more pervasive racial terrorism in Cabarrus County. The early stages of operation at Coleman's mill were nearly simultaneous with the lynching of Kizer and Johnson. And certainly, the lynching remained a dominant topic of diversion among many of the white people interviewed for these pieces. Especially given that the conversation and questions around the Coleman mill were predicated on the problem of race relations, it seems likely that the lynching came up. It would still be many years before talk of the murders was a private subject, rather than one to be detailed and commented upon in open conversation. Likely, this was an intentional omission. Ida B. Wells was among the few journalists to explicitly note the overlaps between white terrorism and white economic anxieties, but other reporters clearly took note of those entanglements in Concord. Despite protestations to the contrary both before and after the lynching of Kizer and Johnson, there is evidence of significant attempts to intimidate, injure, and even kill Coleman and the new class of workers he began to create in Concord.

Even before the mill marked Coleman as a major national success and topic of conversation, there was some intimation in African American publications that one of Coleman's triumphs was over the concerted sabotage efforts of his white neighbors. A comment about his successes notes of the 1885 fire that "he was burned out."[71] This language seems deliberately ambiguous. Perhaps suggestive of arson, it could just as easily refer to the totality of the fire in effecting his near ruin. But other reports from the 1885 fire were less circumspect. One white newspaper noted both that it was "believed to be the work of an incendiary who used kerosene oil freely" and that Coleman's insurance had run out two weeks prior and had not yet been renewed.[72] Both writers were careful to only hint at the truth, though obviously for different reasons. Certainly the Black audience reading the booster pieces about Coleman's mill read between the lines of his phenomenal success and knew the likely toll of intimidation and terror that underlay it.

---

[71] Quick, *Negro Stars*, 118–119.
[72] "Concord's Quiet Warmed into Life," *Raleigh Register*, August 12, 1885.

Such speculation took on more plausibility years later as the mill was in its final stages of development and approaching full operational status. The mill broke ground officially in February of 1898, just three months before the lynching of Johnson and Kizer.[73] By the next year, it was running on at least partial capacity. Toward the end of 1899, a front-page report in the local paper of record noted that the recently finished house of J. A. Lankford, "a colored man who is a machinist at the Coleman mill," had burned to the ground.[74] Lankford was the Tuskegee-trained "master mechanic" at Coleman's mill, and was still in the process of tuning the machinery and getting the mill running at full capacity.[75] His building of a large, two-story house suggests his investment in the new mill and an intention to stay. Indeed, working for Coleman seemed one of the fullest expressions of the skills of newly college-trained Black men, the "engineers, firemen, molders, carpenters, stone and brick masons, tinners, coppersmiths, scientific farmers, dairymen, and horticulturalists who will find a place to use their talent or make a place."[76] White Concordians clearly had other ideas. The account of Lankford's fire reported that "no cause is known for the fire unless it was the work of an incendiary." Further damning was the observation that significant "numbers of persons watched it [the fire] before the alarm was given."[77] The image of expectant white crowds observing, if not actively causing, Lankford's misfortune strikingly recalls the widespread participation in the previous year's lynching. The intimidation was an apparent success. Lankford left town in early 1900, though not before being hassled at the train station by city officials intent on making sure he had paid any taxes due to the city. This final act of intimidation cloaked as bureaucratic officialdom suggests the varieties of terror enacted on Coleman, Lankford, and other upwardly mobile Black people.[78]

It's not difficult to understand why many white Concordians might have hated Coleman. Given that he was one of the largest landowners and shopkeepers in the county, many were in debt to him. Multiple accounts

---

73 "Cotton Mill Owned by Colored Men," *Evening Star*, February 9, 1898.
74 "Dwelling Burned," *Daily Concord Standard*, November 20, 1899.
75 "Clippings from Exchanges," *Daily Free Press*, May 19, 1899, 1; "Merits High Praise," *News and Observer*, October 26, 1901, 2.
76 "Colored Cotton Mills," *Maxton Scottish Chief*, March 3, 1898.
77 "Dwelling Burned," *Daily Concord Standard*.
78 "He Has Departed," *The Standard*, March 22, 1900. At least one historian suggests that another of Coleman's buildings was also the victim of an arsonist: J. K. Rouse *The Noble Experiment of Warren C. Coleman* (Charlotte, NC: Crabtree Press, 1972), 16.

noted both that white people "trade with him and rent his houses" and that he "owns more space in and around Concord than any other single individual, white or black."[79] Coleman both took up significant conceptual space in the county and occupied no small part of it.

Part of the persona-bordering-on-myth of Coleman was the extent of his real estate holdings. The prevailing count held that he "[owned] 350 houses" in and around Concord.[80] The biggest concentrated area of his real estate holdings was in "Coleburg," a section of town apparently named for and concentrated around the plantation of his former owner.[81] Other than profit, few of Coleman's motives for this particular assemblage of property are apparent, though certainly the symbolism of him acquiring and claiming former plantation land for his own ends is hard to ignore. In addition to several other lots and homes owned in the downtowns of Concord, Salisbury, and other local cities, he owned homes and parcels in growing African American neighborhoods in Winston, Greensboro, Monroe, and Albemarle. He also integrated his workforce into a mill village around the site of his factory. In 1902, that village represented "a dozen or more very substantial tenement cottages ... erected and rented to the employees."[82] Employees and others living there were given the designation "near Coleman mill."[83] In short, he was one of the largest landholders in the Carolina Piedmont and built much of his fortune on the purchase and repurposing of former plantation lands.

His real estate investments were not confined only to the growing cities and towns. Coleman owned significant shares of the countryside. Among those were lands immediately proximate to the site of the lynching of Johnson and Kizer. Ninety acres on Little Cold Water Creek next to the Safrit, Barnhardt, and Seamon places. Forty acres "known as the Michael Scott place." A little more than twenty-five acres on the "west side of Little Cold Water Creek," and more than sixty on the Three Mile Branch. Undoubtedly, these locations were incidental to the lynching that occurred

79 "Negro Object Lesson," *New York Tribune*; Eshelman, "Letter from Charlotte."

80 "Butler Denounced," *The Wilmington Messenger*, February 12, 1898; "Wealthy Negro Dead," *New York Times*, April 1, 1904; "Cabarrus County Marriage Register," December 1873, digital image "Jane Jones and Warren C. Coleman," Ancestry.com.

81 "Map of Coleburg," photocopy of original, date unknown, Local History Reading Room, Cannon Memorial Library, Cabarrus County Libraries.

82 Dowd, "Colored Men," 225.

83 Inter-State Directory Company. *Directory of Concord, North Carolina [Serial]*. Charlotte, NC: Interstate Directory Co., 1902, 90, 110, 115, 116, http://archive.org/details/directoryofconcoooointe (accessed April 19, 2022).

on or even within their borders. But these overlaps are instructive in trying to comprehend both the physical and conceptual space lynchings occupied. It is hard to separate Coleman's rural holdings from the pervasive, designed terror that was the space of the public sphere in Concord, in Cabarrus County, and across nearly the entirety of this New South. Control of land and labor both represented footholds against the very real possibilities of material destruction and bodily violence. Nearly all of the profiles of Coleman emphasize the possibilities of textile work not just as a way for African American people to make a living, but as a place where they could be set apart from the restrictions and violence of everyday life.

The long hours and contained spaces represented new forms of bodily immobility to white laborers used to free movement and the farm. White profiles of Black mill work likewise emphasized its limitations in comparison to the supposedly easygoing life of outside work. But this larger discourse around Coleman and the possibility of a Black textile mill implicitly posited the mill itself as a place of safety, even sanctuary. There were certainly many other threads of possibility in the idea of this place, but strongest of these was the notion of it as antidote to compelled spatial segregation, a designed space and place apart. For Black workers, the close confines and compelled community of mill life and work might provide some way of being apart from the tightening Jim Crow structures around them. Amid the tumult of new working roles, uncertain political representation, and the intensifying violence of the era, the Black-owned mill seemed like a credible alternative. It hardly promised equality or much economic gain, particularly when the notion of the Black-run textile mill was generally premised on the competitive advantage of the lower wages its workers could command. But its regular hours, ordered tasks, and strictly regulated space also represented a claim against white assumptions about the unruliness and irregularity of Black life.

This sounds as if I am foreclosing the possibilities of Black life. Surely it was not the case that African American people had recourse only to institutions built on mitigating the ever-expanding structures of inequality. Part of the celebrated potential of Coleman was that his attempts at creating a mill were an extension of the racial mutual aid impulses of the fraternal lodge or insurance group.[84] Grim though it is, this industrial

---

[84] On the role of the fraternal order in this period, see John Giggie, "For God and Lodge: Black Fraternal Orders and the Evolution of African American Religion in the Postbellum South," in *The Struggle for Equality: Essays on Sectional Conflict, the Civil War, and the Long Reconstruction*, ed. Vernon Burton, Jerald Podair, and Jenny Weber (Charlottesville: University of Virginia Press, 2012): 198–218.

work was one of the few opportunities to create succor not just within but from new institutions, turned toward the support of a race that other proponents of the new industrial work wanted to stamp out altogether. For Black workers in Cabarrus County, the tools that give this chapter its title represented some limited possibility. Coleman's model of industrial labor centered on the Black worker seemed to promise the possibilities of self-reliance and of work undertaken for and by Black communities. This promise made even humble tools like the hammer and chisel tenuous symbols of uplift, with physical work as the key to balancing white insistence on the subservience manual labor represented with its potential for further economic gain.

RACE, WORK, MEMORY

This brings us back to the specific tools left behind in the prison after the abduction of Johnson and Kizer. In the turn-of-the-twentieth-century South, the act of using these tools to break into the jail cell and commit a lynching seemed like a reassertion of white manly virtue. As evidenced with Hartsell, the threat of this new work and the promise of lynching constituted a revival of white patriarchy, a salve against the enervating tasks and spaces of the burgeoning industrial order. Certainly, the tools were not the central piece of that performance of masculine strength. But, even unconsciously, they represented a tethering to old ways of adaptable working and to the accomplishments and possibilities of the white male body at work. For the new industrial work, the tools were not the kind of adaptable necessity that they had been for the varied tasks of the farm. But their use in the lynching could be a minor triumph, a way of again demonstrating the prowess inherent in everyday working tasks.

Black work figured here very differently. No accounts explicitly linked the lynching or its victims to the work at Coleman's mill. But they certainly invoked the larger anxieties about Black labor and the threat of Black men not tethered to the routines of the plantation. Women spending the day "alone at home attending to their household duties" were vulnerable to attack while their male protectors "are at work in the fields" or even further away in a factory. This was a seeming change from a would-be "Arcadia" of the antebellum years, when Black men had their movement and routine strictly controlled. In these early accountings of the lynching then, part of the pervasive threat of life was the "lustful brute who may happen to pass along" in the course of his less rigidly controlled working day. Here again, white working men like Samuel Hartsell were presented as the real victims of both lynching and the changing nature of everyday work. Their wives and daughters were subject to attention and attack by underemployed Black men not forced into the routines of daily agricultural labor. Work, and especially the lack of compelled Black labor, seemed like the cause of many of life's woes.[85]

This perception of the dangerous, underemployed class of Black men gradually changed as the lynching became more a part of communal memory than a present danger, and African American workers took on many other forms of employment. As was typical in lynching newspaper articles, some early accounts of the murders of Johnson and Kizer noted that "many negroes took part in the lynching."[86] This was a way of emphasizing the mob's imagined uniformity of purpose and the particular brutality of the crime that preceded it. It was exceedingly unlikely that any African Americans participated in a furious mob of white men, as jokes published making fun of the possibilities of seizing "the wrong negro" suggest.[87] At the outset, this was not a prominent part of the stories told about the lynching, but just another authenticating detail. Still, this piece of the narrative survived in oral tradition, and took on new prominence amid new contexts for Black working men. In 1955–1956, periodic interest in the lynching was aroused once again. An elderly white man, toward the end of a life that had seen him move between farm, factory, and other employment, recalled stories of the lynching from his childhood. His story of the lynching, reflective of a life lived amid evolving community memories, repositioned the Black worker at the very center of the lynching.[88]

In the recollections of Ervin J. Linker, altered by six decades and many retellings, "there was a big yellow Negro in the crowd." As the mob struggled to open the door he demanded: "'Gimme the way' … and he walked up to the jail door with a big hammer and busted the door in."[89] In this telling, it is the seemingly brutal strength of a Black man that is the only key to the jail cell and the men within. This was a folktale born

[85] "Phases of Lynch Law," *Maxton Scottish Chief*, June 16, 1898.

[86] "Life in North Carolina," *Asheville Daily Citizen*, June 3, 1898.

[87] Untitled, *The Standard*, June 16, 1898.

[88] 1900 United States Census, Poplar Tent Township, Cabarrus County, North Carolina, s.v. "Ervin Linker," digital image Ancestry.com; 1910 United States Census, 2nd Township, Cabarrus County, North Carolina, s.v. "Ervin Linna," digital image Ancestry.com; 1930 United States Census, Number 2 Township, Cabarrus County, North Carolina, s.v. "Ervin Linker," digital image Ancestry.com.

[89] Randolph S. Hancock, "Cabarrus Had a Lynching Play," *The Daily Independent*, 1955–1956, clipping, in the Collection of the Eastern Cabarrus Historical Society.

out of several decades of telling and retelling. Linker makes clear to note the man's mixed racial composition, but also his nearly wordless feat of bodily strength and worker's prowess. His labor of just a few seconds is central to the lynching, and seemingly subordinate to the will of the struggling, righteous mob.

Linker's memory, and the contours of the original story, are clearly both malleable. No previous account refers to this character. Instead, he seems to have been an invention of the ensuing years. It seems unlikely that the fourteen-year-old Linker had been at the jail in 1898 to witness the jailbreak, and even more curious that this specific moment would be the one that later became the focus of his telling of the lynching. In true folkloric fashion, a single minor mention ("many negroes took part in the lynching") was distilled into a mythic single figure who stood in for both the mob's unified purpose and the seemingly uncanny ability of Black workers to wield their tools. Here the memory of the turn-of-the-century threat to work and life was inverted. In this imagined recent past, there were again Black bodies eager to do the bidding of white people, and capable of extraordinary effort from their practiced hands. In this minor incident were the seeds of a reenvisioned role for Black labor in a white supremacist society. No longer were Black men solely a threat. Their innate working abilities and animalistic strength could be redirected by mentally strong white men and their natural abilities to lead and direct.

Gone was the early emphasis on the white working man's ability. It was replaced here by a tenuous, imagined racial cooperation where the brute strength of the Black man was repurposed for the white mob's ends.

Within a decade, this invented sketch of a character had assumed John Henryian proportions and a new centrality to the story of the lynching. Like John Henry or other folkloric Black figures, this character was one whose heroism transcended the limitations of white society. Unlike them, he still worked in service to that society.[90] A 1964 article about the mob murders clearly borrows from and expands upon Linker's account. Indeed, the notion that "Even Negroes Took Part in Last Cabarrus Lynching" is the headline and central thesis of the Civil Rights–era article.[91] A "husky

[90] On the Black hero figure and its origins and use in history, see Levine, Black Culture and Black Consciousness, 367–440. Also see Nelson, *Steel Drivin' Man*, 119–142. It seems very likely that the silent strength of the exaggerated Black character here is more than incidentally related to the legend of John Henry. Nelson argues convincingly for John Henry as an ur-figure for heroic Black masculinity in the latter half of the twentieth century.
[91] Ned Cline, "Even Negroes Took Part in Last Cabarrus Lynching," *Salisbury Post*, November 29, 1964.

negro" – presumably the same as the man in Linker's telling – is invoked in the opening paragraphs as not just a participant but the "man who led the lynching party."[92] The story of the break into the jail is explicated in more detail as well:

Those who remember the incident recall that a white man was attempting to burst the cell lock with a hammer when a burly Negro stepped through the crowd and shouted 'Give me that damn hammer.' With one giant whack, the lock was smashed and the pair was dragged to the lynching site...

As a depiction of reality, this beggars belief. It is clearly indebted to the exaggerated oral traditions of folk tales and their larger-than-life characters. The (still unnamed) Black character has apparently unnatural strength, a different kind or at least different purpose for the usual assumption of inhuman strength in Black men. Like other folk tales, it represents the anxieties and interests of the people telling it. Here we see the stereotype of the Black male brute not inverted, but disempowered of his potential harm. His working body is no longer a threat but an asset. The anonymity of the character makes him into a caricature, one who possesses a kind of strength that far exceeds that of the white man futilely attempting his own break-in. It is perhaps too much to say that the crisis of white masculinity here has been resolved. From the retrospective standpoint of those crafting this history in the 1960s, it is fine, good even, that a white man can stand by and allow this kind of work to be completed by a Black man. Far from disempowering or emasculating, this suggests a supervisory power, a managerial vocation that obviates the need for manual labor or physical effort as a marker of and token for patriarchal power. The hammer here returns to the more powerful laboring body, which by this point is assumed, again, to belong to an African American person. Earlier fears of racial corruption and the failures of white male patriarchy linked to the losses of traditional employment had subsided. Decades on, we get a story invented and preserved by farmers and millworkers and a variety of other white people who have come to acknowledge Black work as indispensable rather than uncontrollable. In a sense, these attitudes were perhaps little changed. Black labor had always been the motive economic force of the county, even as it was feared and mistrusted. But now they might regard it as subsumed and controlled, a class of worker to play a part in an all-white drama.

---

[92] Cline, "Even Negroes Took Part in Last Cabarrus Lynching."

CONCLUSION

This chapter has ranged over the territory of the twentieth-century South in ways that perhaps seem far from their subject in anything but time and place. In part, that is precisely the point. Lynching, and the broader networks of racial terror that it accompanied, touched virtually every aspect of what has come to be the region and nation's history. But the connections are much closer than that. The hammer, chisel, and other tools used to break into the jail were utterly ordinary objects. They were little commented upon as the instruments of effecting the abduction or lynching. Their absence from many of the scant historical records around the killings of Joe Kizer and Tom Johnson might otherwise seem to give them a less than central place in that history. And yet, they remind us now of the centrality of both work and conversations about work at the time. And they mark the overlaps between everyday events and actions and the spectacular power of a lynching.

In the immediate moment of the lynching, the use of familiar tools to break a lock was a reassuring reassertion of the abilities of white men to complete a job. A lack of laboring over this narrative is instructive: These were men performing a task, one of a few dozen they might complete in the next week. It was unremarkable excepting the exaggerated nature of its outcome. The surety of minor laborious performances like this one was undermined in the tumultuous years then beginning in earnest. Industrial labor would undermine the assumptions of white masculine control and superiority, and admit whole new classes of people to the promise of economic sustainability and support that a job represented. That the mills so often failed to live up to that potential was another of the disappointments of this new industrial world. Whiteness was not under attack – far from it – but work offered yet another grievance to add to the casualization of white supremacy in these years. At their most exaggerated, those frustrations might become the motive force behind a lynching.

For Black people, these tools and the thoughts about work that they occasioned were even more fraught with complicated meaning. They represented the possibility of threat inherent in the most everyday objects. Hammers might be tools of a working day, but they could also be perceived as weapons in the hands of a Black man. More likely, they could be weaponized against Black men. The restrictive symbolism of laboring tools was complicated and even contradictory, with the only outcome being that Black people imagined as workers lost out. Debates over work brought into sharp relief the activities of everyday life that African Americans were allowed to participate in and on what terms. Lynchings went even further. They marked the ability – or inability in this instance – to take a role in the activities that marked living. Racial violence was the extreme version of this, a way of literally killing people in an immediate eruption of violence. But working life in the South was a form of slow violence. It restricted working possibilities so much that it cut Black people off from the necessities of living. This too is working memory: an imagination of the past so potent and so weaponized that it failed to allow for the imagination, let alone creation, of a better world.

6

The Song

In 1966, J. E. Mainer cut a new record. A long musical career eked out of radio performances and endless touring had made him an excellent promoter, and Mainer managed to get multiple articles detailing his every effort in the local newspapers. But that wasn't enough. From October to December, he placed three versions of near-daily advertisements promoting his single. "New album by J.E. Mainar [sic]" the second of them declared. "You buy the album and you get a record of the murder of Emma Hartsell and a picture of the hanging free!"[1] Mainer was selling the lynching of Tom Johnson and Joe Kizer. His "record" (in both senses) repurposed an old ballad to revive the memory of the lynching and to prop up his claims to an authentic southern sound and image. Fans could buy the single and get an aural and visual memento of the lynching.

Ballads evoke emotion. Story songs about murdered lovers might bring up memories of your own star-crossed affair. Lyrics about a hero sailor who goes down with his ship remind listeners of their own commitments to a righteous cause. The lively melody accompanying the exploits of a badman rouses the audience to indignation before the tune resolves itself and sentences its subject to a violent end. In both lyrics and music, through both performer and audience, ballads center on an "emotional core."[2] Ballads have affective weight, an aural and experiential

---

[1] "Mainer to Cut Record Album," *The Daily Independent*, December 6, 1967; "New 45 r.p.m." *The Daily Independent*, October 27, 1967. The advertisement appeared around fifteen times starting on October 25, 1967.

[2] MacEdward Leach, *The Ballad Book* (New York: Harper & Row, 1955). I am also

resonance. These songs have a peculiar capacity to incite a deep empathic response, to allow reveling in their melodramatic emotionality. Ballads serve as a recitation of memory, desire, and secondhand actions for everyone involved in the performance. Lynching ballads capitalize on this emotion. Songs written about lynchings reduce the narrative complexity of events to an emotive invocation. They then work to perpetuate existing narratives and translate them into the easily digested, emotional reaction. In the years after the lynching of Joe Kizer and Tom Johnson, the story of their murders was fixed in narrative form, but processed, internalized, and enjoyed through song.

"The Death of Emma Hartsell" took the words of a poem about the lynching and set them to the tune of the ballad standard "Barbara Allen." Within little more than a decade, the song had spread across much of the state and entered the repertoires of many singers.[3] It reached further, into the Virginia mountains at least, by the middle 1930s. There it became part of traditional repertoires of the sort embraced by the first generation of folksong revivalists.[4] It was still remembered, though scarce in printed or sung format, nearer to its origins, where "several [older] folks have lately expressed a wish to get possession of the song of which there are but two or three copies."[5] By the time "The Death of Emma Hartsell" made its recorded debut in the 1960s, folksong was again a popular musical expression with renewed audience interest. A new folk revival saw young audiences connect to older sounds in an effort to access a past

relying here on a notion of performance as scholars in folklore and anthropology have defined it. This more formalized set of practices, particularly as they pertain to audience and performer interaction, differ somewhat from the everyday performativity that I deal with elsewhere in this book. For the foundations of this strain of theory, see Richard Bauman, "Verbal Art as Performance," *American Anthropologist* 77, no. 2 (1975): 290–311.

[3] I am grateful for the work of Bruce Baker, who wrote about this particular song in a few venues. My work differs significantly from his in placing it in the broader context of the folk revival movements, and in focusing on its performance and marketing. Baker's work was indispensable in assembling this chapter. See Bruce E. Baker, "Up Beat Down South: 'The Death of Emma Hartsell,'" *Southern Cultures* 9, no. 1 (2003): 82–91; Baker. "North Carolina Lynching Ballads."

Variant texts of the song that I consulted are printed in the *Frank C. Brown Collection*: "Death of Emma Hartsell," *The Frank C. Brown Collection of North Carolina Folklore*, Vol. 2, ed. Newman Ivey White (Durham, NC: Duke University Press, 1952): 684–688.

[4] Arthur Kyle Davis, *Folk-Songs of Virginia* (Durham, NC: Duke University Press, 1949), 277.

[5] Hawkeye, "Among Our Readers," Albemarle News and Press, February 27, 1934.

they liked better than their tumultuous present.[6] It is on this last circulation that this chapter focuses.

The social context for the performance and understanding of the ballad changed dramatically in the first seventy years of its life. Lynching was still prevalent, though it no longer possessed the official social and civic approval it had once enjoyed. Still, the narrative of the lynching as expressed through this ballad found a ready, eager audience. This was an audience newly awakened to the power of this story and its capacity for emotional invocation. The song became in this new, recorded context a sonic arbiter of authenticity. Its affective power connected it to new audiences and new contexts that, despite the temporal and geographic distance from its origins, embraced this narrative arc and its lessons about whiteness, blackness, guilt, and the South. The recorded song – its sound, its packaging, and its accompanying images – served as a material reminder of the lynching and reinforced its meaning to new audiences and in the context of new material understandings of authenticity and the South.

THE BALLAD AND HISTORIES OF RECEPTION

As the ur-folksong form, the ballad has a long history of performance and cultivation of many, varied audiences. Its roots in oral tradition are traceable to the twelfth century, at least. These earliest oral performances gave birth to the printed broadside tradition whose narrative forms similarly

---

[6] There is a vast literature on the periodic folk revivals of the 1930s and 1960s. In my estimation, many of these works suffer from being driven by fandom and nostalgia. See for instance Ronald D. Cohen, *Rainbow Quest: The Folk Music Revival and American Society, 1940–1970* (Amherst: University of Massachusetts Press, 2002) or Dick Weissman, *Which Side Are You On? An Inside Story of the Folk Music Revival in America* (New York: Continuum, 2005). A particularly good work on the 1960s revival that incorporates but also critiques fandom is Robert Cantwell, *When We Were Good: The Folk Revival* (Cambridge, MA: Harvard University Press, 1996). These books also represent different approaches to the history of revivals in the mid-twentieth century and their continuity (Cohen) versus significant change in the early 1960s (Cantwell). My reading of the evidence accords with Cantwell's, but I rely upon both here. I have also found Benjamin Filene's work particularly useful: Benjamin Filene, *Romancing the Folk: Public Memory & American Roots Music*, Cultural Studies of the United States (Chapel Hill: University of North Carolina Press, 2000). An exploration of all the scholarly literature on the topic would take up the remainder of this chapter, at least. Suffice it to say that participants in the folk revival of the 1960s in particular have been their own best documentarians and historians, producing a body of work not always analytical, but exceptionally helpful in re-creating their motives and experiences. The unevenness of books like Cohen or Weissman's makes them more useful as primary sources of the folk revival experience and opinions.

replicated the mix of history, news, and dramatic storytelling. For hundreds of years, ballads were a contemporary form that aestheticized current events and kept significant pieces of the recent past alive. Ballads were also uniquely material, constituted after the rise of print culture as both song and cheap, printed broadsides. These sensational broadside ballads were among the most prevalent and important material media in the English-speaking world well into the nineteenth century. They were both forms of record keeping and, eventually, cultural transmission.[7] For early folklore collectors in the nineteenth century, these ballads and their singers became the remnants of an ancient, nobler past. Both in England and the United States, ballad hunters sought after original, preserved texts that could offer an authentic vision of the past and the emotional lives of those living in it. Ballads carried not just stories, but tradition.[8]

The history of the ballad in America is a history of the search for authenticity. It is impossible to decouple the songs' form from those who sang them, who sought them out, who held them up as representations of race or region. As a systematized form of collecting, ballad hunting, and the late nineteenth-century discipline of folklore that encompassed it, sought after a retrograde authenticity in the mountains of the South.[9] The practice's "very logic maintained that quality folk culture was isolated in the past far from current concerns."[10] The advent of recorded technologies introduced an additional layer of irony into the thoroughly modern forms of documentation and distribution

---

[7] On the ballad and the emergence of popular cultures, see David C. Fowler, *A Literary History of the Popular Ballad* (Durham, NC: Duke University Press, 1968). Patricia Fumerton's recent book definitively catalogs the circulation of ballads and their role in constituting new, visually and materially inflected ways of regarding the world; Patricia Fumerton, *The Broadside Ballad in Early Modern England: Moving Media, Tactical Public* (Philadelphia: University of Pennsylvania Press, 2020).

[8] Ballad collecting was at the core of early folklore collecting and helped it shift from a largely literary pursuit to one based on significant fieldwork. Francis James Child, a professor at Harvard in the late nineteenth century, sought out printed ballad variants and dreamt up categorizations from his office in Cambridge. Though he was obsessed with the survival of English folksong, his interest did not extend to its performers. Cecil Sharp took Child's categories and variants and sought them out in what he regarded as the premodern wilderness of southern Appalachia. See Cecil Sharp, *English Folk Songs from the Southern Appalachians*, 2nd ed., ed. Maud Karpeles (London; New York: Oxford University Press, 1952); *English and Scottish Ballads*, ed. Francis James Child (Boston, MA: Little, Brown, 1857).

[9] David Whisnant, *All That Is Native and Fine: The Politics of Culture in an American Region* (Chapel Hill: University of North Carolina, 1983).

[10] Karl Hagstrom Miller, *Segregating Sound: Inventing Folk and Pop Music in the Age of Jim Crow* (Durham, NC: Duke University Press, 2010), 91.

of these and other folksongs being regarded as somehow out of step with the contemporary world.[11] But despite new and competing forms of entertainment, and periodic revivals of interest in folksong, ballads remained a form of ongoing concern and interest throughout the early twentieth century, long after their initial functional purpose was exhausted. As Benjamin Filene notes, their use in the years around the start of the twentieth century was to present and construct cultural signifiers of an authentic past.[12] More specifically, the songs themselves and particularly the discourses around their collection gave audiences "new ways to talk about racial and cultural authenticity" in constructing both race and region.[13] More than other forms of folksong, ballads were a signifier of practices and forms that sought to historically legitimize the racial order of Jim Crow through the imagined past and created worlds of song.

Lynching ballads were explicit in that aim. Like other cultural productions around lynching, they served to both commemorate and aestheticize the racial violence at their core. Though they were never as commonly documented as other ballads, these songs were commonplace and sung enough to survive for generations in communities across the South.[14]

And in the grand tradition of the form, they were often songs that sought to immediately sensationalize and historicize the horrific events they depicted. That mix of journalistic immediacy and reactive historicism is crucial for our understanding of lynching ballads as a form. Heard through the legitimating lens of historical removal and set to familiar melodies, these ballads turned the fury and trauma of a lynching into entertainment.

The famous folk collector Alan Lomax recorded at least one such song from the Black singer Sid Hemphill in Senatobia, Mississippi. Hemphill recalled the origins of his ballad "The Strayhorn Mob," which he created at the urging of an admitted member of the lynch mob. For at least two generations he played the song for paying customers who "like it too good" and seemed to revel in the brutal work of the mob his song

[11] Jonathan Sterne, *The Audible Past: Cultural Origins of Sound Reproduction* (Durham, NC: Duke University Press, 2003).

[12] Filene, *Romancing the Folk*.

[13] Hagstrom Miller, *Segregating Sound*, 3.

[14] See Bruce E. Baker, "Lynching Ballads in North Carolina," MA thesis, University of North Carolina Chapel Hill, 1995.

described.[15] "Mister Sam House" who commissioned the song, "Mister Norman Clayton ... [who] was in the thing too," and later his daughter, all paid Sid Hemphill to play the song at frequent intervals.[16] Their uproarious laughter as he did so suggests the continual entertainment these multiple generations took from the recollection of their memories (whether firsthand or not) of the event. It was not merely a recitation of the facts of the case but a repeated, enjoyed celebration. The antics and mistakes of the titular mob are played for laughs by Hemphill and his band. But most ballads were less comic. Their enjoyment came from hearing the often grisly details of a crime and the equally violent end for the lynching victims. This was entertainment of another sort.

This seems to be the case with lynching ballads like "The Death of Emma Hartsell." The scrupulous collectors of the North Carolina Folklore Society found at least five variations of the ballad sometime between 1913 and 1942. None is dated, though three come from a single rural county (with a fourth from the county over).[17] This implies that they were collected at the same time, likely by one passing collector. And the fact of there being so many variants within such a small range of space suggests that not only had the ballad been there long enough to have been sung many times, it was ubiquitous enough to invite variation. Given that three of the five variations were also found in a single county (Stanly), it stands to reason that the song was performed in many other places as well. Stanly County is the immediate eastern neighbor to Cabarrus and was perhaps the most demographically similar in the years of the early twentieth century.[18] The ballad's concentration here seemingly stemmed from both geographic proximity and insufficient surveying in each of North Carolina's one hundred counties. Or perhaps the song just took hold in this place, near enough to the site of the lynching that people knew the details, but far enough away that its listeners were not so immediately implicated in the violence. Either way, there was a clear desire and

---

[15] Alan Lomax, *The Land Where the Blues Began* (New York: Pantheon Books, 1993), 323. John Szwed's biography of Lomax is also particularly useful in contextualizing the racial politics of his collecting: John Szwed, *Alan Lomax: The Man Who Recorded the World* (New York: Viking, 2010).

[16] Lomax, *Land Where the Blues Began*, 323.

[17] *Frank C. Brown Collection*, Vol. 2, 685–686.

[18] Indeed, Stanly County was a similar mix of rural farmland transitioning to textile mill work, though it did have a significantly smaller Black population compared to Cabarrus (12% to 29%); US Census Bureau, Population Density, North Carolina, prepared by Social Explorer.

nostalgia for the ballad by the 1930s, when "several [older] folks have lately expressed a wish to get possession of the song."[19]

We can only speculate what the song meant to these particular audiences. As ethnomusicologist Lila Ellen Gray notes, one of the important functions of a communally shared genre like the ballad is the variation and individual response that it invites: "In the ears of one person, one musical moment might simultaneously point to multiple memories or feelings, senses of place or of history."[20] This hints at the broader purpose of lynching ballads that Lomax's documentation reveals. Its intent was to collectively invoke individual memory and serve as a celebratory retelling. "The Death of Emma Hartsell" is a more melancholy song than "The Strayhorn Mob," but that too is part of its function. It means that the audience can be sad together at the details of her murder, righteous at the entrance of the avenging mob, and reminded of their racial solidarity with the closing verse:

> And one thing more my song does lack:
> I forgot to say the men were black;
> Her friends and neighbors will say the same.
> And Emma Hartsell was her name.[21]

These lines at once gave Emma Hartsell a name and some identity, albeit solely as a victim, and rob Tom Johnson and Joe Kizer of the same. Here in its concluding lines, the main emphasis of the song is highlighted: that the lynching was the work of semi-anonymous Black men. As ballads often do, it balanced event specifics with archetypal truths. The truth of this song is one that extends from long-standing beliefs in Black criminality and guilt. Caricatured as stock figures somewhere between badman and bogeyman, Kizer and Johnson became less actual threats than symbolic folk figures. Their identity was paradoxically effaced and made more threatening through this mythic-historical distancing.[22]

The rest of the ballad is far more concerned with the actions of the anonymous mob and the detailed course of vengeance they enacted. Despite the prominence assigned here in the title, the Emma Hartsell of the ballad is little more than an archetype of untrammeled southern womanhood, referred to variously as "poor" and "sweet." The listener

[19] Hawkeye, "Among Our Readers."
[20] Lila Ellen Gray, *Fado Resounding: Affective Politics and Urban Life* (Durham, NC: Duke University Press, 2013), 6.
[21] "Death of Emma Hartsell," *The Frank C. Brown Collection*, Vol. 2, 685.
[22] On the badman figure, see Levine, *Black Culture and Black Consciousness*, 407–420.

mourns her death, but the real point is to revel at the fate reserved for "Tom and Joe" who have "gone to hell below." They are a persistent threat in the song, bogeymen who are waiting to snatch up children and whose other Black male counterparts seemingly haunt the world in search of white women and children. Parents are warned to never leave their children alone "but take them with you wherever you go/and always think of Tom and Joe."[23] In song, the narrative of the lynching became one even more structured by the extremes of good and evil. "Tom and Joe" are exemplars of evil, set against Emma Hartsell's pure light and grace. These were obvious narrative conventions that exaggerated the beliefs of the white southerners who held them. But these archetypes also expressed the deeper-seated fears of a society constructed around the valorization of whiteness and condemnation of blackness.

The same is true with later Jim Crow lynching ballads, like the story of "Gladys Kincaid/who worked in the hosiery mill." Leaving her long shift, she was "all unaware of danger/that stalked along her way." Like Emma Hartsell, she apparently lived in a world where she was under constant threat of attack from lurking Black men. Still, there are meaningful differences between the two lynching ballads. "Gladys Kincaid," written after the 1932 lynching of Broadus Miller, has fewer of the romantic flourishes of its earlier counterpart from Concord. The song is much more matter-of-fact in its statements of both threat and vengeance. Its ballad stanzas are simply a sketch of the whole story of rape and violent revenge, one people knew well from earlier, more sensational songs and stories like "The Death of Emma Hartsell." "Gladys Kincaid" was an encapsulation of both the sensational culture of the nineteenth century and the particular racial prejudices of the early twentieth. In an earlier era, it might have been a more florid and fantastical song. But its creation and performance a little more than a decade after the advent of recorded sound changed its composition significantly. It balanced the exaggerated and spectacular violence of earlier lynching ballads with a sound more rooted in everyday working life. The song was closer to portrayals of the workaday realities of the textile mill that Dave McCarn sang about in "Cotton Mill Colic" than the idyllic rural idylls of Fiddlin' John Carson's "The Little Log Cabin in the Lane." And yet, this heightened realism still saw an imagined, fantastical threat in supposedly rapacious Black men. Kincaid was "all unaware of danger/that stalked along her way." Even in

---

[23] "Death of Emma Hartsell," *The Frank C. Brown Collection*, Vol. 2, 685.

this more straightforward, unadorned ballad, Black men are represented as an impossibly omnipresent threat.[24]

Though the ballad about Kizer and Johnson's lynching seemingly remained popular well into the 1930s and the composition of "Gladys Kincaid," its oral transmission and performance are elusive. I cannot find mentions of "The Death of Emma Hartsell" either in any early recording catalogs or amid the set lists of musicians at early folk festivals. That is likely because it never entered the kind of folk repertoires that signified authenticity in either of those performance modes. Instead, it seems to have remained in circulation in the mill towns and through the Saturday-night dances of the Piedmont, ranging through the set lists of Mainer and other quasi-professional musicians who all aspired to the success of other "linthead" mill workers turned country stars.[25] These early twentieth-century decades of the song's creation and spread saw substantive changes in the perception and reception of vernacular music. What had once been a cross-racial sonic world was increasingly segregated, racialized, and repurposed into signifiers of racial identity. This happened both in the material worlds of the sonic landscape and through the new distribution channels that put those songs on vinyl, wax, and radio. These new recorded technologies were so immediately ubiquitous that the 1930 census added a question asking each household if they owned a radio set. "The Death of Emma Hartsell" then acquired an unusual signification, less a contemporary community song and instead one with its own historical meaning. When people in the 1930s "expressed a wish to get possession of the song of which there are but two or three copies," they were recognizing its scarcity and historical significance in contrast to the widely available new technologies of song.[26]

New technological innovations only helped intensify Crow. Recorded genres of music heightened the artificial distinctions of race and region and allowed the appropriation of Black sounds into white genres. The material world of the song was one that continued to aid in the spread of the

[24] "Gladys Kincaid," *The Frank C. Brown Collection*, Vol. 2, 687–688. On the wider context of mills and early recorded music, see Patrick Huber, *Linthead Stomp: The Creation of Country Music in the Piedmont South* (Chapel Hill: University of North Carolina Press, 2008).

[25] Hagstrom Miller, *Segregating Sound*; Huber, *Linthead Stomp*.

[26] Hawkeye, "Among Our Readers"; "Population Schedule," 1930 US Federal Census, www.census.gov/history/www/through_the_decades/index_of_questions/1930_1.html (accessed April 20, 2022).

now decades-old narrative of the lynching of Tom Johnson and Joe Kizer. "The Death of Emma Hartsell" remained a source of pathos and entertainment. And increasingly, it was indexed to the persistent structures of a Jim Crow society moving ever further into the realization of self-crafted narratives of racial prejudice, landscape, and sound.

THE BALLAD, AFFECTIVE DESIRE, AND JIM CROW

Everyday actions help constitute larger social structures, though the significance of even minor activities is often lost to observers and participants alike. Our every interaction exists within and performs hierarchies of power. This is most particularly true of expressive culture and the moments we see as most divergent from the world around us.[27] Even (or perhaps especially) entertainment has a relationship to hegemonic power. Music served this function in the Jim Crow South by reinforcing an artificial "sonic color line."[28] Singing, listening to, and internalizing ballads allowed white people to imagine themselves as part of a collective that was at once more tragic and heroic, more courageous, and more deeply embattled than they actually were. With lynching ballads, this performance of pleasure and pathos only served to deepen the persistent, adaptive meaning of the lynching, while further obscuring any conflicting details. "The Death of Emma Hartsell" existed in a world of sound, noise, and narratives all competing for the attention of consumers. Its clarifying purpose as a function of this sonic world was to uncritically cut through the increasingly complex understandings of lynching and serve as a bulwark against any attempt to rethink the simplified meaning of Emma Hartsell's death and the reactive lynchings of Tom Johnson and Joe Kizer. It assured the maintenance of a simplistic white supremacist narrative.

Jennifer Lynn Stoever insists that we regard Jim Crow "listening as a racialized bodily discipline."[29] Jim Crow's sensorial focus landed not just on the visual signifiers of race, but increasingly on aural difference as well. African diasporic contributions to traditional American music got

---

[27] I am relying here on writing on affect and its relationship to the everyday, in particular Kathleen Stewart *Ordinary Affects* (Durham, NC: Duke University Press, 2007).

[28] Jennifer Lynn Stoever, *The Sonic Color Line: Race, and the Cultural Politics of Listening* (New York: New York University Press, 2016).

[29] Stoever, *Sonic Color Line*, 4.

subsumed by the obliterating vagaries of genre.[30] The various technological and material impacts of the decades of Jim Crow singing, recording, and hearing added up to audible perceptibilities of racial difference that reinforced the hierarchies of the period. Music marketed to white people could sound "Black" but only to certain extents, and only when its performers were not themselves visually Black. Those material impacts – among them segregation and lynching – constituted a form of "sonic terrorism" whose broadcast was made all the easier by the adaptive technologies of recorded music, and its distribution mechanisms through the radio and record store. We can compare these auditory impacts to the other visual, perceptual, and material ones enacted for and against Black people, rendered always as bodies in need of discipline, punishment, correction. This sonic terrorism added another layer of aggression to the indignities of Jim Crow life.[31] But like lynchings themselves, music and other sonic aggressions had a dual audience on both sides of the Jim Crow color line. They could serve at once to intimidate African Americans and to entertain whites. Songs (and particularly lynching ballads) were at once repositories for white pleasure and for Black intimidation. Recall Sid Hemphill's command performance of "The Strayhorn Mob" and his white audience's mirth in its details. Even to Alan Lomax, an uncertain white ally at best, Hemphill admitted that his audiences "like it too good."[32] In that small admission there was a vast world of prejudice, coercion, and concealed fear.

The ballad form helped to create an affective material world that allowed for the development of a particular set of sonic, aesthetic categories. They reinforced both the existing narrative of the lynching and the meaning that had been made from it. Its reaching this level of cultural ubiquity and performance made it a material force amid the restrictive

[30] In particular, there is a broad literature on the banjo and its material and cultural roots in African and African American traditions. It serves as an excellent case study for the ways in which musical conventions served to erase any of these deep linkages. First in minstrel shows and then in Appalachian and "old-time" musical circles, banjo became an instrument that was intimately associated with white people and white sounds. See Cecelia Conway, *African Banjo Echoes in Appalachia: A Study of Folk Traditions*, Publications of the American Folklore Society (Knoxville: University of Tennessee Press, 1995); Dena J. Epstein, "The Folk Banjo: A Documentary History," *Ethnomusicology* 19, no. 3 (1975): 347, https://doi.org/10.2307/850790; Shlomo Pestcoe and Greg C. Adams, "Banjo Roots Research: Changing Perspectives on the Banjo's African American Origins and West African Heritage," in *Banjo Roots and Branches*, ed. Robert B. Winans, Music in American Life (Urbana: University of Illinois Press, 2018), 3–18.
[31] Stoever, *Sonic Color Line*, 184; Eric Lott, "Back Door Man: Howlin' Wolf and the Sound of Jim Crow," *American Quarterly* 66, no. 3 (2011): 704.
[32] Lomax, *Land Where the Blues Began*, 323.

white citizenship where it circulated. That circulation, more even than others chronicled in this book, has to be measured by its engagement in what one scholar of sound and affect calls "bodily ways of knowing and being in the world."[33] Ballads in particular represented a materialization of emotion, a means of performing the affective work of mourning, vengeance, and celebration that a lynching represented to white communities. Even in listening, the song invited a transhistorical participation in the crowds of people who participated in the lynching. It collapsed the distance of time and space and allowed its listeners and singers to place themselves amid the mob. The performance of the ballad was a re-creation of the emotions of the lynching in miniature, making it seem at once historical and of the present moment.[34] Amid the other sounds and noises of a region whose nineteenth-century quietude was beginning to admit the sounds of industrial work, the premise of an authentically old-fashioned ballad offered a means of sonic escape.[35] Ballads sounded like an earlier time. They had familiar melodies and song structures that built tension only to resolve it. Ballads were miniature worlds that evoked an actual past but characterized it through fairytale evocations of good and evil. First at house parties, in small performances, and eventually via recording, folk ballads offered an emotionality that blended nostalgic recall with the pleasures of an audience that reveled in the imagined past worlds of these songs. The ballad was a vehicle for nostalgia, a grasping after an imagined history translated into an emotion.[36]

This sense of the past created the ballad as a potent technology of nostalgia. In "The Death of Emma Hartsell" and other songs like it, listeners and singers both could project themselves into another place and time. In its earliest versions, the song about Kizer and Johnson's lynching referred to the local particularities of the lynching site and its surroundings. It invoked local landmarks, and included specific details derived from local newspaper accounts.[37] This early version of the ballad established not just the relationship of the performing or listening individual to the story

---

[33] Steven Feld, "Sound Worlds," in *Sound*, ed. P. Kruth and H. Stobart (Cambridge, UK: Cambridge University Press, 2000), 173.

[34] In this, I am invoking the earlier and expanded definitions of lynching explored earlier in this book, and in particular Ashraf Rushdy's "complicity model" of lynching: Rushdy, *The End of American Lynching*.

[35] Mark M. Smith, *Listening to Nineteenth Century America* (Chapel Hill: University of North Carolina Press, 2001), 13.

[36] Gray is again useful here in thinking about the affective impacts of traditional music in particular. She characterizes her own subject of study, fado, as "history ... rendered as a feeling." Gray, *Fado Resounding*, 9.

[37] Baker, "North Carolina Lynching Ballads," 223–224.

of Tom Johnson and Joe Kizer's lynching, but to the landscape of the lynching in all of its particulars.[38] As time passed and the ballad was distributed more widely, even these minor details were mostly excised in favor of a cleaner narrative arc and resolution.

J. E. Mainer's 1960s version cuts out nearly half of the original verses. By the time of his recording, the original story of the song was entangled with his projection of a rural, mountain authenticity. The place of Kizer and Johnson's lynching that he invoked was just another abstractedly southern one. Like other ballads, "The Death of Emma Hartsell" stood in for a regional authenticity and mostly placeless southernness. It signified at once the particular affective response of the individual listening to or performing it, the larger system of Jim Crow whose history it mined, and the sense of regionality that the moniker of folk ballad signified. Karl Hagstrom Miller notes that commercialized "coon songs" created a vicarious attack on Black bodies within the space of a listener's home.[39] Lynching ballads took it one step further, inserting the listener as part of the avenging mob. Violence here was more literal and bodily, and appeared without the jaunty melodies or obfuscating lyrics of minstrel show songs.

Lynching ballads brought racial violence into the white home as a product for both emotion and entertainment. When coupled with their broader regional signifiers, this created a whole world that invoked authenticity and the southern past through sonic markers. Such songs are "objects of emotion that circulate … saturated with affect" and sticky with the resonance of collective past and individual response colliding.[40] The distribution of the ballad did this work for decades. It nostalgized the lynching of Johnson and Kizer for relatively local audiences who might only vaguely recall the crime, but were nonetheless roused to fury by its invocation in song. Nearly seventy-five years later, the material and conceptual world of Jim Crow seemed to be cracking. What once seemed like fringe movements for civil rights had invaded the mainstream, with landmark court cases and legislation promising long-delayed protections for Black citizens. But amid these changes, white southern cultural power was as strong as ever. In its perceived backwardness and anti-modernity, the South represented a bulwark against larger societal changes.[41] "The

[38] Dell Upton, "Sound as Landscape," *Landscape Journal* 26, no. 1 (2007): 24–35.
[39] Hagstrom Miller, *Segregating Sound*, 43.
[40] Sara Ahmed, *The Cultural Politics of Emotion* (Edinburgh: Edinburgh University Press, 2004), 11.
[41] Zachary J. Lechner, *The South of the Mind: American Imaginings of White Southernness, 1960–1980* (Athens: University of Georgia Press, 2018).

Death of Emma Hartsell" reified the cultural basis of Jim Crow. And in
its new guise as an authentic old-time tune, it spread the justifying logic
of lynching well past its origin point, into the ears and onto the record
players of a new generation.

DISTRIBUTING JIM CROW AUTHENTICITY

By the 1960s, local memory of Tom Johnson and Joe Kizer's lynching
was fading. After the 1930s, each decade would see a brief revival of
the old story in a local newspaper, one of a familiar category of nostalgic "remember when?" stories. But the 1950s and 1960s – when
J. E. Mainer seems to have been playing the song – saw a slight shift
in how the lynching was understood in the context of challenges to Jim
Crow apartheid. Local people were beginning to rethink the meaning
of the lynching in an era where overt racism gave way to protestations
about interracial cooperation and friendship. Lynchings generally, and
this lynching particularly, were no longer easily justifiable as a category
of white supremacist rule. Instead the lynching of Johnson and Kizer
was transformed into an exceptional instance of lynching, justified by
the particulars of the crime.

   The logic of these narratives is best exemplified by a 1964 *Salisbury
Post* headline, "Even Negroes Took Part in Last Cabarrus Lynching."
The article is premised on a vision of the lynching that reads the supposed
racial harmony of the present back into the lynching of Kizer and Johnson. As I discuss in Chapter 5, this narrative relied upon invented Black
characters whose participation in the lynching characterized both its
supposed cross-racial justice and the long-standing cooperation between
Black and white residents of the county. This was a new vision of the past
in other ways as well. That same article notes that "the incident embedded so much fury and fear" in people that it lingered still, even amid
the "often spotty" remembrance of other details.[42] This is the perhaps
the clearest statement of the affective power of lynching that I have yet
encountered. It was emotionally charged, even many decades later when
its principal remainders were feelings. We might call this *memory*, with
all the omissions and erasures that label entails. But actual details of the

[42] Ned Cline, "Even Negroes Took Part in Last Cabarrus Lynching," *The Post*, November
   29, 1964.

past played little part in the perception of the lynching. As it had been with the ballad for many decades, the past was now mostly a feeling. Scholars of memory suggest that, the past is often made up of a mixture of facts misremembered, elaborated, or even invented. The ballad of Kizer and Johnson invoked the past as a series of emotions for the performer and audience to experience. This was a step farther from other invocations of memory, the creation of a past that trod the line between literal myth and historical fact.

Other contemporaneous articles made sure to draw a distinction between the current status quo and that of this imagined earlier era. A 1955 article noted that "Negroes didn't come to white people's homes back in those days."[43] As with the narrative of the African American man with the hammer in Chapter 5, newspaper accounts added additional, often dubious details. They helped preserve and enliven the narrative for an older generation who might remember it and furthered it for younger people who had only heard of it through family stories, if at all. Readers learned in the 1955 article, in details never reported beforehand, that Johnson and Kizer watched the Hartsell house for hours, before they "stealthily ... crept out of the woods" and chased Emma Hartsell around the house.[44] But they also read additional descriptive details like those of an earlier era. E. J. Linker, a young boy at the time of the lynching, noted that the men were big and powerful "with black skins."[45] Whether his observation came from firsthand experience of the men in life or death he does not say. And the article's writer, Randolph S. Hancock, similarly rearticulates some of the earlier sensationalistic language of reportage. He notes that the men were filled with "brutal strength," "hungry lust," and a kind of stealthy cunning.[46] This was both the same old linguistic tropes, and a newer form of justification that spoke to a perceived shift in relationships between Black and white residents of the county. Though no Black voices were present to justify the claims of their participation in the lynching, they were nonetheless invoked now as at once a mass of indistinguishable people, and a differentiated class with some "bad Negroes" spoiling the name of the rest.

[43] Randolph S. Hancock, "Cabarrus Had a Lynching Play," *The Daily Independent*, 1955–1956, in Emma Hartsell Lynching Scrapbook, Collection of the Eastern Cabarrus Historical Society.
[44] Hancock, "Cabarrus Had a Lynching Play."
[45] Hancock, "Cabarrus Had a Lynching Play."
[46] Hancock, "Cabarrus Had a Lynching Play."

It was a subtle shift in rhetoric, but one that met the particular needs of the era. These new articles rearticulated old tropes and ensured that the lynching remained part of local consciousness and feeling, if not an officially recognized part of its past.

These local changes were set among larger trends that renewed a national interest in the lynching and its cultural productions. Amid the turmoil of the late 1950s and 1960s, there was a revival of folksongs and folkways. A young generation not raised on old-time traditional music found the playing, hearing, and collecting of this music outlets for their longings for an authentic cultural self. The mainstreaming of this music was carried out through a huge number of artists. There were slick but faithful performers of old standards like the Kingston Trio, interpreters and adapters of folksong forms like Bob Dylan, and then the old-time players that these younger musicians sought to emulate. J. E. Mainer fits into this last category as a performer who had spent his whole career selling himself as one of the last purveyors of the old-time mountain music. He found his late-career audience in the most ardent of these new folk music fans.

As Robert Cantwell notes, this generation sought out authenticity in both folk music and folk musicians. New fans went so far as "to dress, groom, speak, comport themselves, and even attempt to think in ways they believed compatible with the rural, ethnic proletarian."[47] Most of these young people were content to listen to recordings, collect records, and style themselves after their new heroes. The more intrepid (and often wealthier) few might trek to the Newport Folk Festival and see their idols on stage. And the most dedicated fringes of this new revival were a group of collector-musicians who heroized the collecting Lomaxes as much as the musicians, and sought out "the old, weird America" of early recorded folksongs.[48] These (mostly white, mostly) men sought out old recordings and the people who made them. Striving to emulate both the musicians and their earlier collectors, they ventured again into thrift stores and warehouses, and then the hills, hollows, and clubs, in a re-creation of earlier collectors and an embodiment of tropes about the location of

---

[47] Cantwell, *When We Were Good*, 2.

[48] Greil Marcus, *The Old Weird America: The World of Bob Dylan's Basement Tapes* (New York: Picador, 2001). Though Marcus is referring specifically to Harry Smith's *Anthology of American Folk Music*, his phrase represents the broader world of this music and the role of anthologies like it in serving as the inspiration for a new generation of collectors.

authenticity. The South, an imagined, primitive, mythic place, was their lodestar. Like previous generations, they invested the region with an originary cultural power. And like some of their most intrepid progenitors, they sought out this authenticity firsthand.

That quest differentiated these new fans from their predecessors of the previous two decades. From the 1930s to the mid-1950s, folk music fandom was linked to leftist politics of the Popular Front, trade unionism, or similar movements. The revivalists of the 1960s rejected those institutions and their ideologies. As collector and musician John Cohen noted in a frequently cited defense of his contemporaries, "our emphasis is no longer on social reform" but instead on a "search for real and human values."[49] They found those values in places unfamiliar to them. The backroads, mountain woods, or even more apparently ordinary places of the South seemed to allow them access to a deep well of authenticity. In summarizing Cohen's recollections during an interview, the historian Scott L. Matthews notes the collector's awe at hearing Flatt and Scruggs on a radio outside a gas station in Virginia. Even this most routine encounter was enough for him to feel "close to the source" of the music and feelings he had spent so much time seeking out on records.[50]

Uniting each of these wings of folk revivalism – the popular and the underground – was a focus on the people and places of authenticity. For this new group of old-time collectors, musicians, and eventually distributors, the value of authenticity was their chief inspiration and organizing principle. This was the world inhabited and created by this new generation of revivalists, people like John Cohen and Chris Strachwitz, outsiders to the South but fascinated by its cultural roots as expressed in traditional music. As they evolved from fans into active promoters of these sounds, they departed from an earlier generation of folklorist-collectors and sought after the people who produced this music, marking them as survivals of a sort too, rather than simply vessels for the music. Some performers might have remained shy and retiring, but many fit the mold of Concord's J. E. Mainer. He cannily understood his changing audience and the necessity to perform a vision of authenticity

[49] John Cohen, "In Defense of City Folksingers," *Sing Out!* 9 (1959), quoted in Cantwell, *When We Were Good.* Cohen's article assumed centrality as a defense of the new revivalists. For broader context, see Mikiko Tachi, "Commercialism, Counterculture, and the Folk Music Revival: A Study of Sing Out! Magazine, 1950–1967," *Japanese Journal of American Studies* 15 (2004): 187–211.
[50] Scott L. Matthews, interview with John Cohen, undated, quoted in Matthews, *Capturing the South,* 118.

that would play well with his young audiences outside the South. Mainer cultivated this image for decades, but the crowning example of it was his recording his own version of "The Death of Emma Hartsell" and reclaiming its meaning for the purposes of cultivating his new audience.

J. E. MAINER AND THE SELLING OF SOUTHERN AUTHENTICITY

Joseph Emmett Mainer was born around Weaverville, North Carolina, in July 1898, making him an almost exact contemporary of the lynching of Tom Johnson and Joe Kizer.[51] Like many other rural mountain families, Mainer's moved to so-called public work in the burgeoning mill towns of the Carolina Piedmont when he was a child. Mainer first worked as a doffer at Glendale Mill in Spartanburg, before crossing back over the state line and settling in Concord as a young man.[52] He worked frequently in the mills there for spells, though he tried to make his living both on the local dance circuits and through radio gigs, recording, and festivals.[53] He played his music at WBT in Charlotte in the early 1930s, and at XERA, the famous strong-signal radio station on the Texas–Mexico border, in the late 1930s, and was "continuously active through the forties and fifties" trying to make a living.[54] Mainer's initial recorded output was full of early tropes of recorded country music. Songs like "Maple on the Hill" or "Where the Red, Red Roses Grow" represented the pervasive nostalgia for rural life that drew so many new town dwellers in the 1920s and 1930s to Mainer and his more famous contemporaries like Charlie Poole.[55]

But Mainer's reputation came from his live show. Unsurprisingly, his performance style was built on the persistent tropes of blackface minstrelsy. Like performers for a century or more, Mainer had a repertoire largely comprising crude attempts at imitating Black cultures and sounds. One well-advertised local affair in Sumter, South Carolina, saw Mainer and his band perform a dialect show, "Sambo and Liza Goes to Court."

[51] J. E. Mainer, "J.E. Mainer of Concord, North Carolina," *Sing Out!* 18, no. 1 (1968): 22–27.
[52] Mainer, "J.E. Mainer of Concord, North Carolina."
[53] Ivan M. Tribe, Liner Notes, *J.E. Mainer at Home (With Friends and Family)*, Vol. 1, Old Homestead Records, 1983, Southern Folklife Collection, Wilson Library, University of North Carolina at Chapel Hill.
[54] Tribe, Liner notes; Marvin Eury, "Mountain Music Man." *The Daily Independent*, April 23, 1967, sec. C.
[55] "New Bluebird Records," *Kingsport Times*, April 9, 1936, 9.

Though no accounts of this fundraiser for the "Ladies Missionary Society of Broad St. Methodist Church" survive, it seems likely that the performers donned blackface. It would perhaps have been more notable if they did not.[56] Certainly, Mainer and his band styled themselves after minstrelsy in their performances. One account of a Charlotte concert in 1935 notes that the band "fiddled and strummed and sung and also clowned like noody's [sic] business."[57] Whether the band was in blackface or not, these performance tropes clearly evoked the world of the minstrel show. A century old by Mainer's 1930s touring, it was both a popular and immediately recognizable style of performance, despite having moved away from its centrality as the most popular of American entertainments. It persisted in venues like the ones Mainer played, and in the sound of bands like his who combined older folk forms with their earliest commercial adaptations of the minstrel show. Blackface eventually went away, but Black sound was persistent and adaptable.[58]

Mainer went on to record numerous dialect songs in his prolific recording career.[59] At least part of his professional identity was built on this exploitation of caricatured and dehumanized blackness. He was hardly alone in these efforts. The transformation of blackface during the twentieth century was in large part to obscure its avowedly racist origins by subtracting the most visually racist elements of the practice.[60] What remained was the sound and style without the visual evocation of stereotyped blackness. It allowed again for the consumption of Black culture in avowedly white supremacist formations and, especially, under the guise

[56] "Presenting J.E. Mainer's Crazy Mountaineers," *The Item*, July 22, 1938.

[57] "The Wayside Mailbox," *The Charlotte Observer*, February 18, 1935, 16.

[58] See Cantwell, *When We Were Good*, 24–26, on the persistence of minstrelsy both in rural places and as part of folk traditions. A broader exploration of the topic is Rhae Lynn Barnes, "Darkology: The Hidden History of Amateur Blackface Minstrelsy and the Making of Modern America, 1860–1970," PhD dissertation, Harvard University, Graduate School of Arts & Sciences, 2016. The earliest origins of minstrelsy and African American culture's prevalence more generally are well documented in Roger D. Abrahams, *Singing the Master: The Emergence of Afro-American Culture on the Southern Plantation* (New York: Pantheon Books, 1992).

[59] Indeed, one of his earliest recordings was a minstrel tune in dialect. That song, "Watermelon on the Vine," was only the most overtly stereotypical and earliest of the minstrel and dialect songs that he recorded. J.E. Mainer's Mountaineers, "Watermelon on the Vine/Johnson's Old Grey Mule," Bluebird Records, October 7, 1936, *Discogs*, www.discogs.com/J-E-Mainers-Mountaineers-Watermelon-On-The-Vine-Johnsons-Old-Grey-Mule/release/9357492 (accessed September 2, 2020).

[60] Eric Lott, *Love and Theft: Blackface Minstrelsy and the American Working Class* (New York: Oxford University Press, 1993).

of a Jim Crow authenticity. Mainer mined the sounds of the mountains and the minstrel show alike, all under the guise of a genuine rural persona. He made himself into a figure emblematic of the sound and image of a deracinated, paradoxically placeless South.

Mainer's carefully honed sound and image finally paid off in the last decade of his life. From 1961 through 1972, folk revivalist labels helped him put out a slew of releases.[61] His fame never translated to the kind of crossover appeal of earlier old-time turned country performers, but at least in the estimation of his admirers, he led "one of the best loved string bands."[62] It was amid this resurgence of a nearly four-decade career that Mainer recorded and laid claim to what he variously called the "Song of Emma Hartsell" or "The Story of Emmer Hartsell."[63]

Mainer's version of the song opens with a brief spoken introduction where he addresses his audience: "friends I'm gonna tell you a story about Emma Hartsell who was murdered between Concord and Charlotte."[64] Never minding his muddled geography, his invocation makes the song about Hartsell, rather than Johnson and Kizer, and places it outside of any specific time in the past. Then, to a variant of the tune to the folk standby "Barbara Allen," he recites almost verbatim lyrics from the long-circulating "Death of Emma Hartsell." His version leaves out a few of the minor details of earlier documented versions, particularly the references to the specific place of Cold Water that Bruce Baker identifies in his study. But this is probably due to variations over time as much as any authorial intent. The ballad, the narrative it presents, even its tune are all repurposed from earlier cultural circulations. Much more interesting is the fact that Mainer claims authorship of the ballad, even going so far as to claim copyright in his songbook from around the same time. There he claims that "this was written by J.E. Mainer

---

[61] These started with the release of an LP for King Records in 1961, for Arhoolie in 1962, and then a sixteen-volume set for Rural Rhythm throughout the decade.

[62] Chris A. Strachwitz, "J.E. Mainer's Mountaineers," in *Songs as Sung by J.E. Mainer and His Mountaineers*, ed. J. E. Mainer (Concord, NC: self-published, date unknown), in the collection of the author.

[63] The former title appears in his self-published songbook, *Songs as Sung by J.E. Mainer and His Mountaineers*; the former is the title given on one recording of the song from 1966: J.E. Mainer and His Mountaineers, "Julie Ann/The Story of Emmer Hartsell," Blue Jay Records, Salisbury, NC 1966. He also apparently self-released the song on a 45 single with the title "The Murder of Emma Hartsell," as documented in the front of his previously cited songbook. I have not been able to locate a surviving copy of that release.

[64] J.E. Mainer and His Mountaineers, "Julie Ann/The Story of Emmer Hartsell," Blue Jay Records, Salisbury, NC, 1966, 45 rpm single, in the collection of the author.

and is Copywritten."⁶⁵ He even adds a brief commentary on the song: "Crime doesn't pay."⁶⁶ In this whole pamphlet, a collection purporting to be a comprehensive catalog of Mainer's songs, this is the only additional commentary on a song, and the only song to bear a legal claim to authorship.⁶⁷ Mainer's claims to the song are bolstered by his including a photograph of the lynching in his booklet. Like the supposed copyright, this authenticates his claim to the distribution of not just the song, but the story of the lynching. For Mainer it is a straightforward narrative of murder and justice, and an easy song and message to lay claim to. His purported authorship allows him to add another song to his repertoire, and to further establish a public reputation in keeping with the highly cultivated image he created and maintained in these years.

That persona was clear in his 1960s-era recordings, and in the variety of authenticating testimonials he sought from the folk revivalists then becoming interested in his music. He had seemingly always had a flair for self-promotion, a necessary characteristic for a mill worker–musician working the radio and dance circuits. He intensified that impulse in this latter stage of his career. For his Arhoolie debut in 1963, he and his band were billed on the front cover as "the Legendary Family from the Blue Ridge Mountains."⁶⁸ This was despite the fact that he had not lived in those or any mountains for forty years, and the family referred to were his children, all born in Concord or other mill towns.⁶⁹ In that same release, his new friend and promoter Chris Strachwitz further emphasizes

⁶⁵ J. E. Mainer, "Song of Emma Hartsell," in *Songs as Sung by J.E. Mainer and His Mountaineers*, in the collection of the author.
⁶⁶ J. E. Mainer, "Song of Emma Hartsell."
⁶⁷ I can find no evidence that Mainer actually filed a copyright to the song, though it's possible that he did. He claims authorship over a handful of other songs in the book, but never to the extent of seeking copyright.
⁶⁸ J.E. Mainer's Mountaineers, ["The Legendary Family from the Blue Ridge Mountains"], Berkeley, CA: Arhoolie, 1963, in the Southern Folklife Collection, Louis Round Wilson Special Collections Library, University of North Carolina at Chapel Hill.
⁶⁹ Unsurprisingly, biographical materials written by record promoters are less forthcoming about Mainer's Blue Ridge residency than even the typically fawning journalistic coverage he received. Marvin Eury's "Mountain Music Man" is the most comprehensive biographical portrait of Mainer, though it suffers from some awe at his many accomplishments and strong personality. The last census showing J. E. Mainer living in what can be considered the mountains is 1920, when he was living in Buncombe County, outside of Asheville, North Carolina, and, according to Eury, working in a mill to help his father financially. Emmitt Mayner, 1920 Federal Census, Buncombe County, North Carolina, digital image, Ancestry.com, 1940, shows Mainer married and his children, ranging from three to sixteen years old, living with him and his wife Sadie at Poplar Tent

Mainer's authentic, rural, mountain roots. He let the reader know that Mainer "has made a living playing his fiddle but life hasn't always been so pleasant." He was "born in a one room country shack," and struggled to build a reputation and make a living from those humble origins.[70] Strachwitz was calling on old tropes used by promoters from the very beginnings of recorded music. Polk Brockman made the virulent racist Fiddlin' John Carson arguably the earliest recording star by capitalizing on rural identity and nostalgia. Carson was not the first recorded country music artist, but he was certainly its earliest success story. The genius of early country music lay with promoters like Brockman and Ralph Peer, who managed to commercialize regional and rural longing in their marketing of an old sound. Carson was adept at playing the character and capitalizing on the promotional opportunities of radio, records, and live shows. From the beginning, then, the old-time sound was a product of commercial expectations and a creation of consumer demand. The new generation of fans and promoters coming of age in the 1950s and 1960s were no less canny, though they resisted the label "commercial."[71]

J. E. Mainer's genius lay in recognizing this longtime trend and, like his predecessor Carson, playing to expectations. His career, particularly in the 1960s, was an active process of authentication with eager collaborators bent on preserving the old-time sound. Mainer clearly understood creating authentic sounds as a larger cultural process. He went out of his way to present himself as the real thing, and to aid the new revivalists in telling his story in the broad tropes of the authentic mountain musician.

Besides his identification as a Blue Ridge musician, the record cover photographs made in the last decade of his life show a musician who understands new perceptions of himself, but is still slightly invested in the image of the slick, professional performer. Take for instance *The*

outside of Concord. Sadie was employed as a spinner, and each of the family members alive in 1935 had been at the same location then. Finally, Sadie and J. E.'s middle child Carolyn noted in her social security application that she had been born in Concord in 1930; Carolyn Maxine Mainer US Social Security Applications and Claims Index, digital image, Ancestry.com. All available evidence suggests that the family was rooted in Cabarrus County and its textile economy for decades.

70 Chris Strachwitz, Liner notes, J.E. Mainer's Mountaineers, ["The Legendary Family from the Blue Ridge Mountains"], Berkeley, California: Arhoolie, 1963, in the Southern Folklife Collection, Louis Round Wilson Special Collections Library, University of North Carolina at Chapel Hill.

71 Richard A. Peterson, *Creating Country Music: Fabricating Authenticity* (Chicago: University of Chicago Press, 1997), 12–32; Bill C. Malone and Jocelyn C. Neal, *Country Music, U.S.A.*, 3rd rev. ed. (Austin: University of Texas Press, 2010), 33–36.

Legendary J.E. Mainer, the eighth volume in his series of releases for Rural Rhythm. The cover focuses on Mainer in the foreground. He's older and a little haggard looking and wearing a cuffed, brand-new pair of overalls. He's posed just slightly on his heels, grabbing at his waist where a gun would be. Mainer is clearly in a barn, and there are fresh bales of straw immediately behind him. It all projects a particular kind of rural signifying, not necessarily that of a musician so much as a relatively prosperous farmer. Mainer throws a wrench into this image with an incongruous scene partner. Also in the background is a much younger woman with teased blonde hair and tight clothes. She's looking at his back coyly while hugging a post, turning her body in profile toward the camera (Figure 6.1). Mainer used this kind of imagery on other covers like *The Fiddle Music of J.E. Mainer and the Mountaineers* (Rural Rhythm Volume 19) or *The Legendary J.E. Mainer and the Mountaineers with Morris Herbert* (Rural Rhythm Volume 16).[72] The former featured an elderly Mainer (in the last year or two of his life) posing as if playing a fiddle against a log cabin while another blonde woman in bathing suit top faces him, profile to the camera.

The album billed with Morris Herbert shows a sickly, elderly Mainer with Herbert and another musician. They are outside at a modest house – likely Mainer's on the outskirts of Concord – with their instruments and an array of carpentry tools laid out on sawhorses in the yard. The notes on the back are penned by the self-styled "Uncle" Jim O'Neal, founder of Rural Rhythm. He invokes the stereotypes of Mainer and mountain music, claiming that "'bout the only pleasure them mountain folks ever knew was moonshine makin', huntin', romancing', praising the Lord and playing mountain music which was great."[73] Each of these records represents the contradictory persona of Mainer. He was a thoroughly modern musician who lived in an urban place and cultivated his reputation through whatever technological and social networks he could bend to his own interests. But at the same time, like other country and old-time

[72] J. E. Mainer, The Fiddle Music of J.E. Mainer and the Mountaineers, Vol. 19 (Arcadia, CA: Rural Rhythm, 1972), Southern Folklife Collection, Wilson Special Collections Library, University of North Carolina at Chapel Hill; J. E. Mainer, J.E. Mainer and the Mountaineers with Morris Herbert, Vol. 16 (Arcadia, CA: Rural Rhythm, 1972), Southern Folklife Collection, Wilson Special Collections Library, University of North Carolina at Chapel Hill.

[73] "The Legendary J.E. Mainer and the Mountaineers with Morris Herbert, Vol 16," Rural Rhythm, 1972, in the Southern Folklife Collection, Louis Round Wilson Special Collections Library, University of North Carolina at Chapel Hill.

FIGURE 6.1 Cover art from *The Legendary J.E. Mainer*, 8th volume, Rural Rhythm

musicians, that reputation and much of his income came from playing to ideas of rurality and backwardness. That kind of *authentic modernity* was central to the folk revival of the 1960s. The seeming contradiction of that phrase best represents the constant creation of structures of authenticity in the period. Like the notion of modernity, authenticity was one to be policed and defined frequently. Neither label was a given. Authenticity was determined in large part by sonic, visual, spoken, and written signifiers.[74] Mainer was a master of cultivating each one of these

[74] I am relying here on literature on both authenticity and modernity. In particular see Bruno Latour. *We Have Never Been Modern*, trans. Catherine Porter (Cambridge, MA: Harvard University Press, 1993); Miles Orvell, *The Real Thing: Imitation and Authenticity in American Culture, 1880–1940* (Chapel Hill: University of North Carolina Press, 1989).

cultural forms. Indeed, particularly with "The Death of Emma Hart-sell," he helped push this new generational embrace of authentic culture past broad rural signifiers and into the specifics of racial violence and white supremacy.

As I have suggested above, this was a generation primed for a deeper authenticity, and who prided themselves on not being fooled by slick marketing or image creation. Eschewing the explicitly leftist politics of earlier revivals, Cohen and his cohort "were putting our stamp of approval on these white guys who until that time had been stereotyped as racists, lynchers, and all these nightmarish things about the South."[75] On one hand, Cohen's intention was to resist the kind of caricatures of white southernness that had grown up in the several decades prior to the 1960s. But he and other revivalists also willfully ignored and even embraced those same characteristics in Mainer, who recorded minstrel songs for them and who forthrightly embraced racism, lynching, and other "nightmarish" things about the South.

When Cohen and Mainer first got in touch, Mainer was in the middle of a career revival. After a 1961 release on King Records, the new label Arhoolie put out a Mainer release in 1962. Mainer was fully enmeshed in these revivalist circles by the time that he contacted John Cohen in 1968. Cohen promptly published their correspondence in the movement's paper of record, *Sing Out!* There Mainer pitched his bona fides and launched a plan to "have a songbook printed with 30 songs in it," funded by Cohen and sold by each of the two men. The books represented the first foray in their partnership, one that would help Cohen stay on the map of his fellow revivalists and bring Mainer both a new audience and more money. Though there's little private correspondence – Cohen effectively published verbatim the first letter the two exchanged – both men seem to have recognized the other as a worthwhile and equal partner in their dual authenticating project.[76] Perhaps surprisingly, they looked to lynching as the means to help prove their bona fides to this new audience. But they were following in a long pattern of cultural usage of both the

---

[75] Cohen quoted in Matthews, *Capturing the South*, 116.

[76] As of the writing of this book, John Cohen's personal correspondence and other materials have been donated to the American Folklife Center at the Library of Congress. Due to the conditions of writing this book during a pandemic, I was not able to visit the collection. Assistance from the archivists there suggests that there were not other copies of correspondence between the two men.

lynching and the ballad written about it. As I have noted elsewhere in this book, the lynching was long used as a symbol of local, state, and regional identity. Mainer and his collaborators collapsed these identities into the persona of J. E. Mainer, mountain musician and defender of the white South.

Mainer and Cohen likely corresponded in greater depth about the proposed publication of the former's songbook. Though those letters were not published, evidently the two worked out a plan for publication. If Cohen's professed lack of remuneration and Mainer's promotional flair are any indication, Cohen likely footed the bill and offered his voice to the homegrown publication. Indeed, Cohen's standard defense against any criticism was the penurious nature of the work that he undertook. Throughout his career, he put pen to paper to defend himself against charges of exploitation. By his logic, his motives were pure because they were not avowedly commercial (or at least his attempts at commercialization failed). In place of dollars, Cohen's currency was authenticity. This is important for the larger understanding of folk revivalism and authenticity. For Cohen, an Ivy league–educated son of upper-middle-class parents, an unsuccessful record release only allowed him to be closer to the rural poverty that he and others of his generation romanticized. This was important to the images they crafted for themselves and for the artists that they worked with. Cohen and Mainer were an excellent pair, equally adept at promotion.[77]

In the first paragraphs of Mainer's songbook, Cohen writes a laudatory introduction, calling the Concord fiddler "one of the best in music." The rest of his description relies on familiar tropes of Mainer as "an honest to goodness musician to the old timey music," with multiple mentions of his Blue Ridge provenance and the authenticity implied by it. More interesting is the second paragraph, where Cohen turns to a full-scale marketing of Mainer and his music. The first product on offer is a 45 rpm single with Mainer's original Dave McCarn copy "Hard Times in a Cotton Mill" on one side and "Train No. III" on the B-side. Cohen passes by this record quickly, moving onto and repeatedly mentioning the other single on offer, "another 45 rpm with 'The Murder of Emma Hartsell' on it." The main selling point of this is seemingly that with

---

[77] See for instance John Cohen, "A Visitor's Recollections," in *Long Journey Home: Folklife in the South* (Chapel Hill: Southern Exposure, 1977), 115–118. Here he mentions repeatedly how few copies his records sold and how little money they made him.

it "you will receive a picture of the hanging of Tom and Joe, the two negroes who killed her." Cohen goes on to specify various configurations of records that you might buy from Mainer, either at his "record shop" in Concord (a small cinderblock building in back of his house) or by mail from either man. Any purchase you make came with "the small one free and a picture of the hanging of Tom and Joe." In the eyes of both Mainer and Cohen, this is clearly a major selling point. You get not only the single – one that Mainer kept claiming as his own – but a lynching photograph that represented an added visual authenticity to the sonic one of his recordings. Here, visual and aural authenticity worked in tandem as portals to the past. The listener and viewer could re-create in their own homes the experience of being in the crowd at the lynching, of plucking a souvenir from the scene.

For Cohen and the customer base he helped cultivate for Mainer, this kind of object authenticity, a physical image you could hold and regard, was a unique representation of the broader cultural basis that they were so eager to collect and channel through the music. Cohen himself had a long relationship with this sort of authenticating objecthood, writing in his earliest visits to the South of attempts to "experience Appalachian music first hand."[78] He found that, apparently, amid even the most cursory experiences of the landscape, like hearing Flatt and Scruggs blasting from a car radio at a gas station in Virginia.[79] Though Cohen eventually became an experienced documentarian of the region and its culture, he still maintained many similarly totalizing totems of the culture under his scrutiny. He writes of a particular photo as a "talisman image," evoking a fuller perception of the real and otherwise inexpressible.[80] So this kind of fixation on the lynching photograph was not unexpected. Revivalists sought the sound of an older South. The 45 was a way of mediating that sound, confining it to a tenuously modern format that allowed for a briefly transporting experience. But combined with the image, this well-circulated marker of white southern culture, it might allow its consumer to imagine themselves as more fully immersed in the society that they were so fascinated with. Likely many of them did not display or even look at the lynching photograph. Its talismanic properties were enough. But this circulation and possession of the image were authentic in other ways too. They replicated the collecting processes of an earlier generation, and put

[78] John Cohen, *There Is No Eye* (New York: PowerHouse, 2002), 25.
[79] Cohen, "A Visitor's Recollections."
[80] Matthews, *Capturing the South*, 133.

these young, largely northern consumers into a well-established pattern of meaning making from the remainders of Tom Johnson and Joe Kizer's murders.

To be sure, J. E. Mainer had been an earlier audience for this same photograph. Made in the year of his birth some 150 miles distant, the photograph undoubtedly was a later acquisition. Mainer probably procured his copy as a young man playing at house parties in mill villages. Its titillating content could serve as a kind of wink and nod of white insiderness, one that Mainer projected to his new, young audience decades later when he distributed it as well. His reproduction of the image does not bear any printer's marks, so it's possible that it was not a commercially produced image. More likely, he obscured the photographer's marks altogether, an act that made it for his audience too a kind of shibboleth for entrance into a club of onlooking consumers. His is the most widely distributed of the surviving copies, but others were collected and preserved as well. One such, brought by a family named the Browns when they moved to Indiana, suggests both its local and national circulations. Before they moved west, the Browns lived in nearby High Point and bought the photograph from Z. E. Scott.[81] Whether they purchased it at his shop over Marsh's Drugstore on Union Street, or at one of the many stops this early itinerant photographer made across the region, they invested enough in the reproduction financially and emotionally to bring it across the country and keep it in the family for the next century.[82] Certainly by 1989, when a local college student wrote a report on Emma Hartsell's death, copies of the photograph extant locally. Her copy came courtesy of "Mrs. Ira Dayvault," suggesting both that she knew enough to inquire about the lynching and that there were enough people preserving the contours of its narrative to fill her ten amply illustrated pages.[83] That this grisly image could be included in a college term paper suggests too the ubiquity and everydayness of both the lynching narrative and its objects. For locals, it was a piece of "the historical record" and local lore.[84] But the folk revival

[81] Steven E. Keefer to Kathryn L. Bridges, April 7, 1994, Local History Room, Cannon Memorial Library, Cabarrus County Libraries.

[82] Entry for Z. E. Scott, *Directory of Concord, North Carolina*, Charlotte: The Interstate Directory Company, 1902; "Short Locals," *Daily Concord Standard*, November 7, 1898; "Personal Pointers," *Daily Concord Standard*, October 17, 1898.

[83] Rebecca Jones, "The Murder of Emma Hartsell," Local History Room, Canon Memorial Library, Cabarrus County Libraries.

[84] Jones, "The Murder of Emma Hartsell."

audience could regard it with fresh eyes. For those buying it from Cohen in New York or via mail from Mainer, the song and image together were the strongest material reminder of the lynching and the one that traveled the farthest from its origins. This combined sonic and visual material created, if not a new narrative, a new means of distributing and understanding it. Its centrality and inextricability from the pitching of Mainer's music and Mainer's persona suggested how closely lynching had come to be associated with southernness and southernness with whiteness.

Cohen was more explicit in that regard than Mainer, and more carefully policed those boundaries. Witness his comment cited earlier: "we were putting our stamp of approval on these white guys who until that time had been stereotyped as racists, lynchers, and all these nightmarish things about the South." He was invested in recuperating and defending southern white men in particular, not just folk singers. Mainer seemingly felt no such compunction, perhaps because he knew that despite old stereotypes, he and his kind were still among the most admired and protected of American classes. Historian Zachary Lechner suggests as much, noting that even amid the white southern reprisals against Black freedom struggles in the period, white southern men were still simultaneous exemplars of both rural backwardness and a liberated, authentic sense of self.[85] Mainer's genius was in understanding this desirous complexity and profiting from it. He projected it in the image he cultivated, and the songs he recorded. We need look no further than the dialect and minstrel show songs that he recorded during his prolific output in the last years of his life. On 1968's *The Legendary J.E. Mainer, Volume 5*, he includes both the mock-spiritual minstrel tune "Jordan Am A Hard Road to Travel," and his slightly cleaned-up version of The Skillet Lickers' "N*gger in the Wood Pile." Both of these songs remained staples of his legacy career long after his death. They were included on the twenty-song retrospective of his career released on Rural Rhythm in 1998. This is yet another example of the less overt racism of the late Jim Crow period, where the visual and linguistic markers of the more openly violent earlier years were masked by niceties and substitutions.[86]

---

[85] Lechner, *The South of the Mind*.
[86] J. E. Mainer, *The Legendary J.E. Mainer*, Vol. 5, 33 rpm (Nashville, TN: Rural Rhythm, 1968), Southern Folklife Collection, Louis Round Wilson Special Collections Library, University of North Carolina at Chapel Hill. Mainer's version of the profane early hillbilly tune is cleaned up to "Man in the Wood Pile," though in melody and lyrics it is otherwise nearly identical; J. E. Mainer and the Mountaineers, *Twenty Old Time Favorites* (Nashville, TN: Rural Rhythm, 1998), in the possession of the author.

Mainer knew that white singers had built much of their popularity on the sites and sounds of minstrelized Black identity. By the 1960s, blackface was less acceptable in even the underground commercial worlds Mainer was distributed in. But the *sound* of Black voices was more popular than ever. In the most popular rock and roll acts from Britain, or the most obscure folk performers from the Piedmont, musicians were adapting Black sounds and styles to enormous acclaim and significant amounts of money. Mainer was one of many thousands of white men in a variety of genres who profited from their articulation of those long silenced and marginalized voices. This was a transformation both conscious and largely unacknowledged. We have to view his recording, promotion, and distribution of the Concord lynching ballad and its accompanying photograph in this light. Americans had not lost their taste for the violence of southern portrayals of Black life. Mainer trafficked in both the demeaning caricatures of Black actions, and the sonic, visual, and material invocations of their torture and death.

The more salient issue here is not this rearticulation of old forms of racism as entertainment. Minstrelsy presented as a realistic portrayal of southern life had a long history by the mid-1960s. Mainer's use of the ballad's recording and imagery had a different functionality. It showed not only that the savagery and cruelty of the white supremacist South was in full force, but that it had come to be embraced as a representation of the region and its people. It's not that Cohen and others intended to recuperate southern white masculinity as something other than racist and backward, but that they embraced and presented it partially *because of* those flaws. In Mainer's era, the region was slowly eking toward progress through the sustained efforts of Black activists. During the seven decades since the murders of Johnson and Kizer, activists throughout the nation had remained committed to what had seemed like a lost cause of civil and human rights.

Their incremental progress was countered by the further and continued spread of lynching as a tool for both terror and the building of white community. Through the efforts of activists like Ida B. Wells Barnett, lynching had decreased in scope and frequency since its height around the years when Johnson and Kizer were killed. But it never really stopped as a practice.[87] And its presence in material form was even more prominent. Lynching's material culture changed in meaning and form, but persisted as public displays of exclusionary visions of the past.

---

[87] Rushdy, *The End of American Lynching*.

Conclusion

Archival Remains

The material culture of Tom Johnson and Joe Kizer's lynching circulated throughout the landscapes of the twentieth-century South. Transferred from person to person, these things had an outsized impact on the way people understood not only lynching, but their own place within the larger racialized hierarchy of Jim Crow society. The gradual evolution in meaning of these objects that began when they were first transformed into things of resonance and value continued throughout the following decades. Alongside that shift came a larger cultural evolution in the meanings of lynching. Ida B. Wells, Walter White, and a myriad of others completely transformed public discourse, making lynching a furtive, secretive practice rather than the public spectacle it had long been. Few people with mainstream opinions would outright defend lynching as an effective and necessary practice.

And yet, this material culture persisted, still circulated and preserved. My focus to this point in the book has been on the public lives of these objects. Even at times when the lynching seemed by many outward appearances to have been forgotten, I have argued that its material remains kept the lynching of Tom Johnson, Joe Kizer, and many thousands of other lynching victims an active presence in a variety of public spheres. But those public faces concealed more secret histories. Some of the objects related to lynching were things hidden, lost, or forgotten. In private hands, they might be the inherited legacy of an earlier generation, illegible, unknown, or even shameful to their recipients. Eventually, these private objects began again to enter more fully into the public realm. As donations to archives and museums, they were transmuted into *historical objects*, things that were meant to inform their users about the racial violence of the past. But this institutionalized historicity did not eliminate the many other pasts of these objects.

By way of concluding this book, I want to further explore that process of historicization. The remainder of this chapter will focus on the historical objectification of lynching objects. I ask how objects of lynching became the materials of history, and how historians and other consumers of the past understand lynchings through their material culture in the context of institutional archival and museum collections. What pasts do we produce from things recontextualized by their accession into institutionalized collections? And how do these histories persist amid continued violence and disregard for Black lives? What happens when decades of accrued meaning are decontextualized for inclusion in a museum collection? Do those narratives remain attached to the object, or does this new setting somehow obliterate them? And, perhaps most crucially, how do we as researchers, visitors, and new kinds of consumers encounter and understand these objects and images?

Objects of racial violence have power as a form of witness. In archives and through their studied application, that power can be put to use not just to observe but to *tell* history. The history of lynching would remain at least partially untold without the efforts of scholars, building on a long history of telling the stories of lynching.[1] But these archival objects may also re-create the trauma of encounter and reify the prurient interest of white consumers. Every time we access archival objects – the physical materials of historical production – we also access their other pasts and other uses, whether we acknowledge it or not. We have seen that the meanings of these objects, even while changing their specific valences, have remained stable signifiers for white supremacist ideologies. Not inert objects, lynching souvenirs, mementos, and relics bring their own contexts and build on the institutional frameworks in which they are placed. As heritage institutions have begun to resist and restructure their foundational racist origins, so too can they help us rethink the politics of lynching's material culture. I want to turn now to a few short case studies of archival circulation and museum exhibition to think further about the politics of display, interaction, and use.

---

[1] In this, scholars are following the footsteps of earlier intellectuals and activists who insisted that revealing the hidden complexities of a lynching would expose the practice to additional scrutiny and fuller understanding.

INSTITUTIONALIZING COLLECTIONS

The rise of the professional museum and archive was contemporaneous with the most intensive period of racial terror lynching. Particularly in the South, formalized and public institutions for preserving history and memory were being painstakingly established while the larger society was still structured by white supremacy and the cultural logics of lynching. This overlap was not wholly incidental. These new institutions of the early twentieth century sought to embed larger societal beliefs into their formation, and in so doing legitimate racist structures through their association with the past. Professional history became a legitimating tool in much the same way southern memory had been. As with other southern-led efforts to commemorate the past, these turn-of-the-century movements toward professionalization of history were monuments to the South's structures of inequality.

At their founding, these new professionalized archives and museums capitalized on late nineteenth- and early twentieth-century obsessions with objects, and desire for rational order. The neat and decontextualized display cases of the museum, and the complex organizational system of the archives, appealed to these cultural demands.[2] At the same time, association with and ingestion into these institutionalized collections established a new legitimacy for the interpretation of the past. The new History supplanted the memory work that had been largely the domain of amateur women. Professionally trained and university-legitimated men lent the credibility of their education and expertise. In Alabama, for instance, the lawyer and bibliographer Thomas Owen directed his considerable energies toward the establishment of an archive that would deepen the quality of research underpinning the Lost Cause. His lobbying led to the establishment of the first state archive in the United States, and blazed a trail for the establishment of southern historical institutions.

---

[2] On the development of the postbellum museum and its departures from previous epistemological frameworks of knowledge creation and interpretation, see Steven Conn, *Museums and American Intellectual Life, 1877–1926* (Chicago: University of Chicago Press, 1998). I here conflate the museum and the archive as a matter of historical development with their linkages coming through the similarities in framework that Conn identifies. Later parts of this chapter will explore, though not at sufficient length, the developing distinctions between these two cultural institutions through increasing generations of professionalization. My point here, though, is more to think about the endurance of these turn-of-the-century models in the contemporary institution. I do this with apologies to my archival and museum colleagues, and the very real distinctions that now exist between their professional practices.

Between 1900 and 1910, every state in the South forged some institutional presence for the preservation and interpretation of its part of the southern past.[3]

In North Carolina, the emerging professional historical industry was particularly robust. Its state history museum grew out of a private collection of Confederate relics that included a gun from Antietam and the bullet-riddled smokestack of the CSS *Albemarle*. The first, impermanent exhibition of these collections went up in 1898, the same year as the Wilmington massacre and the Johnson and Kizer lynching. The museum was officially established in 1902 as a "Hall of History," in chronological order through the state's perceived human history. It began with ancient "relics of the Indians" and proceeded to early examples of when "the whites appeared, and as is their wont, took charge of affairs." Many of the museum's contents still bore the traces of both antebellum museums of entertainment and Victorian practices of bodily object association. Personal effects of the Confederate generals James Johnson Pettigrew and Bryan Grimes occupied a case apiece. The equivalent space was given to dozens of Indian relics representing many hundreds of years. Pettigrew's case held a handkerchief "dyed by his blood" and the uniform he wore when killed. These were objects that did not meet the increasingly stringent standards of scientific historical practice. They revealed instead the continuing structures of feeling attached to Confederate history. These contents were preserved in "cases … of North Carolina oak, cherry, and walnut … each [with] a triple locking device, and is dust and moth proof." And the museum's director, Frederick Olds, detailed the taxonomic structure of the new space, proceeding from the earliest Indian history on through to the historic triumphs of the white race. These early historians built the old structures of relic veneration into the emerging professionalism of the past.[4]

3 Brundage, *The Southern Past*, 105–137; Daniel Cone, "The Cause Archived: Thomas Owen, the Alabama Archives, and the Shaping of Civil War History and Memory," PhD dissertation, Department of History, Auburn University, 2020.

4 Frederick Olds, "North Carolina's New Hall of State History," *The News & Observer*, December 28, 1902, morning edition; Harry S. Warren, "North Carolina Museum of History," in *NCPedia*, 2006, www.ncpedia.org/north-carolina-museum-history (accessed April 20, 2022); "117 Wonderful Years: A History of the Museum," *North Carolina Museum of History*, 2019, www.ncmuseumofhistory.org/history-of-the-museum (accessed April 20, 2022). On the nineteenth-century origins of the museum as an entertainment, see Andrea Stulman Dennett, *Weird and Wonderful: The Dime Museum in America* (New York: New York University Press, 1997).

But the most dominant of these new institutions, and the one that would have the most impact on the future production of a unitary, white supremacist southern past, was the archival collections at the University of North Carolina (UNC). There the Southern Historical Collection (SHC) emerged from the efforts of the white supremacist and student of the notorious William Archibald Dunning, Joseph Grégoire de Roulhac Hamilton. "Ransack Roulhac" roamed around the South, securing collections from prominent families with the shibboleth of his own august family names as a badge of entrance. He sought to form a full-scale record of southern civilization, one that would expand upon the open racism of his mentor's "Dunning School" of Reconstruction history with a comprehensive primary source base for the study of white southern civilization. It would become, and remains, precisely that.[5]

Though today it is a diverse and pathbreaking archive committed to community participation and curation, its physical collections are still dominated by the records of the planter class and their descendants. As archival scholar Alex Poole notes, the university and particularly its archives were among the most fervently opposed to segregation in the entire South. Into the 1950s, at least, access to these collections was uneven at best for Black scholars seeking to use them. Employing the obfuscating language of bureaucratic policy, this and other library collections at UNC sought in 1952 to limit what were theoretically public holdings to students, faculty, and staff. This was a clandestine way of effectively barring African American researchers.[6] These exclusions reified earlier visions of southern history as white and exclusive. Though white women were allowed to participate in the production of southern history, it was most often as helpmeets to the supposedly brilliant scholars they had wed. Black men (and even more rarely women) could conduct historical research too, but only with permission and much self-congratulation on the part of southern whites for their largesse.[7] Institutionalization and

---

[5] Brundage, *The Southern Past*; Alex H. Poole, "The Strange Career of Jim Crow Archives: Race, Space, and History in the Mid-Twentieth-Century American South," *American Archivist* 77, no. 1 (2014): 23–63; John Herbert Roper, "Ransack Roulhac and Racism: Joseph Grégoire de Roulhac Hamilton and Dunning's Questions of Institution Building and Jim Crow," in *The Dunning School: Historians, Race, and the Meaning of Reconstruction*, ed. John David Smith and J. Vincent Lowery (Lexington: University Press of Kentucky, 2013), 179–202.

[6] Poole, "The Strange Career of Jim Crow Archives," 49–50.

[7] Roper notes that Hamilton's wife, Mary Cornelia Thompson, was his equal partner and collaborator on many of his projects, though she was not credited as such: Roper,

professionalization had calcified earlier divisions of race and gender and delimited the scope of southern history and its practitioners.

These histories of archival formation and accumulation continue to structure access to the past. Archives are not prescriptive, but they do restrict the contours of the work historians are able to do. Without extant sources or even knowledge of their existence we are often left to speculate idly and imagine histories. I have done this many times for Tom Johnson and Joe Kizer, though my own work here was ultimately dictated by the materials of history and memory that I did have access to. There are counterhistories too: Monroe Work at Tuskegee assembled an archive of lynching victims with a conscious evocation of their use for history.[8] Other Black intellectuals likewise responded to both crises of the present and the preservation of the past. But they were exceptions in a southern historical industry that made life difficult for anyone outside its heavily policed borders. Each of the institutions mentioned above is today an exemplar of contemporary professional practice. And in their own ways, each has confronted the exclusionary nature of its origins.[9] But our knowledge of the past is limited by the materials that

"Ransack Roulhac and Racism," 192. Likewise in Alabama, Marie Bankhead Owen expanded her late husband's archival practices and kept a close watch on Black researchers aspiring to make use of the archive. When John Hope Franklin made use of the archives, she was by turns welcoming, racist, and dismissive, using a racial epithet to refer to him and condescendingly attributing his manners to education in the South: Poole, "The Strange Career of Jim Crow Archives," 31. The broader point is that women were still allowed to police the boundaries of historical production, though increasingly through the imprimatur either of a male-dominated profession or through their husband's name. A notable exception to the general rules about white maleness and exclusive access is evident in the work of Helen Edmonds, the pioneering historian of the post-Reconstruction-era South. See Edmonds, *The Negro and Fusion Politics in North Carolina*. Edmonds was able to do the work she was partially out of the genteel racism of archival access, but also because there was less interest in the source base that she was the near-exclusive user of for decades.

8 On Monroe Work's career and life, see Linda O. McMurry, "A Black Intellectual in the New South: Monroe Nathan Work, 1866–1945," *Phylon* 41, no. 4 (1980): 333–344. R. J. Ramey does an excellent job setting out the context of Monroe Work's historical work and its continued value: R.J. Ramey, "The Profundity of Your Archive Doesn't Want to Live in Boxes Anymore: An Introduction to Monroe Work Today," *Preservation, Digital Technology & Culture* 48, no. 2 (2019): 61–68.

9 For the SHC, particularly in recent years, this has meant a significant commitment to seeking out and archiving community collections and cultivating new audiences among atypical archives users. I know of few other archives that have undergone such a transformation. The SHC's current archival staff consists almost exclusively of archivists tasked with outreach, public programming, and community engagement; "Staff," *Southern Historical Collection*, https://library.unc.edu/about/dept/university-libraries/wilson-library/

we can access. For the material culture of lynching, the vast majority of would-be archival objects are likely lost. Either through nonpreservation, outright destruction, or simply the lapse of time that renders a thing like a scrap of cloth back into a quotidian object, they have not been accessible as objects of study. But occasionally, these materials have made their way into archival collections or under the soft glare of the museum case. It is in these spaces that they begin the transition into objects of history, and through which we can read them in the context of the history of racial violence still unfolding.

FAMILY HEIRLOOMS IN THE PUBLIC ARCHIVE

Among the numerous and typically voluminous archives of the SHC are a number of so-called z-files. These are the otherwise unclassifiable, extraordinarily small, often single-object collections that do not quite fit elsewhere. Amid archival abundance, they often contain documentation from the peripheries of events. One of these noncollections is the "Sabine County (Tex.) Lynching postcard, 1908."[10] Though I discuss this postcard as an object earlier in this book, it warrants particular attention as an archival object. As Michel-Rolph Trouillot suggests, meaning attaches to historical objects at every moment of their creation and use. The process of an object being deemed worthy of archival value builds on its initial acquisition, the decision to save it, and the will to preserve it. At many points in the life cycle of such a thing, it could be destroyed, discarded, forgotten. Its survival is an act of conscious preservation. The accrual of meaning of such an object, through many dozens of years and perhaps a nearly equal number of hands, stays with

southern-historical-collection (accessed October 8, 2020). The SHC has also received significant funding to model this community-driven archival practice: "Southern Historical Collection Receives $877,000 from Andrew M. Mellon Foundation," *Southern Historical Collection*, https://library.unc.edu/2017/04/southern-historical-collection-receives-877000-from-andrew-w-mellon-foundation (accessed October 15, 2020). The Alabama Department of Archives and History responded to the uprisings and other protest movements of 2020 by releasing a thoughtful statement on the burden of its own past. This "recommitment" both acknowledged the role of Owen and others in perpetuating a white supremacist vision of southern history, and established a plan for improving the diversity of its representation; Steve Murray and the Alabama Department of Archives and History Board of Trustees, "Statement of Recommitment," *Alabama Department of Archives and History*, June 23, 2020.

10 Like the majority of the rest of the SHC, it is discoverable via an online catalog search and readily accessible in the search room. Its finding aid can be found at https://finding-aids.lib.unc.edu/05694 (accessed April 20, 2022).

things like the Sabine lynching postcard in ways both materially evident and largely conjectural. Historians note or bypass evidence every time we seek to retrieve information from "the archive," its collections, and the individual objects within them.[11] Archival things may not have their own agency, but they do have histories. And consciously or not, historians access those histories every time we make use of an archival object.[12]

The Sabine County lynching postcard exists in multiple printings and at least two archival collections.[13] The one I originally consulted in the SHC was printed by T. DeBenning and donated by Jordy DeBenning (presumably a descendant) in 2016.[14] On its face, this is not unusual. The SHC is an important archive for southern objects, and any number of donors find it via internet searches or some form of personal connection. What is more unusual is the postcard's status as a solo object. The donor could easily have found another home for it or, indeed, thrown it out. Instead, he opted to seek out an archive and donate it. Doing so suggests the historical weight of the object and the significance attached to it. The objects we hold in our own collections of family ephemera may have significance to us as individuals or to the communities we reside in, but legitimation as an object of History most often requires that they be donated to an institutional collection. It is such places, in both popular and scholarly understanding, where Historical meaning and significance are created.

The process of deciding to donate the DeBenning postcard, seeking out an archive to send it to, forging a relationship with the receiving archivist, and finally delivering the object all take time. Perhaps it was

---

[11] "The archive" has been an area of interest for the past several decades, owing in large part to the theoretical work of Foucault and especially Derrida. They were both concerned with the forms of knowledge produced by the abstraction of archival collections. Their concern then was not primarily with assembly, but with knowledge as it was produced from the archive. Trouillot deepened this discussion considerably by focusing on the assembly of archives, insisting that the particularities of place, time, and occasion are essential in understanding archives, rather than the singular archive. Carolyn Steedman usefully intervened in this literature with her meditations on archival assembly and use by historians. See Jacques Derrida, *Archive Fever: A Freudian Impression*, trans. Eric Prenowitz, Chicago: University of Chicago Press, 1996); Michel Foucault, *The Archaeology of Knowledge*, trans. A. M. Sheridan Smith (New York: Pantheon Books, 1972); Carolyn Steedman, *Dust: The Archive and Cultural History* (New Brunswick, NJ: Rutgers University Press, 2002); Trouillot, *Silencing the Past*.

[12] Trouillot, *Silencing the Past*.

[13] In addition to the postcard I accessed in the SHC, there is an alternate version archived at Yale: "Harkrider Drug Company Postcard: The Dogwood Tree: Lynching Scene in Sabine County, TX, June 15, with White Supremacist Poem," postcard, Sabine County, Texas, 1908, Visual Resources Collection, Yale University Library.

[14] Personal communication with Chaitra Powell, July 3, 2017.

done with a sense of reverence for the postcard and its potential use to future researchers. More likely, I think, it was a way of exorcising a family demon and finally ridding it of the legacy of a small object with an immense metaphorical weight.[15] As Susan Stewart notes, "the function of the heirloom is to weave, quite literally by means of narrative, a significance of blood relation at the expense of a larger view of history and causality."[16]

In other words, the significance of these objects resides in their relationship to our individual pasts, rather than the larger, collective history. Eventually, the world of historical significance intrudes on these objects. In the case of Kizer and Johnson's lynching, "The Song of Emma Hartsell" morphed into a means of justification and historicization. In other lynchings, these objects being subjected to larger historical significance might force recognition of the complexities of family inheritance. Objects we possess are entangled in lynching and racial violence. But those entanglements are not always easy to confront.

Heirlooms and other objects of memory become historical only when they no longer belong to individuals. Archives and museums offer justifying frameworks for the historical importance of an individual object. In the act of donation and accession, the Sabine lynching postcard became an *historical object*. This implies that the collected, preserved, and now donated object becomes part of the materials of historical production, a status that privately held things cannot normally aspire to. The status conferred by historicity is one that implicitly strips each of these earlier narratives and the intention behind its collected status. We are left then with an object whose meaning comes largely from its survival, rather than the many narratives that have been attached to it. Indeed, historical objects in museums and archives most often leave behind their particular histories and implicitly represent their moment of creation, rather than their use since. Consider for instance the archived letter. As

[15] The archivists at the SHC were immensely helpful in providing me with information about this archival donation. Particularly since this is well outside the range of their usual work, I am grateful for the extra effort that Chaitra Powell and Biff Hollingsworth went to to assist me. I would argue that we need more of these kinds of studies that look not just at the content or composition of archival objects, but at the ways in which they are formed. My reading of the motivations for donation are based on my understanding of the object itself, their recollections of the process, and a small part of my own judgment and conjecture. Hollingsworth did attempt to put me in touch with the postcard's donor, who did not respond to requests for an interview.

[16] Susan Stewart, *On Longing: Narratives of the Miniature, the Gigantic, the Souvenir, the Collection* (Durham, NC: Duke University Press, 1993), 137.

researchers, we re-create and conceptualize the moment of its creation. We might even mark its circulation from individual to individual. But we most often fail to think about its afterlives, its time spent piled on a desk, locked in a steamer trunk, stored in an attic. The interstitial lives of objects are lost to us. We see them marked only by the epochs of their most legible interactions with humans: their creation, collection, circulation, sale, or inheritance. What fails to enter the historical record are the furtive glances at the lynching postcard, its passing around to family or guests like a whispered secret, its shame hidden away with a stack of other family ephemera. Even those more public afterlives of the Sabine lynching postcard in the SHC are lost to us.

But some duplicates of the postcard have resurfaced in public. One such postcard was passed down to Peggy Womack in Fort Worth, Texas. Unlike the SHC postcard, this one has been both sent and preserved, revealing some measure of both its original use and the meanings it has held in subsequent years as part of a collection of family heirlooms. The origins of this particular postcard differ from the formally archived one. It was purchased at Harkrider Drug Store, forty miles away from the scene of the Hemphill lynching in Center, Texas. These surviving postcards are likely only two examples of a bigger industry related to this lynching. Clearly they moved in a circuit up and down east Texas, at least. As circulating objects, they could bridge these geographic gaps with the shared intimacy of regarding the pictured scene together.

Peggy Womack's postcard indexes the social relationships that this shared viewing occasioned. Her grandfather received the postcard in the mail from a childhood friend in Brookeland, right on the border of Sabine and Jasper counties, where he grew up. The friend sent the postcard all the way across the state to Coleman, the west Texas town where Womack's grandfather was living. In these early days of its existence, the postcard made its way across the state in the context of an existing relationship, a casual overture of renewed friendship based on the shared pleasure of regarding a lynched body.

The beginning of the message is like any other short note on a postcard. The friend remarks that he missed seeing him when he had recently been back in their hometown. Amid his casual message, and in the transcribed conversational style of the infrequent writer, the friend calls attention to the content of the card: "'say, look at this picture at the other side and see how they do negros in this county.'"[17] In the context of the rest of the note,

[17] Bob Ray Sanders, "Postcard Offers Look into Deplorable Past," *Star-Telegram*, April 17, 2005, sec. B.

this seems like an expression of pride in their shared home region and its treatment of Black people. "Look," the friend seems to be saying, "we still know how to treat them here. Don't you wish you were back home?"

We cannot know the full intentions of the writer. Just as surely, we do not know why Womack's grandfather kept the postcard. Perhaps it was nostalgia for his hometown, or for his old friend. Maybe he got a vicarious thrill out of viewing the image of the lynched men, as so many others did. He clearly attached some value to it, historical or otherwise. He kept the postcard and then passed it down in the family, first to his daughter, and then to his granddaughter. By the time Womack received it "when she was 10 or 11 years old" in the mid-1930s, it clearly had the sentimental value of a family heirloom. Reflecting years later, Womack was hard pressed to think ill of her family. She claimed that they kept the card "'not out of curiosity, but to remember how things were then.'"[18] This is an intriguing expression of a familial relationship to the past, and how significance accrues in objects as we hold on to them. When Womack's grandfather first received and kept the card, it was still newsworthy and an object of contemporary significance. Maybe he did keep it as a visceral reminder to himself – and subsequent generations of his family – of the casualization of such violence. More likely, I think, Womack was projecting her own memory practices onto those of her ancestors. Though the newspaper article about Womack's postcard portrays her locating it as a chance discovery, her own account of the postcard disputed that. She noted that "'this particular card is something I've looked at frequently and could never understand why we did things like that.'"[19] In this telling, she viewed the postcard often out of a kind of incomprehension of its content and purpose. It was a random inheritance, not something that built on generations of investment in racist violence.

Bob Ray Sanders, the journalist interviewing her, seemed to agree. In a follow-up to his initial column on Womack and her lynching postcard, he describes the scene depicted as "unlike any you can imagine."[20] Except, of course, his interviewee was living proof of the visual and material memories preserved from this lynching and countless others like it. It took very little imagination to depict the scene of the lynching or its ideological underpinnings. It was comprehensible and legible to both

[18] Sanders, "Postcard Offers Look into Deplorable Past."
[19] Sanders, "Postcard Offers Look into Deplorable Past."
[20] Bob Ray Sanders, "Image Shows One Episode in Our Tragic History," *Star-Telegram*, April 20, 2005, sec. B.

its original recipient and the two generations that intentionally passed it down. Sanders valiantly links it to his contemporary moment and the lynching of James Byrd, Jr., in Jasper, the town of Womack's family origin. Womack herself tries to historicize the postcard. She reflects that "that part of history is terrible … you wonder why people didn't do more." This happens even as both journalist and subject discuss the lynching of Byrd, an event so proximate in time and space that, like the original postcard when Womack's grandfather received it, it could hardly be deemed historical. Sander's linking of the two tries to refuse that distancing. At one point he forthrightly claims that "lynchings are not a thing of the past in America."[21]

But undoubtedly many of his readers wanted to be reassured that this kind of collecting was morally acceptable, and the furtive preservation of such materials within the family was only a case of innocuous inheritance, memory work without nefarious intention. Perhaps others knew better and wondered at the lack of cultural comprehension of Womack who would reverse the transformation of a public object made private. These keepsakes had once been objects to proudly share and display. But over time they had become things to keep and not refer to, to enjoy or be ashamed of in the private domain of the home. Undoubtedly some readers had their own inheritances that they understood were better left hidden, looked at, speculated about, regarded in secret. The historicity of these objects then is contingent and tenuous. Even made public or ingested into the quasi-public space of the archive, they still hold their power as objects, as heirlooms, as inherited things.

In the case of the Sabine postcards, their historical meaning comes in large part from their having been preserved, rediscovered, and again made public. It was this period of preservation of the material that gave it its historical meaning. By virtue of its survival, and its performative "discovery," it was now old enough and apparently rare enough to be deemed worthy of status as an historical object.

This kind of historicity tends to apply to archives, and allows for the recontextualization, if not decontextualization, of the objects within them. But as Trouillot reminds us, archives are political projects.[22] Historicity is not necessarily a positive judgment, but it does impart a value of sorts to an object. Viewed as historical objects, their power to induce trauma or reinforce communal definitions of white supremacy

[21] Sanders, "Image Shows One Episode in Our Tragic History."
[22] Trouillot, *Silencing the Past.*

is implicitly voided. But as I have shown to this point, historical distance from an event does little to mute the potency of objects associated with it. Temporal distance and the remove implied by it do not always translate to material objects. An object's origin date tends to dictate the historical frame that the archive and scholar put it in, which ignores the subsequent use value and accrual of meanings. This is certainly the case with the vast array of lynching photographs held in the Library of Congress (LOC). Their accession into one of the nation's official archival repositories and subsequent use help suggest the literal value attached to images of lynching and the means by which archiving might help shield and preserve that value.

COMMERCIAL VALUE AND INSTITUTIONAL COLLECTIONS

Lynching objects always held a peculiar valuation. Some souvenirs taken from bodies and sites might have monetary value. But as they cycled from person to person, their worth became more individual and familial, lessening their exchange value as objects of monetary worth.[23] These multiple spheres of value are ones that accumulate in objects throughout their various existences. Even in institutional collections and with the imprimatur of history, they never fully lose either their monetary worth or the other valuations they are freighted with. Indeed, they are held there in part because of those intersecting regimes of worth.[24] The collections of lynching photographs at the LOC literalize that process of valuation. The LOC holds dozens of images of lynchings. Perhaps more importantly, they too have a recognizable (if short) chain of custody that reveals the significant cultural and financial investment in objects and images of lynching. Almost invariably, these objects came to the LOC as part of copyright registrations. Their origins then are in attempts to monetize scenes of suffering and torture and claim it as intellectual property. That basis of archival preservation necessarily provides a contextual frame for their meaning and access and has colored their usage since.

---

[23] Kopytoff, "The Cultural Biography of Things."
[24] Steven Conn hints at this kind of valuation; see Conn, *Museums and American Intellectual Life*, 23. For the term itself, I am grateful to Karen Bassi and her insights into this important but understudied distinction. Indeed, much of my thinking in this chapter comes from an extraordinarily generative month thinking about museums in a National Endowment for the Humanities Summer Institute led by Bassi and Gretchen Henderson.

The LOC grew exponentially in the late nineteenth century as a direct result of the process that brought these photographs into the collection. Under Ainsworth Rand Spofford, from 1864 onward, the library added significant amounts of material under new copyright registration requirements. As the first professional head of the LOC, Spofford lobbied Congress for the passage of two acts to strengthen copyright registration requirements. These laws made copyright enforceable if not properly registered.[25] This helped make the modern Library and massively grew its collections – particularly in the burgeoning field of commercial photography – in the years leading up to the twentieth century.[26]

These dozens of lynching photographs arrived in this wave of registrations. And while patron access to these materials has varied significantly in the century since, they have been made readily available as objects of interest to study. Indeed, this overlap between their commercial potential as demonstrated by their patent registration and their interest and availability to researchers suggests the continued investment in these things as both object and image. Take, for instance, one of the more extensive collections from an individual lynching in these photographic holdings. Submitted for copyright in 1897, the objects in the "Series of fifteen stereographs relating to the murder of a woman in Tyler, Texas" hold a remarkable narrative of both creation and use. Through a series of sequential images, they tell the story of Henry Hilliard and his unlawful public murder in 1895.[27] There's an oddity to this collection, even

[25] In addition to some firsthand information from archivists at the LOC, the bulk of this information comes from Peggy Ann Kusnerz, "Picturing the Past: Photographs at the Library of Congress, 1865–1954", PhD dissertation, Department of American Culture, University of Michigan, 1992. I use "professional" here in recognition of Spofford's role as the first trained head archivist at the LOC, as opposed to earlier heads who were purely political appointees.

[26] Reese Jenkins, *Images and Enterprise: Technology and the American Photographic Industry, 1839–1925* (Baltimore: Johns Hopkins University Press, 1975); Carl Ostrowski, *Books, Maps, and Politics: A Cultural History of the Library of Congress, 1783–1861*, Studies in Print Culture and the History of the Book (Amherst: University of Massachusetts Press, 2004).

[27] It's worth noting that none of the materials explicitly identifies him as such, either in the descriptions or in the metadata of the finding aids. I found Hilliard's identity and a description of the lynching in "Burn Him at the Stake," *Chicago Tribune*, October 30, 1895, 2. This suggests that the identity of the place where he was lynched had more value than the victim himself. This is particularly the case since his identity was both not disclosed and was replicated by someone else for the majority of the photographs that formed the basis of this collection.

amid the other stereoscopic views of lynching in the LOC. They do not merely illustrate the hanging itself, or its immediate aftermath. Instead, these images purport to show the lynching as a whole, from the alleged attack on a woman to the aftermath of the lynching and its impact on the landscape. Intermingled with actual images of Hilliard, his torture and death are staged, hand-colored re-creations of his supposed crime. It's a highly curated, largely invented visual tale that is powerful both for its projection of the imagined narrative of a lynching, and for what it suggests about research and viewing practices both at its creation and in the generations since.

The set of stereoscopes was created by an enterprising local businessman – C. A. Davis – in Tyler. On the verso of each image in the set, he advertises "an unlimited supply of Stereoscopic views of the city on hand" in his shop. Holding pretensions to being both artist and businessman, he also promises that he can do commissioned works, though they will be *"views* [emphasis his] not portraits." Indeed, he seems to have cultivated a reputation as the local documentarian of important personal and civic affairs, noting in the last line of his advertisement that he gives "special attention to picnic parties."[28] This calls attention to the imagery on the front, both in its depiction of the massive crowds at the lynching and of the stereograph's uses as a form of social pleasure. The alternating images of large crowds and close, immersive views of the crime suggest the social function of both the original lynching and its stereographic reproduction. These are objects meant not for inert display, but rather to serve as the center of a social occasion. They were diversion and entertainment. As Sheenagh Pietrobruno notes, stereoscopes "tantalized viewers with … three dimensional effects and visual immediacy."[29] These lynching stereoscopes tell a story in visual form that helps each individual viewer project themselves into the scene as somewhere between spectator and participant, inhabiting a floating omniscience. This is a situation suited to the consumption of stereoscopes. You can

---

[28] If surviving records are any indication, Davis too was trying to set himself apart as a commercial photographer in and around Tyler. His main competition in the area seems to have been Henry York, who has many surviving photographs in the Smith County Historical Archives in Tyler, Texas. They also hold some of Davis's images, though the archives were not able to confirm that they held one of his lynching postcards. See Richard Pearce-Moses, *Photographic Collections in Texas: A Union Guide* (College Station: Texas A&M University Press, 1987), 285.

[29] Sheenagh Pietrobruno, "The Stereoscope and the Miniature," *Early Popular Visual Culture* 9, no. 3 (2011): 171.

at once isolate yourself in the scene they create and then pull out of it to engage with the others around you, to give them a turn to take a look and inhabit the world for a moment. Stereography is premised on this suspension of disbelief, a desire for both experience and the "illusion of reality interrupted by the very medium delivering it."[30] This kind of intentional sharing and disruption created the rhetorical space for a collective processing of the lynching. Together, then, group members could relay and digest their experiences. For those buying these sets, they were a promise of the re-creation of an experience. This could either be an experience you actually had, as in the case of Davis's picnic images, or one you could not hope to actually experience except through the imagined and created landscape of the stereoscope. The Hilliard lynching exhibit was the latter, a projection of the imagined crime and criminal and its very real consequences. Even those who attended or participated in the lynching could not hope to have had the experience projected in these re-created images of the lynching. They created an immersive and imagined world that allowed for the communal and individual sharing of the lynching.

In a sense, this collection literalizes the imagined formulaic narrative of a lynching. It contains fifteen images that capture every step of the process. This offers an expanded framework by which people understood the lynching, an example of the wider geographic and temporal contours of individual lynchings that I have explored in this book. Rather than just depicting the aftermath, these images show a double of Henry Hilliard lying in wait for his victim and then assaulting her in graphic, simulated detail. Other images depict mobs hunting Hilliard down, capturing him, and bringing him to the purported justice of the lynching rope. Of the fifteen images in the series, four come from the actual lynching. The eleven additional stereoscopes are artist crafted. Perhaps they are at the original site, or one that looks like it. They certainly do not show the purported victim or Hilliard, both of whom were dead by the time this series was created. Instead, they represent a close double that literally projects the larger imagination of how the events happened. In so doing, they allow not the usual form of nostalgic recall, but instead a wholly new experience that is irreplicable even for those who might have served in the lynch mob, who might have taken their own memento, who might have their own story of the day of the lynching. This then offers something

---

[30] Emily Godbey, "'Terrible Fascination': Civil War Stereographs of the Dead," *History of Photography* 36, no. 3 (2012): 270.

unprecedented even among the many dozens of such images produced during the nineteenth and twentieth centuries. It's a re-creation – or, more aptly, a creation – of the experience of a lynching from the impossible vantage point of observation of the entire imagined crime. These stereographs are an extension of the bodily technologies of the genre as nineteenth-century Americans understood it. They "brought before the eye images that unaided sight could never have."[31] And indeed, they were not just visual, but something like a facsimile of experience. They place us, the consumer, as observer and participant in each step of a process where even our imagined intervention might change the event's outcomes. But they also disallow any form of action, taking away our complicity as viewers either for the alleged crime of sexual assault or of the lynching-murder itself. It is a brilliantly curated set of images for the forms of license that it grants by the poetics of implication.[32] We are allowed to view, to observe, to study each minute detail, so long as we do not intervene.

This complex form of meaning persists even amid the implied recontextualization of the archive. The immersive aim of the stereoscope fits somewhat uncomfortably within the intensive concentration and repeated examination of our archival research practices. Viewed now in a reading room, through a newer stereoscopic viewer and amid the low hum of other researchers and archivists working, this collection seems even further removed from the imagined landscapes of its creation. But its use and value sit uncomfortably close to those original intentions, both because of the commercial intent behind its archiving and because of the process of value assigned to objects in institutions. They are valued here for research potential, for the belief that close study of their content and form can teach us something about the past. That's true, but also an incomplete assessment of the work these objects continue to do even when their meaning is seemingly reframed. They continue to be used, repeatedly and intently, in a form whose physicality replicates their original intent.

When I received the twelve photographs of Henry Smith's lynching, they were out of order. Another infamous Texas lynching, the 1893 mob murder in Paris, was well documented with a dozen photographs sent to the archive for copyright protection. I found the photograph captioned

---

[31] Robert J. Silverman, "The Stereoscope and Photographic Depiction in the 19th Century," *Technology and Culture* 34, no. 4 (1993): 749.
[32] St. George, *Conversing by Signs*.

"The Torture Begun" at the top of the folder, out of the collection's narrative sequence. Clearly, the last researcher had focused on this, the most gruesome of the images and most explicit in its violence-invoking caption.[33] In the Hilliard lynching collection, some cards likewise show more intensive use and a fuller story of their archival consumption. Cards twelve and thirteen ("The Torch Applied"; "First Fire Withdrawn") have clearly been studied for longer and at greater depth than the other thirteen objects in the collection (Figure C.1). They bear wear marks at the corners – some splitting and cracks, as well as what appears to be a repair on card thirteen.

Likely this damage came from the routine use of the items. This involves putting them into and then withdrawing them from the stereoscope. These are sturdy objects, designed for just this kind of repeated use. But it's still easy to catch a corner on the brackets of the viewer, particularly when the printing stock of the card is worn down from repeated use. This could have happened to any of the cards in the collection over their 125-year archival life, but it has happened only to these two, the two images of Henry Hilliard undergoing torture and death. Perhaps not coincidentally, they are two of the "real" images of the lynching, rather than the staged reproductions of the process. That can hardly be a coincidence. Instead, it seems like the researchers using these collections were drawn to the images of Hilliard's torture and death. These have clearly been the objects in the set most studied, a supposition supported by the significant interest in images of lynching over the last several decades.[34]

---

[33] "Paris, Tex., Feb. 1893. Lynching of the African American murderer of a child," Twelve black and white photographic prints, Library of Congress Photographic Archives, accessed July 18, 2019.

[34] I am thinking here principally of the *Without Sanctuary* exhibition and the exhibition book, which purports to use the decontextualizing space of the exhibition to force a reckoning with lynching photographs and postcards. In rendering these objects in an almost fine art exhibitionary context, I believe it actually forces them back into the realm of the spectatorial. This is only exacerbated by the project's website, where you can buy multiple editions of the book at a variety of price points based on edition. This kind of connoisseurship only reifies the original intention of these images. It is easy to imagine the large, handsomely bound book sitting on a coffee table for visitors to flip through, unconsciously invoking earlier generations of lynching photograph consumers as they do; "Books," *Without Sanctuary*, https://withoutsanctuary.com/product/without-sanctuary-lynching-photography-in-america (accessed June 26, 2020). In a retrospective evaluation of the significance of Brundage's *Lynching in the New South*, Amy Louise Wood rightly points out that *Without Sanctuary* helped revive the study of lynching's artifacts as a central piece of lynching's seemingly vanished rituals. I hope this book has built on Wood's suggestion that these rituals did not disappear, but instead took other forms. See Wood, "Without Sanctuary: The Symbolic Representation of Lynching in Photography," 88.

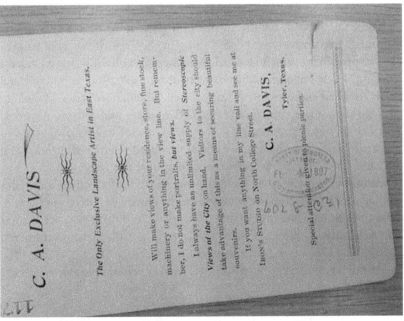

FIGURE C.1A AND C.1B Wear marks on images of torture in an archival lynching collection

Perhaps this use of the objects mirrors that of its original consumers. Maybe they too passed over the narrative arc of the collection to fixate on its conclusion, the torture and murder that resolve the story. Without other existing copies of this stereoscopic exhibit in archival collections, it's difficult to say how and when it got used. But we should bear in mind that at least part of the original intention of objects like these was to elevate the importance of the event that they documented. Stereoscopes and other images like the Hilliard one historicized lynchings. They sought to both preserve and enlarge their significance, documenting them for the sake of posterity. In the largely imagined narrative of the lynching in Tyler, the mob got portrayed as heroic defenders of white womanhood and a way of life. Whether mob members intended it or not, the stereoscopic collection puts them, Henry Hilliard, and everyone else involved into the realm of history. Davis was filing his images in the archives as a claim to copyright protection. But that seemingly simple act is laden with other intentions. Archiving suggests a valuation of the object, one that protects it from the commercial incursions of other entrepreneurs by placing it into the official record. In the archive, it continues to accrue meaning and significance, becoming an historical object used to understand the past. In this way, historians are not immune from its histories of reception. Indeed, we are an integral part of an object's becoming historical. Every time we access a thing in the archive, we help to produce its historicity. When I looked at the stereographs of Henry Hilliard's lynching, I felt uncomfortably close to the people who purchased and preserved their own copies. Perhaps Davis intended someone like me to one day view these stereographs and write them and him into history. Whether or not that is true, the collection clearly has its own sense of history. It is one that marginalizes Henry Hilliard in favor of the mob and the viewer.[35] We are both subject and creator of this history.

Intention clearly matters amid the complexities of an object's use. But scholarly intention does not account for the particular affective power of these objects. Holding, examining, viewing each of them puts the scholar simultaneously in the mindset of the creator and the viewer, all filtered through the lens of our own attempted objectivity. This is a hard balance to strike. Inured by access to dozens of other comparable objects in

---

[35] On the historical imaginations of historical actors, see Steedman, *Dust: The Archive and Cultural History*, 30. Steedman directs historians to think about the specific posterity that their historical subjects imagined and the other conscious acts of historical production that they engaged in.

archival collections, and many thousands more of contemporary images of racist violence, the tension between our scholarly selves and our consumer selves begins to break down. This is exacerbated even more by the access we have to digital facsimiles of comparable historical objects. The Tyler, Texas exhibit is among the very few lynching objects held in the LOC that are not digitized and accessible to anyone with an internet connection and basic knowledge of search functionality. Access and democratization of information are good, but how do we maintain that connection between scholarly inquiry and prurient interest? Particularly, how do we do so in a world where images of dead Black people rendered as bodies – Michael Brown, Philando Castile, Eric Garner, George Floyd, Ahmaud Arbery – have become omnipresent?[36] How might the institutional framework of the archive or museum be more than implied context?

Part of the argument of this book has been that objects are not inert and that their meaning changes over time. That ontological shift is not permanent. Instead, these are things that take on more resonance at particular times. Objects go through life cycles. Their categorization as historical does not foreclose the additional meanings they have accumulated and may continue to accumulate. We are constantly engaged in historical production, the contemporaries of the pasts we create.[37]

That contemporaneity feels all the more evident now. In the time that I have worked on this book, the long-standing spectacle of state and personal violence against Black men in particular has achieved prominent attention, arguably unprecedented since the height of the first anti-lynching movement. That attention has come in the mobilization of protestors and the building of movements. But it also comes in the form of people regarding images of bodily harm and death. Looking becomes a substitution for action, or indeed for reaction. As Susan Sontag notes, this viewing forces us again into the historical condition of spectatorship.[38] The shock

---

[36] Tonia Sutherland notes that the virality of violent images of the deaths of African American people has become familiar, even if unintentionally. More particularly, she claims that the process of accessing these images blurs the lines between commemoration and commodification, a familiar tension for those similarly accessing lynching photography. Her testament to the personal and professional trauma of these media encounters is an important caution about the power of such objects. Tonia Sutherland, "Making a Killing: On Race, Ritual, and (Re)Membering in Digital Culture," *Preservation, Digital Technology, and Culture* 46, no. 1 (2017): 32–40.

[37] Trouillot, *Silencing the Past*, 16.

[38] I am combining several points from Sontag here. Her larger argument is that images of suffering and death are tied to photographs as a consumer product, and as such we view them principally through the frame of seeking out ever more shocking materials. We

of a gruesome image is a momentary feeling that nonetheless gives the viewer a sense of having *done* something, rather than merely reacted.

The study of history seems to offer few antidotes for this condition. Part of the argument of this book has been that objects are not inert and that their meaning changes over time. That ontological shift is fluid. The material culture of lynching is composed of things that take on more resonance at particular times. At this moment in history these are objects that seem to have a new narrative function that might better take advantage of the countermemories of lynching and help propel us into a new understanding of their legacy. The framework we currently have, the one that makes these objects comprehensible, is one inherited from centuries' worth of reducing images of suffering to little more than observation and interest. Even our most intense visual scrutiny is lacking a fundamental recognition of the traces of personhood left behind. It's not enough to see.

LANDSCAPE AND THE ARCHIVES OF LYNCHING

The National Memorial for Peace and Justice opened in 2018 in Montgomery, Alabama. This so-called lynching memorial functions as a commemorative space for each of the thousands of known, post-Reconstruction lynching victims in the United States. The memorial itself is meant, more even than other commemorative spaces, to be a materialization of the emotional weight of lynching. It is a place for commemorating the extraordinarily traumatic weight of one aspect of the Black past, a partial fulfillment of Toni Morrison's desire for a spot of remembrance and reflection on the Black past.[39] More than that, it extends the

---

might feel compassion for the subjects of such a photograph, but are just as likely to feel that flood of compassion dry up and be forgotten. I argue that this is all the more the case for historical subjects, distanced from us by space and time. See Sontag, *Regarding the Pain of Others*, particularly 21, 33–34, 79–80.

[39] Morrison is most often quoted as desiring "a little bench by the side of the road" for such purposes, though her historical and commemorative imagination was actually a bit more ambitious. The quote has given rise to a project to place reflective benches at places like Sullivan's Island, where many thousands of enslaved peoples were brought into the United States; "Bench by the Road Project," *Toni Morrison Society*, www.tonimorrisonsociety .org/bench.html (accessed October 27, 2020). She was talking more specifically about the history and legacy of slavery, but her larger point, and larger call, applies to the ambition of the Memorial: "There is no place you or I can go, to think about or not think about, to summon the presences of, or recollect the absences of slaves; nothing that reminds us of the ones who made the journey and of those who did not make it. There is no suitable memorial or plaque or wreath or wall or park or skyscraper lobby. There's no 300-foot tower. There's no small bench by the road. There is not even a tree scored,

commemorative practices of the memorial into the rest of the world. The space reminds us that we dwell constantly among the traumas of racial violence embedded in the landscape.

In the memorial itself, visitors are presented with looming monuments, first just over eye level, and then eventually hanging suspended more than a dozen feet above their heads. Their presence obviously evokes bodies hanging. But that literal reading is almost too simple. As a collective, the hanging markers take on a kind of grandeur that repurposes the familiar shape and figuration of hanging masses. Visitors come to be overwhelmed by a collective sense of loss, and by the terribly stark beauty of the lost lives represented.

The individual markers for each lynching are simple objects. Huge, rusting steel slabs with various counties and the names and dates of people lynched there. Kizer and Johnson's memorial is almost at the halfway point, just high enough that I needed most of the reach of my arms to trace the outlines of their names. In the months it has been there, I imagine others have done the same, if not to this, then certainly to others of the six-foot-long markers. I have not been witness to many overt rituals of memorial, but have occasionally seen flowers left behind, a couple lingering near a marker, an individual touching an engraved name. It is one of the few ways to be proximate to a representation of lynching victims.[40] Taken together, the memorial is overwhelming in scope. But at the level of the individual, it can be almost intimate, our best and closest substitute for the many unmarked graves of victims like Joe Kizer and Tom Johnson.[41]

This main section of the memorial evokes awe at the grand scope of a collective, largely forgotten historical trauma. Exiting from the structure enclosed by the hanging markers, visitors are greeted first by a massive concrete wall bearing a Toni Morrison quote, and then an almost incongruously small sign: "Monument Park." Beyond this sign, in rows neatly

---

an initial that I can visit or you can visit in Charleston or Savannah or New York or Providence, or better still, on the banks of the Mississippi"; Toni Morrison, "Melcher Book Award Acceptance Speech," *UU World Magazine*, August 11, 2008 [1989], www.uuworld.org/articles/a-bench-by-road (accessed April 20, 2022).

40 My observations here are based on more than a dozen visits to the National Memorial for Peace and Justice since its opening in April 2018.

41 On the uses of contemporary monuments and memory, see Erika Doss, *Memorial Mania: Public Feeling in America* (Chicago: University of Chicago Press, 2010); Marita Sturken, *Tangled Memories: The Vietnam War, the AIDS Epidemic, and the Politics of Remembering* (Berkeley: University of California Press, 1997).

arranged in alphabetical order by state and county, lie duplicates of the hanging markers, here laid out like many thousands of coffins waiting to be claimed by loved ones. It's worth dwelling on the incongruities of this space. Its name suggests something far grander than its reality. The evocative grandeur of the earlier section is absent. This looks like a warehouse, or the images of war dead arrayed in their coffins and awaiting formal ceremonies of repatriation and burial.

These duplicates are meant to be distributed to the communities where these lynchings were held as part of a process of reckoning. Coalitions of community members are now working to research and commemorate the lynching, with the end result being the distribution of this duplicate marker for display. To date, none of the markers has been distributed, though there are dozens of community remembrance projects ongoing around the country.[42]

This last section with the duplicate monuments is the most transformative of the entire space. These are things designed to be removed, to be marked by their absence in one place and presence in another. They are an acknowledgment that memorialization occurs not just in the locations we build and prescribe for those purposes, but in all of the places that surround us. Our landscape is a memorial. The places we dwell in are inextricable from the racial terror that occurred there, that made use of the landscape as both backdrop and fundamental symbolic element. The National Memorial for Peace and Justice only makes that connection explicit. For many Black people, it has never been hidden. Remember the observation of the newspaper editor who knew that a lynching "carries with it a grewsomeness which Negroes for fifty miles around do not forget for a generation."[43] Or the Mississippi leader who knew that the very threat of a lynching meant it was time to get out of the South. In response to questions about safety, the man noted "there was nothing I could answer … and so I have not again urged my race to remain."[44] People in his community were among the millions fleeing the South in the first half of the twentieth century. Though it has become a truism that this Great Migration was motivated in part by racial terror, it's impossible to quantify that motivation. We still do not know the full extent of

---

[42] "Community Remembrance Project," *Equal Justice Initiative*, https://eji.org/projects/community-remembrance-project (accessed March 5, 2021).

[43] Quoted in Trotti, "The Scaffold's Revival," 208.

[44] Isabel Wilkerson, *The Warmth of Other Suns: The Epic Story of America's Great Migration* (New York: Random House, 2010), 43.

lynchings undertaken by mobs in the South. And we will almost certainly never have an accounting of the larger terror and trauma they caused. Still, it is apparent that the South is a landscape marked by the scars of these events. There are few places not proximate to a would-be memorial for a victim of racial terror lynching. Just as southerners still live in places where claims to ownership rest on Native removal, so too do we live, work, and play amid the unmarked graves of our victims.

But perhaps we can call this landscape an archive too. Memorial implies commemoration, even veneration. An archive is something that allows for repurposing and education, a redirection toward both analysis and action. I am critical of the pasts of such formulations of historical material. But perhaps like all historians, I am in awe of their potential. If you dig into this spatial archive a little, you find indigenous removal, claims by wealthy settler colonists, literal transformations by the hands, backs, and minds of enslaved people. We know all of this, those of us who study this place. But perhaps we could be better reminded of how visceral and how proximate that violence is. It surrounds and encompasses us, built into our landscapes and enacted continually through both the "slow violence" of land loss and climate change, and the more immediate horrors and terrors of the continually renewed violence against Black people.[45] Every day we inhabit the archives of these violent southern pasts. We live in a world made by lynching.

---

[45] Rob Nixon, *Slow Violence and the Environmentalism of the Poor* (Cambridge, MA: Harvard University Press, 2011).

Index

Printed in the USA
CPSIA information can be obtained
at www.ICGtesting.com
LVHW050823161023
761116LV00073B/59